Railroad Mergers and Abandonments

RAILROAD MERGERS and ABANDONMENTS

by Michael Conant

PUBLICATIONS OF THE INSTITUTE OF BUSINESS AND ECONOMIC RESEARCH
UNIVERSITY OF CALIFORNIA

UNIVERSITY OF CALIFORNIA PRESS

1964 BERKELEY AND LOS ANGELES

UNIVERSITY OF CALIFORNIA PRESS
BERKELEY AND LOS ANGELES, CALIFORNIA

CAMBRIDGE UNIVERSITY PRESS
LONDON, ENGLAND

LIBRARY OF CONGRESS CATALOG CARD NUMBER: 64-22705

MANUFACTURED IN THE UNITED STATES OF AMERICA

Acknowledgments

This study was made possible by two major grants of financial assistance which enabled me to secure partial relief from teaching duties. The first was from the Institute of Business and Economic Research of the University of California which allocated funds from the generous gift of the Pacific Telephone & Telegraph Company. The second was from the Institute of Governmental Studies of the University of California, which supported the research for eighteen months beginning in 1962. I am indebted to the general counsels of most Class I railroads for supplying me with materials from their files and to the Secretary of the Interstate Commerce Commission for reports and data assembled by the Commission. I wish to thank Dean John W. Cowee and all colleagues at the University of California who so unselfishly offered critical assistance. Their comments greatly sharpened the quality of the analysis and exposition. My special debt is to Professors John P. Carter, George W. Hilton, Tillo E. Kuhn, Julius Margolis, and Dow Votaw. The directors of the Institute of Business and Economic Research, Professors Joseph W. Garbarino and Lee Preston, were continuously helpful and encouraging in their assistance to the publication, as were the editorial and typing staff of the Institute. For permission to reprint parts of my earlier articles, I thank the editors of the *Stanford Law Review*, *Minnesota Law Review*, and *Land Economics*.

MICHAEL CONANT

Berkeley, California
January, 1964

Preface

This study was conceived as an example of economic criticism of the administrative regulation of resource allocation. Railroad mergers, abandonments, and service discontinuances were chosen as the specific topics because they are interrelated aspects of business policy toward remedying the excess capacity and overinvestment in railroad lines and terminals. It is therefore appropriate to begin this work with a detailed estimate of route capacity, excess capacity, and overinvestment.

A major impediment to railroad mergers has been the alleged competition between railroads. Chapters II and III examine this allegation in detail and render a judgment on the effectiveness of interrailroad competition as an impetus to adjustment of investment to changes in technology and shifts in demand.

Chapter IV follows logically as an evaluation of the economic impact of recent railroad mergers. In reporting annual net savings of more than $7,000 per mile of line abandoned when traffic is transferred to a parallel line with excess capacity, these mergers demonstrate a clear relationship between traffic density and cost.

Chapters V, VI, and VII are concerned with the problems of reallocation of resources through disinvestment in fixed plant. The emphasis is on the regulatory aspects of joint use and abandonment of facilities.

The plan of this study was to deal only with those regulatory problems of combination and disinvestment that were peculiar to the railroad industry. Since the special problems of freight-car supply have been treated by other economists, they are only noted incidentally herein. Issues relating to labor productivity, such as work rules and dismissal pay, are not unique to railroads but are special problems of adjustment to technological change which can be better studied by labor economists.

Contents

Tables

I

Route Capacity, Excess Capacity, and Overinvestment

The regulation of railroad consolidations and abandonments of railroad lines must be viewed in its economic setting of an industry which, relative to the general economy, is declining.[1] Investment in railroad lines during the period of local monopolies resulted in an industry structure which has not been adjusted to the more recent rivalries of highway and air transport.[2] Optimum operating units in railroads today require the reorganization of the industry both in number of firms and investment in rights of way. Underlying the railroad-consolidation movement are specific economic problems of excess capacity and overinvestment. These issues will be analyzed as a prologue to developing public policies relating to combinations and to disinvestment in railroad lines.

CAPACITY

A microeconomic concept of the capacity of fixed plant and equipment is not easily formulated.[3] Yet such a concept must un-

[1] See U.S. Congress, Senate, Committee on Interstate and Foreign Commerce, *National Transportation Policy* (Doyle Report) 58–67 (87th Cong. 1st Sess. 1961).

[2] Nelson, *Railroad Transportation and Public Policy* 151–157 (1959).

[3] Stigler, *The Theory of Price* 276 (1946). Most literature on industrial capacity is macroeconomic and based on historical peak outputs. See bibliography in de Leeuw, "The Concept of Capacity," *1961 Proceedings of the Business and Economic Statistics Section*, American Statistical Association 320–329, and de Leeuw, "The Concept of Capacity" 57 *J. Am. Stat. Ass'n.*, 826 (1962).

derlie any discussion of long-run excess capacity in a regulated industry and any policies for its reduction. The simplest approach to the problem is to equate plant capacity with output at the minimum point on the average total cost curve.[4] This solution is reasonable if average cost declines over most of its range and reaches a minimum at or near the physical limit of the equipment.[5] It is not useful if average cost is constant or is slightly rising over a substantial portion of its range.[6]

A more general economic concept of capacity must combine the engineering definition with the cost constraints. An engineer would define capacity as that output which can be produced with a given plant under a normal organization of production with an uninterrupted and unlimited flow of variable inputs.[7] Normal organization would presume technical efficiency and operation for 168 hours per week minus necessary shutdown time for repairs and maintenance, unless labor could not possibly be hired at an economic wage for such continuous production.[8] As the engineering capacity output is neared, the marginal physical product of additional units of the variable inputs will approach zero. In this area of operation, marginal cost will begin to rise rapidly and will approach infinity. This is the key component of a definition of economic capacity.[9] It is a maximum output consistent with a finite marginal cost, with allowance for maintenance of fixed plant. Hence, capacity can be defined as the output where average total cost is at its minimum or as the output where marginal cost begins to rise rapidly, whichever is larger.

Theoretical route capacity.—Traffic or output capacity in number of trains per day which can cross a line is the important eco-

[4] See, e.g., Klein, "Some Theoretical Issues in the Measurement of Capacity," 28 *Econometrica* 272, 273 (1960); Committee on Price Determination, *Cost Behavior and Price Policy* 234 (1943).

[5] Dean, *Managerial Economics* 304–305 (1951).

[6] See Bain, *Industrial Organization* 152–155 (1959). For a summary of the empirical evidence that average and marginal costs are constant over wide ranges in manufacturing industry, see Heflebower, "Full Costs, Cost Changes, and Prices," in National Bureau of Economic Research, *Business Concentration and Price Policy* 370 (1955).

[7] Hickman, "Capacity, Capacity Utilization and the Acceleration Principle," in *Problems of Capital Formation* (National Bureau of Economic Research Studies in Income and Wealth, Vol. 19), 419, 420 (1957).

[8] Compare Haines, "Capacity Production and the Least Cost Point," 38 *Am. Econ. Rev.* 617, 618–619 (1948); Clark, *Studies in the Economics of Overhead Costs* 91 (1923).

[9] Bishop, "Cost Discontinuities, Declining Costs and Marginal Analysis," 38 *Am. Econ. Rev.* 607, 616 (1948).

nomic question.[10] Following the definitions of capacity in the previous section, the theoretical traffic capacity of a railroad route or line will be reached when the number of trains per day is so great that it begins to cause congestion, that is, material delay of a substantial number of trains on the line. Ideal traffic capacity estimates presume adequate departure and receiving yards for all trains to be carried on a line. They also presume that traffic will be evenly spaced in time throughout the day and that sidings will be long enough for trains of optimum length.

On a single-track line, with trains running in both directions, the trains in each direction would have to be spaced two sidings apart. Presuming sidings long enough to hold any train dispatched, equal distance between sidings and all trains with the same speed, capacity in trains per day would be:

$$\frac{\text{Speed (MPH)}}{\text{Distance in miles between sidings}} \times 24$$

If the speed of all trains was 40 miles per hour and the sidings were ten miles apart, capacity would be 40/10 x 24 or 96 trains per day. This traffic or output capacity in trains per day is not dependent on the length of the line but only on the length of single-track sections between sidings. Disregarding delay from switching and running through sidings and presuming uniform speeds, capacity of a rail line will be primarily a function of the speed of trains, the distance between sidings, and the efficiency of the signaling system.

Ernest C. Poole has stated this ideal capacity formula on the alternate assumption of sidings uniformly spaced on a running-time basis.[11] His formula is $C = 1440/t$, where C is capacity in trains per day and t is the running time in minutes for a train between siding centers. As an example, if trains took 15 minutes to run between sidings, capacity would be $1440 \div 15$ or 96 trains per day. Poole has developed the more complex versions of this formula which account for deceleration and delay at sidings, and for passing of slower trains by faster trains. For most single-track lines with sidings five or more miles apart, the ideal theoretical capacity is fewer than 200 trains per day.

---

[10] This is in contrast to the static capacity of a line at any one moment, a basic engineering factor which underlies economic capacity. See "Train Capacity and Train Performance," 48 American Railway Engineering Association, *Bulletin* 462, 125–144 (1946); Hay, *Introduction to Transportation Engineering* 271 (1961).

[11] Poole, *Costs—A Tool for Railroad Management* 147 (1962).

Double-track railroad lines have no problem of trains meeting, but only one of sufficient cross-overs for faster trains to pass slower ones. On many modern lines, such cross-overs are six to eight miles apart. The theoretical capacity of a double-track line with all trains operating at the same speed (no passing) and one mile headway between trains is:

$$\frac{\text{Speed of trains (MPH)}}{L_t + 1} \times 24$$

where L_t is the length of one train measured as a fraction of a mile. As an example, if trains move at 40 miles per hour, each train is one-fourth mile long, and headway between trains is two miles, then the theoretical traffic capacity of a line is 40.24 ÷ 2.25 = 426 trains. Considering the safety requirements for railroad operation, few double-track lines would have an ideal theoretical capacity of more than 400 trains per day.

Theoretical capacity is thus based on the assumption that all trains will travel at the same speed. Delays caused by operation of high-speed trains which pass slower trains and by bunching of trains at certain hours of the day greatly reduce capacity. The Russian experience in planned operation of all trains at uniform speed confirms this capacity theory.[12] Theoretical capacity also assumes that on single-track lines, where train meets must occur, the best signaling system possible has been installed. At the present state of signal engineering, the best signal system is centralized traffic control. Engineering studies show that centralized traffic control will increase the capacity of a single-track line by 75 to 80 per cent over systems used previously on the same lines.[13] This is accomplished by enabling nonstop meets of the majority of trains.

Actual route capacity—first estimate.—The chief obstacle to estimating the capacity of American railroads is the lack of data classified according to type of line and location. Information on the number of tracks, types of sidings and cross-overs, grades, curvatures, local speed restrictions, and signaling systems for each segment of railroad line in the United States is not available. Hence, only aggregate estimates can be made from published statistics.

[12] Williams, *Freight Transportation in the Soviet Union* 98–103 (1962).

[13] 80 *Electrical Engineering* 650 (1961). See Association of American Railroads, *American Railway Signaling Principles and Practices: Principles and Economics of Signaling* (rev. ed. 1955); Schwendt, "Economic Relation Between Signals, Track Arrangement, Motive Power, and Method of Operation," in Association of American Railroads, Signal Section, *Economics of Railway Signaling* 447–499 (1937).

Since route capacity is determined by the number of trains that can pass over a railroad line in a given period of time, increased capacity of freight trains means increased route capacity. More powerful engines, larger cars, and longer trains have had the effect of increasing output per train and thereby increasing capacity.[14] As shown in Table 1, the average load per train (net ton-miles per train-mile) has doubled between 1930 and 1962. Since the sizes of cars and average load per freight car have both increased, the average number of cars per train has had to increase only 50 per cent to accommodate the doubled load.

Another indication of route capacity, though of limited value, is the peak output carried by railroads in World War II. As shown in Table 1, the net ton-miles per mile of road per day on freight trains reached a peak of 9,446 in 1944. The 1962 figure of 7,657 represents a decrease of 18.9 per cent. An alternate measure is the average number of trains to cross a single mile of track per day. As shown in Table 1, this figure was 8.3 freight trains per day in 1943 and 1944, whereas in 1962 it was 4.9, or 40 per cent less. The peak number of passenger trains on the lines offering passenger service, as shown in Table 1, was 8.2 trains per mile of road per day in 1945. By 1962, this figure dropped to 6.1 trains per mile of road per day, a drop of 26 per cent. Table 1 indicates that this drop in average passenger train density took place in spite of the great number of complete cessations of passenger service on lines with the fewest trains. Miles of road in passenger service dropped from 161,499 in 1945 to 86,028 in 1962, a drop of 47 per cent.

Aggregate wartime peak traffic densities are not indicative of total route capacities because most routes were not operated to capacity. The available locomotives and cars were only a fraction of the number which could have been handled by the existing routes. Furthermore, most railroad lines do not follow the shortest routes between key industrial cities, and their capacities were never required to be tested during the war. A reasonable estimate of the proportion of total railroad lines which was operated at capacity during World War II would, at maximum, be 10 per cent.

[14] The average capacity of box cars rose from 41.5 tons in 1930 to 46.4 tons in 1946 and to 49.6 tons in 1961. The average capacity of gondola and hopper cars rose from 53.9 tons in 1930 to 56.8 tons in 1946 and to 61.9 tons in 1961. The tractive effort per steam locomotive in 1930 was 45,225 pounds, while the tractive effort per diesel locomotive was 55,872 pounds in 1946 and 61,749 pounds in 1961. The average number of cars per freight train was 47.9 in 1930, which rose to 51.8 in 1946 and to 71.0 in 1961. Association of American Railroads, *Railroad Transportation: A Statistical Record, 1921–1961*, at 8, 12, 28 (1962).

TABLE 1

MILEAGE AND TRAFFIC DENSITY IN FREIGHT AND PASSENGER SERVICE
CLASS I RAILROADS IN THE UNITED STATES (1930–1962)

	Freight Service					Passenger Service		
Year	Miles operated[a] (excluding trackage rights)	Freight train-miles (thousands)	Net ton-miles per train mile	Net ton-miles per mile of road per day	Trains per mile of road per day	Mileage operated in passenger service[a]	Passenger train-miles (thousands)	Trains per mile of road per day
1930	230,602	539,392	784	4,815	6.1	n.a.	542,914	n.a.
1935	225,170	430,009	734	3,625	4.9	n.a.	388,091	n.a.
1940	220,288	481,892	849	4,792	5.6	170,226	391,597	6.3
1941	219,445	567,727	915	6,107	6.7	167,652	400,841	6.6
1942	217,358	666,437	1,035	8,143	7.9	163,829	427,588	7.2
1943	216,825	701,212	1,116	9,291	8.3	162,330	463,391	7.8
1944	216,188	698,761	1,139	9,446	8.3	161,833	476,093	8.0
1945	215,488	652,250	1,129	8,763	7.8	161,499	481,385	8.2
1946	215,213	590,413	1,086	7,664	7.0	161,174	448,247	7.6
1947	214,776	616,071	1,146	8,451	7.4	160,654	414,909	7.1
1948	214,726	584,671	1,176	8,221	7.0	159,751	407,133	7.0
1949	214,510	498,573	1,138	6,814	6.0	156,798	380,253	6.6
1950	214,066	514,971	1,224	7,569	6.2	146,266	357,545	6.7
1951	213,921	528,573	1,300	8,262	6.4	139,067	355,128	7.0
1952	213,580	502,891	1,296	7,836	6.0	132,851	344,468	7.1
1953	213,105	492,409	1,301	7,745	5.9	128,846	333,128	7.1
1954	212,698	447,122	1,287	6,979	5.4	124,533	317,141	7.0
1955	212,250	476,444	1,374	7,964	5.8	119,545	298,838	6.8
1956	211,102	475,561	1,422	8,234	5.8	115,749	289,866	6.8
1957	209,965	446,733	1,439	7,884	5.5	112,522	274,789	6.7
1958	209,529	400,420	1,430	7,050	4.9	106,929	246,402	6.3
1959	208,592	414,133	1,443	7,385	5.1	100,049	225,045	6.2
1960	208,043	404,464	1,466	7,324	5.0	93,893	209,367	6.1
1961	207,621	386,410	1,507	7,237	4.8	89,120	198,443	6.1
1962	206,386	393,346	1,557	7,657	4.9	86,028	193,211	6.1

SOURCE: U.S. Interstate Commerce Commission, *Statistics of Railways in the United States* and *Transport Statistics in the United States* (1930–1962).
[a] Average mileage operated during each year.
n.a. = not available.

Average output or traffic density figures, as shown in Table 1, are useful as a first approach to estimation of railroad line capacity, but these figures are deceptive because of the highly uneven distribution of traffic on the different lines. The only empirical study of traffic density by miles of line for the whole United States was done in 1953 for President Barriger of the Pittsburgh & Lake Erie

Railroad.[15] The results of this study are summarized in Table 2. They show that 10.1 per cent of total mileage, or 22,500 miles of railroad line classified as heavy density, produced 50 per cent of the total or 316 billion ton-miles of freight service in 1953. The

TABLE 2

DISTRIBUTION OF FREIGHT TRAFFIC DENSITIES OF RAILROAD LINE (1953)

1	2	3	4	5	6 = 4 ÷ 2	7	8
						Range of densities within class	
Density classification of railroad line	Miles of line in class	Per cent of total lines	Traffic density in net ton-miles (billions)	Per cent of total output	Average density in ton-miles per mile of line per year (thousands)	Maximum ton-miles per mile of line per year (thousands)	Minimum ton-miles per mile of line per year (thousands)
Heavy	22,500	10.1	316.00	50	14,044	60,000	4,000
Medium	133,500	60.1	303.36	48	2,272	4,000	400
Light	66,000	29.8	12.64	2	192	400	0
TOTALS	222,000	100.0	632.00	100	2,847		

SOURCE: Totals from U.S. Interstate Commerce Commission, *Statistics of Railways in the United States*, 1953. Distribution in Columns 3 and 5 derived from data in Barriger, *Super-Railroads For a Dynamic American Economy* 8 (1956).

range of density within this highest 10.1 per cent was from a low of 4 million ton-miles per mile of line to a high of 60 million ton-miles per mile of line. Average density on the heavy-density line was 14.04 million ton-miles of freight per mile of line in 1953. This was equal to an average of 38,500 ton-miles per mile of line per day or about 30 freight trains of average load per day.

The next 60 per cent of route mileage or 133,500 miles of line carried 48 per cent of total freight or 303.4 billion ton-miles in 1953. The range of densities on this second group of lines was from a low of 400,000 ton-miles to a high of 4 million ton-miles per mile of line per year. Average density in this 60 per cent of route-miles was 2,272,000 ton-miles per mile of line or one-sixth of the average on the high-density lines. This annual density was equivalent to 6,200 ton-miles per mile of line per day or about 4.8 trains of average load per day.

[15] Barriger, *Super-Railroads For a Dynamic American Economy* 8 (1956).

The lowest density, 30 per cent of route mileage or 66,000 miles of line, carried only 2 per cent of total freight or 12.6 billion ton-miles in 1953. The range on these low-density lines was from none up to 400,000 ton-miles per mile of line per year. Average density was 192,000 ton-miles per mile of line. This annual density was equivalent to 526 ton-miles per mile of line per day or about two and one-half trains of average load per week.

A conservative estimate of the actual route capacity of American railroads can be made by extension of the cited data. It requires the presumption that the main or through lines of all railroads, about 110,000 miles of line, could be maintained or reconditioned so that at peak utilization they could carry on the average as much as did the high-density lines in 1953. This was 14.04 million ton-miles of freight per mile of line in 1953 or about 30 freight trains of average load per day in addition to the passenger service carried on some lines. The branch and secondary lines, which constitute the rest of the route miles, can carry only a fraction of the trains carried on main lines since they are dependent functions of main-line traffic. They could be expected, however, to carry at capacity on an average at least as much as the medium-density lines carried in 1953. This was 2.27 million ton-miles of freight per mile of line in 1953 or 4.8 freight trains of average load per day. At this estimated peak capacity, the total freight traffic to be carried on all lines, main and secondary, would be 1,799 billion ton-miles per year. This freight-traffic capacity, which could be carried in addition to the scheduled passenger trains, was 2.8 times the amount actually carried in 1953.

Actual route capacity—second estimate.—A second approach to practical capacity is based on a sample of wartime estimates of when specific lines have become congested by a substantial number of trains subject to excessive delay. Excessive delay can be said to exist when the net revenue (revenue minus direct costs) from sending an additional train along a line is exceeded by the additional costs to the carrier resulting from delays of other trains. Since marginal costs of additional delays are not accurately measurable and difficult even to estimate for an entire line, excessive delay has usually been estimated on a time basis. Generally, delay of a substantial number of trains for more than one hour for every 10 miles of line traveled was considered excessive in the wartime reports.

The practical capacity of a railroad line on which high-speed passenger and freight trains must meet and pass slower trains can be only a fraction of theoretical capacity.[16] It is limited by the fact that even among the three classes of trains—passenger, fast freight, and dead freight—individual trains will travel at different speeds. As a result, meets and passes cannot be scheduled accurately by timetable and train orders. Stops at sidings and grades and curves of lines restrict the speeds of individual trains differently, depending on the weight of the train and the motive power employed. Therefore, sidings on single-track lines and cross-overs on double-track lines cannot be equally spaced on a time basis for all trains. Some delays are inevitable. Capacity, as defined in terms of the onset of excessive delay, can only be estimated by a study of actual operations.

The great traffic increases during World War II tested the capacity of many railroad lines. A few rough generalizations can be made. For comparatively level single-track lines (grades of less than .5 per cent) with few sharp curves and with block signaling, capacity is 40 to 50 trains per day. On a 27½ mile single-track section of the Missouri Pacific, for example, 55 trains per day exceeded the capacity.[17] Some coal trains took three hours to cross the line because they had to yield the right of way to passenger trains. Excessive delays were encountered on a 121-mile single-track section of the St. Louis Southwestern carrying a wartime maximum of 45 trains per day.[18] Similar capacity figures were reported on single-track segments of the Nickel Plate, the Nashville, Chattanooga and St. Louis, the Chesapeake and Ohio, the Denver & Salt Lake, and the Baltimore & Ohio.[19]

On single-track lines with steep grades and sharp curves, operated by timetable and train orders, the capacity is approximately 25 to 30 trains per day. Excessive delays on the Norfolk & Western's Shenandoah Valley Line were encountered before reaching the 1944 peak of 33 trains per day.[20] On one 26-mile line of the Louisville & Nashville carrying heavy coal trains of 120 cars, grades and curves limited train speeds to 18 miles per hour.[21] Before the installation of centralized traffic control, this part of its route

[16] See "Notes on the Determination of the Traffic Capacity of Single and Multiple Track Railways," 22 American Railway Engineering Association, *Proceedings* 744, 746–748 (1921).

[17] *Railway Age*, Nov. 7, 1942, at 724.

[18] *Ibid.*, Jan. 26, 1946, at 232.

[19] *Ibid.*, July 17, 1943, at 89; Oct. 23, 1943, at 640; Aug. 24, 1946, at 340; April 6, 1946, at 725; Sept. 6, 1954, at 46.

[20] *Ibid.*, July 29, 1944, at 192.

[21] *Ibid.*, Oct. 2, 1943, at 519–521.

created a bottleneck with 34 trains per day. Similar capacities on severe grades were reported on the Virginian, Union Pacific, Santa Fe, Western Pacific, and St. Louis-San Francisco.[22]

On double-track lines which are relatively level and with few curves, and on which trains are authorized by timetable and train orders, actual capacity is about 90 to 100 trains per day.[23] Steep grades and sharp curves will reduce double-track capacity as much as 50 per cent below the 100 train per day ideal. Thus the Union Pacific double-track line between Cheyenne and Laramie reached capacity with 76 trains per day plus 20 helper-engine movements.[24] And the 98-mile, double-track line of the Santa Fe from Holliday to Emporia, Kansas, with 54 regularly scheduled trains, encountered excessive delays moving extra trains during fruit- and grain-harvest seasons.[25]

Actual track capacity is greatly increased by the installation of centralized traffic control, though it is doubtful that the 80 per cent increase which is estimated for ideal conditions can be reached. The Missouri Pacific reported the scheduled movement of 77 trains per day on a single-track line equipped with centralized traffic control.[26] Before this installation, excessive delays were experienced with 50 trains per day on the line. On a single-track line with steep grades, the Southern Pacific was able to move 60 trains per day after the installation of centralized traffic control.[27] And a Seaboard single-track line with bad grades and curves was able to carry 50 trains per day after the installation of centralized traffic control.[28]

Estimated actual capacity of double-track lines with bidirectional centralized traffic control is 150 to 160 trains per day for lines without steep grades. Railroads report the regular movement without substantial delays of 100 trains per day on double-track with centralized traffic control.[29] On these lines, the bunch-

---

[22] *Ibid.*, Jan. 23, 1943, at 249; Sept. 4, 1943, at 371–375; March 31, 1945, at 591; June 23, 1945, at 1108; Sept. 22, 1945, at 485.

[23] See report on wartime experience of the Richmond, Fredricksburg & Potomac. *Railway Age,* Dec. 5, 1942, at 927; Richmond, Fredricksburg and Potomac Railroad Co., *1944 Annual Report,* at 6.

[24] *Railway Age,* Nov. 7, 1955, at 24.

[25] *Ibid.*, June 1, 1959, at 16.

[26] *Ibid.*, Nov. 7, 1942, at 724.

[27] *Ibid.*, Jan. 27, 1945, at 236.

[28] *Ibid.*, June 20, 1942, at 1181.

[29] See report on the Rock Island in *Railway Age,* Oct. 13, 1952, at 132; report on New York Central, *ibid.*, Nov. 21, 1955, at 28.

ing of trains in periods of 1½ to 2½ hours has demonstrated that 140 trains could be handled on these lines without the delays encountered under less efficient signaling systems.

Information on the grade and curvature of each mile of railroad line in the United States is not available. Consequently the data on actual capacity of railroad lines just reported have been reduced to conservative estimates of average daily line capacities for insertion in Table 3. After separation of secondary from main

TABLE 3

ESTIMATED CAPACITY OF RAILROAD LINES IN THE UNITED STATES (JANUARY, 1962)

Type of line and signaling system	Miles of line	Estimated average total capacity (freight and passenger) in trains per day	Estimated total capacity in train-miles per day
I. Main lines:			
A. Block-signal system with train orders:			
Single track	53,115	30	1,593,450
Two or more tracks	18,926	60	1,135,560
B. Centralized traffic control:			
Single track	26,772	65	1,740,180
Two or more tracks	5,728	120	687,360
II. Secondary and branch lines: No signals—trains authorized by timetable and train orders only:			
Single track	104,782	5	523,910
Two or more tracks	680	10	6,800
TOTALS	210,003	—	5,687,260

SOURCE: Miles of Line: U.S. Interstate Commerce Commission, *Tabulation of Statistics Pertaining to Signals, Interlocking, Automatic Train Control, Train Operation By Timetable and Train Orders and Train Communication Systems* (1962).

lines, these estimated average capacities are multiplied by the miles of each type of line to give the estimated daily line capacities in train-miles. The grand total capacity of 5,687,260 train-miles per day is approximately 3.5 times the actual total train-miles of Class I railroads in the United States in 1962.

Yard and Terminal Capacity.—The actual line capacity of railroads cannot be fully determined by the number of trains the lines can carry because yards may be inadequate to receive that many trains.[30] For this reason, the optimum economic size of classification yards is another significant factor in railroad merger decisions. Beckmann, McGuire, and Winsten have analyzed the cost elements of freight classification yards in terms of sets of policies relating to receiving, grouping, makeup and scheduling of trains.[31] The interdependence of costs in yards in dispatching and receiving cities means that sets of policies must aim to minimize system costs. This factor alone is strong ground for merger of yards of railroads serving common cities. The minimization of accumulation delay and the extension of preclassification at the large and most efficient yards in major cities can best be achieved if all freight cars going to each smaller town are assembled in the same yard in each major city.

The capacity of a classification yard cannot be measured simply in terms of the number of cars which can be received in and dispatched from the yard in a given period of time. The factors which together determine the capacity of a particular yard are complex. Among the component parts or operating conditions that may be the limiting factor on capacity of an individual yard are the following:

1. The layout of the yard: the location of lead tracks, running tracks, and of repair, storage, and icing tracks, and the extent to which operations on these various tracks interfere with the basic function of classification.

2. The location and length of receiving and departure tracks in relation to train lengths, and the extent to which arrival, doubling, and dispatch of trains may interfere with the function of classification.

3. The condition of rails, ties and ballast: the possibility of yard derailments, and the consequent effect upon classification activity.

4. The number of classification (class) tracks available in relation to the number of classifications required.

5. The amount of special services; e.g., icing, required.

6. The kind of car repairs (heavy or light) for which the yard is responsible, and the incidence of bad order cars.

7. The incidence of cars which involve holding for billing or diversion orders, as in, for example, the wheat traffic. (From a classification standpoint, hold cars are particularly onerous, since the cars on the

[30] For report on bottlenecks in railroad yards during World War II, see Nelson, *op. cit.*, note 2 *supra*, at 162–164.

[31] Beckmann, McGuire and Winsten, *Studies in the Economics of Transportation* 156–163 (1956).

hold tracks usually must be classified at least once each day to pull out the ones ready to go forward.)

8. The amount of local industry siding and transfer traffic handled by the yard.

9. The efficiency of yard communication systems.

10. The availability of alternative leads in the event the normally-used lead becomes blocked.

11. The extent to which traffic comes to the yard in blocks, or, conversely, the extent to which each car classified requires a separate switching move (in the case of a retarder yard, the extent to which each car requires a separate "cut" on the hump.)

12. The extent to which train arrivals are staggered or bunched.

13. The promptness (or lack of it) with which departure tracks are cleared when trains are ready. (The incidence of worry concerning this factor appears mainly in yards at junction points where connecting lines may fail to take cars promptly, because of insufficient road power or crews, inadequate receiving tracks, or for other reasons.)[32]

Since there are no assembled data on the sizes and types of railroad yards in the United States, no estimates of total yard capacity can be made. Most railroads do not share yards with others, however, so that aggregate yard capacity would not reveal the likelihood of bottlenecks on any particular line. The limited sharing of railroad yards is illustrated by the fact that of the 59,146 miles of yard tracks operated by Class I railroads in 1961, only 5,948 miles were operated under trackage rights.

Table 4 indicates that the yard tracks owned or leased by Class I railroads and mileage owned by switching and terminal companies have changed little in the past twenty-five years. Yet because of declining passenger service and technological changes, yard capacity of railroads for freight operations in many major cities has increased greatly in the postwar period.[33] The key technological advance has been the construction of many electronically controlled hump yards.

Automatic switching was introduced in 1950 and automatic retarder controls in 1953. Although exact data are not available, a panel of the American Railway Engineering Association estimated

[32] U.S. Interstate Commerce Commission, Bureau of Transport Economics and Statistics, *The Capacity and Capital Requirements of the Railroad Industry*, 106–107 (Statement No. 5227, 1952).

[33] For data on the decline in locomotive hours in switching service, increasing excess capacity in yards for freight operations, see Nelson, *op. cit.*, note 2 *supra*, at 167–168.

TABLE 4

	Class I Railroads		Switching and Terminal Railroads		
Year	Number	Yard-switching tracks owned and leased (miles)	Number	Mileage owned	Mileage operated
1936	139	54,256	219	n.a.	7,415
1941	132	52,872	245	5,955	7,444
1946	130	53,355	253	5,953	7,395
1951	127	54,236	255	6,066	7,632
1956[a]	113	54,060	234	6,219	7,690
1961[a]	103	53,198	219	6,170	7,552

SOURCE: U.S. Interstate Commerce Commission, *Statistics of Railways in the United States* (1936, 1941, 1946, 1951), and *Transport Statistics in the United States* (1956 and 1961).

n.a. = not available.

[a] In 1955 and earlier years Class I railroads were those with more than $1 million annual revenues. Since 1955, Class I railroads are those with more than $3 million revenues.

that $300 million was spent by railroads on such yards between 1950 and early 1958.[34] Between 1950 and 1961, more than 45 hump retarder yards were built.[35] The minimum traffic required in order to make an economic investment in an electronically controlled yard is 1,200 to 1,500 cars per day.

One recent example is the Bison Yard, completed in 1963 at East Buffalo as a joint venture by the Erie-Lackawanna and the Nickel Plate railroads. The $13 million electronic yard has 49 classification tracks and 17 receiving and departure tracks, and its estimated capacity is 3,000 cars per day.[36] This estimate of capacity for a single-hump classification yard is confirmed by a switching time study done by Ernest Poole.[37] A sample of 223 cuts of cars showed that it took on an average .29 minutes per car to switch all cuts over the hump. When allowance is made for "dead" time between cuts, it can be estimated that a total time of hump-

[34] See *Railway Age*, April 28, 1958, at 13.

[35] McKnight, "Automatic Classification Yards: What They *Will* and *Won't* Do," *Railway Age*, February 20, 1961, at 16.

[36] Erie-Lackawanna Railroad Company, *1962 Annual Report*, at 4, 7 (1963). See *Railway Age*, April 29, 1963, at 13.

[37] Poole, *op. cit.*, note 11 *supra*, at 156.

ing would be about one-half minute per car, or 2,880 cars per day.

Electronic hump yards with automatic retarders have a dual economic effect. By saving in labor and locomotives, they markedly reduce the cost of car classification. By speeding the classification process, they reduce total transit time. The Missouri Pacific's $13.5 million double-hump yards, for example, opened in 1959 in Kansas City with 72 classification tracks and an estimated capacity of 6,000 cars per day; humping cut in half the time for a car to get through the Kansas City yards, formerly 19½ hours.[38]

The increased capacity and cost savings are illustrated by the New York Central Railroad's construction of four modern electronic classification yards to replace 60 smaller, obsolete yards.[39] These yards at Buffalo, Youngstown, Elkhart, and Indianapolis were expected to reduce by as much as 24 hours the time needed to move freight cars from St. Louis or Chicago to New York. The $11 million cost of automating the 490-acre Indianapolis yard was estimated to reduce costs sufficiently so that the investment would be recouped in three years. The 3,000-car daily capacity of the Indianapolis yard is illustrative of the national increase in railroad yard capacity because of automation. The New York Central officers maintained that this yard could handle, in addition to its own peak traffic, all the parallel traffic of the Pennsylvania Railroad. The New York Central-Pennsylvania proposed merger plan called for abandonment of the major parts of the Pennsylvania's Indianapolis yards.[40] The recent petition of the Illinois Central to control the Chicago & Eastern Illinois is also illustrative of this growing yard capacity. Illinois Central asserted that its Chicago and East St. Louis yards could easily handle the additional traffic now carried by the Chicago & Eastern Illinois to those cities, enabling abandonment of the C. & E. I. yards.[41]

EXCESS CAPACITY

Excess capacity has been defined as the difference between the output that a productive agent is capable of producing and the

---

[38] *Railway Age,* Dec. 21, 1959, at 46.

[39] New York Central Railroad System, *1962 Annual Report,* at 3. See *Railway Age,* Oct. 10, 1960, at 30.

[40] See *Wall Street Journal,* July 18, 1962, at 22.

[41] *Illinois Central Railroad Company—Control—Chicago & Eastern Illinois Railroad Company,* I.C.C. Finance Docket No. 21980, Report of Hearing Examiner Hyman J. Blond, September 26, 1963, at 48.

output it is actually called on to produce.[42] In terms of the economic definition of capacity developed in the preceding section, excess capacity is the difference between the output at minimal average cost or, if larger, that output where marginal costs of the firm begin to rise rapidly and the lesser output the productive agent will be required to produce at the expected seasonal or cyclical peak demand.

The more elementary theoretical concept of excess capacity is that of fixed factors of production of the individual firm in the short run where such factors are specialized to one particular product or service. Under competition such excess capacity could not prevail in the long run, since no factors are fixed in the long run. But railroads have both statutory and institutional barriers to mergers and abandonments which would reduce capacity. These factors, together with the indivisibilities of railroad lines and yards, mean that some railroads or particular routes of railroads may have excess capacity of lines and yards in the long run.[43] A railroad line must have roadbed, rails, sidings, and signals adequate to enable the carrier to transport freight cars at about the same speed as other railroads between common terminals. Depending on grades and curves, such a minimal single-track main line will still be likely to have a capacity of from 20 to 45 trains per day. Since only 20 per cent of the main lines (22,000 miles) carry more than 16 trains per day (freight and passenger), and since most of these lines are double-tracked, there is more than 50 per cent long-run excess capacity on most railroad lines in the United States. The capacity estimates of the previous section, in ton-miles and train-miles per day, confirm this by showing aggregate United States route capacity to be from 2.8 to 3.5 times the actual traffic densities of recent years.

A more complex concept of excess capacity is that of all factors of production in a group of firms serving a particular market. This is the Chamberlin concept of long-run excess capacity.[44] Under imperfect competition with collusive pricing or tacit understandings of firms not to cut prices, entry of new firms will cause

[42] Cassels, "Excess Capacity and Monopolistic Competition," 51 *Q. J. Econ.* 426, 427 (1937). For analysis of the concept of optimum overcapacity based on expected growth in demand, see Chenery, "Overcapacity and the Acceleration Principle," 20 *Econometrica* 1 (1952).

[43] See Comments of Professor Heflebower in *Transportation Mergers and Acquisitions* 159–173 (Burnie, ed. 1962). See Lerner, *Economics of Control* 174–185 (1944), on the nature of indivisibilities.

[44] Chamberlin, *The Theory of Monopolistic Competition* 104–109 4th ed. (1942).

all firms to operate at an output less than that of minimum long-run average costs. Although no individual factors of production are underused, each firm is smaller than optimum long-run size, and thus each firm has a combination of productive resources which is non-optimum as compared with competitive markets. As a result, there would be a greater amount of general productive resources in the industry than would be necessary to produce the same output if they were efficiently employed in optimum-size firms.[45]

In the United States, the railroad industry is encumbered by both types of excess capacity. Many railroads have excess capacity in the fixed factor, railroad lines. Many market areas also have a general excess capacity of railroads, in that fewer, optimum-size railroad lines and yards would have substantially lower average costs. The two types of excess capacity are interrelated in that a number of carriers in one market, each with insufficient traffic to approach capacity on a single-track line, would also mean excess capacity of all factors in that area. In economic terms, under conditions of oligopoly the railroads each maintain a plant (lines and yards) that is larger than the optimum size for their peak demand. Yet their plants may be smaller than the long-run optimum size for the market area if conditions of competition existed which would drive higher cost firms out of business.

TABLE 5

PARALLEL RAILROADS BETWEEN CHICAGO AND OMAHA

Carrier	Length of line: Chicago to Omaha (miles)	Distance from Rock Island Line at Des Moines (miles)
Chicago, Burlington & Quincy R. R. Co.	496	42, south
Chicago, Rock Island and Pacific R. R. Co.	493	
Chicago and North Western Ry. Co.	488	23, north
Chicago, Milwaukee, St. Paul and Pacific R. R.	488	33, north
Illinois Central R. R.	515	67, north
Chicago Great Western Ry.	508	84, north

Particular studies of excess capacity in main lines of railroads, other than the converging routes entering a major city, must concern the parallel routes between two industrial centers. The six roughly parallel railroad lines between Chicago and Omaha are

[45] See Cassels, *op. cit.*, note 42, *supra*, at 431.

listed in Table 5, together with the distances on each line between the two terminals. None of these distances shows the shortest rail route between Chicago and Omaha, since a combination of Rock Island and North Western segments could reduce the total through route to 470 miles (by building 13.5 miles of connecting track). Since the Illinois portions of these railroads carry trains from many other areas, this discussion of the capacity will center on the Iowa portions of these lines. Through Iowa, the Rock Island is the most important of these carriers, since it is the direct connection between the industrial centers of Davenport and Des Moines and Omaha.

Table 5 shows the distances south or north of the Rock Island line of the other parallel railroads measured at Des Moines in the center of Iowa.

The total number of scheduled freight and passenger trains on the Iowa portions of the six railroads shown in Table 5 is less than 100. It is clear that in a state which is now well supplied with paved highways, investment in six main-line carriers from eastern Iowa into Omaha represents substantial excess capacity in railroad lines. Three of these carriers could easily handle the east-west traffic of all major towns in Iowa. Together with their north-south connecting lines, they could serve the smaller towns and easily move the agricultural crops during peak harvest season. A program of consolidation or coördination through trackage agreements would require detailed studies, commodity by commodity, of traffic movements. Such a study would undoubtedly reveal the possibility of abandoning some of the main lines across Iowa and relegating others to the status of low-maintenance branches.

OVERINVESTMENT

Overinvestment exists in an industry if the investment exceeds the ideal amount which results from the competitive distribution of resources among all the different industries contributing to the national product.[46] If the rate of return on investment in a specific fixed plant in an industry is less than the return in the rest of that industry or in other industries with relatively similar patterns of market uncertainty, there is overinvestment in that plant. Cassels demonstrates that under imperfect competition with inelastic demand for the product or service, economic theory would

---

[46] *Ibid.* at 440.

lead one to expect overinvestment in an industry. Given the railroads' unique efficiency in carload freight at the present relative rates, which are below the cost of highway transport, the demand for this main service of the railroads is inelastic. The general low rate of return on investment in the railroad industry as compared with other regulated industries also supports the conclusion of overinvestment.[47] Although there seems to be substantial overinvestment in railroad lines, generalizations about overinvestment in all railroad plants would be erroneous. The low per-diem rate for freight-car rental has surely resulted in underinvestment in freight cars.[48] Overinvestment in railroad lines, however, has contributed to the poor general financial condition of railroads and has thus been another cause for underinvestment in railroad equipment.

There is substantial evidence of overinvestment in railroad lines.[49] The traffic density study by John Barriger reports that the least-traveled 30 per cent of railroad route-miles carried only 2 per cent of the total annual ton-miles of freight traffic.[50] If applied to 1961 rail statistics, this would mean that on 64,933.5 miles of railroad only 174,423 ton-miles of freight was carried per mile of road. If average freight revenue and cost data from Class I railroads (the only data available) are applied to this figure, there is strong evidence of overinvestment. Average 1961 freight revenues of $.013737 per ton-mile less average variable costs (transportation and maintenance of equipment)[51] of $.007671 per ton-mile leaves only $.006066 per ton-mile to pay for maintenance of way, traffic, miscellaneous and general expenses. On the least traveled 30 per cent of route-miles, this remainder to cover over-

---

[47] For analysis of data of railroad earnings, see Doyle Report, *op. cit.*, note 1 *supra*, at 50–57.

[48] See Grunfeld, "The Effect of the Per Diem Rate on American Railroad Freight Car Fleet," 32 *J. of Bus.* 52 (1959); Church, "Railway Freight Car Problem," 21 *Survey of Current Business* 10 (1941); Pegrum, "Investment in Railroad and other Transportation Industries under Regulation," 47 *Am. Econ. Rev., Papers and Proceedings* 416, 421–424 (1957); U.S. Cong., Senate, Committee on Commerce, *Hearings on Freight Car Shortage* (87th Cong. 1st Sess. 1961). For a general survey of railroad equipment capacity, see U.S. Interstate Commerce Commission, Bureau of Transport Economics and Statistics, *The Capacity and Capital Requirements of the Railroad Industry* (Statement No. 5227, 1952).

[49] See Clark, *op. cit.*, note 8 *supra*, at 109–113.

[50] See note 15, *supra*.

[51] Account numbers 301–337 and 371–413 in the ICC Uniform System of Accounts. See U.S. Interstate Commerce Commission, *Transport Statistics in the United States* 122–128 (1961). The ICC separation formula for joint costs with passenger service probably understates the true freight service costs.

head would average only $1,058.05 per mile for 1961. Since average maintenance of way and structures on branch lines carrying only slow freights is estimated to range from $1,100 to $1,800 per mile per year,[52] these lines would fail to earn their maintenance costs and contribute nothing toward traffic, miscellaneous or general expenses. They are clearly operated at a loss. Furthermore, the average transportation costs on Class I railroads used in the calculations probably underestimate the actual costs on lightly traveled lines. Such lines usually have shorter-than-average trains, resulting in higher-than-average transportation costs.

The changing technology of transport and the regulatory system have been the primary causes of the overinvestment in railroad lines. Before intensive highway, water, and air-line competition, parallel railroad lines 30 miles apart were in many instances profitable. But even then, a regulatory system which attempted to guarantee a return on all investment by permitting high and discriminating monopoly pricing (value of service rate making) was an inducement to overinvest.[53] The present overinvestment in railroad lines is thus a consequence of the failure to disinvest, as road and air transport diverted much traffic and also lowered revenue by rate competition for transport of some commodities. But a railroad cannot by itself disinvest in a segment of its single-track main line without going out of business. The indivisibilities of railroad plant make disinvestment by one railroad in main lines impractical. Only through consolidation or agreements for joint use of lines, accompanied by abandonments, can such main line disinvestments be effected.

The abandonment of 49,374 miles of railroad lines in the United States between 1920 and 1963 is evidence of attempts by the carriers to reduce the overinvestment.[54] Because of the economic and regulatory impediments to main line abandonments, almost all the mileage abandoned was of branch lines. The recent entire abandonments of the New York, Ontario and Western, the Rutland, and the Chicago, North Shore and Milwaukee indicate that

[52] American Railway Engineering Association, *Bulletin* 574 at 115 (November 1962); Poole, *op. cit.*, note 11 *supra*, at 23–27. Since these studies are calculated as maintenance per mile of track, the sum of the lengths of sidings would have to be added to a single-track line to calculate the maintenance per mile of road. See Meyer, Peck, Stenason and Zwick, *The Economics of Competition in the Transportation Industries* 49–54 (1959).

[53] See Averch and Johnson, "Behavior of the Firm Under Regulatory Constraint," 52 *Am. Econ. Rev.* 1052 (1962).

[54] U.S. Interstate Commerce Commission, *77th Annual Report* 215 (1963).

main-line abandonments of net loss railroads are increasing. The failure to disinvest in railroad lines when technological change encouraging intensive investment in a few lines and shifting demand both make for increased excess capacity can only lead to consumption of capital and eventual bankruptcy of many railroads. This is clearly illustrated by the history of the electric interurban railroads.[55]

CONCLUSION

Excess capacity and overinvestment in railroad lines and terminals waste economic resources in two ways. The first is the original cost of underused lines and terminals which, of course, cannot be recovered. The second economic waste is the cost of maintaining and servicing this excess capacity, which is reflected in unnecessarily high railroad rates. This can be remedied only by consolidations or coördinated joint use of facilities. The joint use of the Pennsylvania passenger station in New York during World War I illustrates the possible savings.[56] President Miller of the Maine Central Railroad has estimated that the volume of traffic on his line is one-ninth its actual capacity.[57] He further estimated that if volume of traffic on the Maine Central doubled, rates could be reduced by 20 per cent and the carrier would still be better off financially. The 1962 traffic densities of major railroads are shown in Table 6.

Chronic excess capacity and overinvestment in railroad lines increase as more efficient signaling systems and larger, faster engines increase the capacity of lines. The financial problems of overinvestment in lines become more acute as rising wages cause operating and maintenance costs to increase[58] and as the rates on some commodities are lowered to meet highway and water competition.[59] Furthermore, railroad technology of the future seems directed toward super-railroads which will meet and overcome the rivalry of high-speed highway transport.[60] Such super-railroads

[55] Due, "An Empirical Study of Abandonment Decisions," 14 *J. of Finance* 361–372 (1959); Hilton and Due, *The Electric Interurban Railways in America* 240–251 (1960).
[56] See Hotelling, "The General Welfare in Relation to Problems of Taxation and of Railway and Utility Rates," 6 *Econometrica* 242, 265 (1938).
[57] See report in *Railway Age*, Sept. 14, 1959, at 67.
[58] See Horowitz, "Some Effects of Labor Costs On the Railroad Industry," 8 *Labor Law Journal* 105–116 (1957); Harbeson, "Some Aspects of Wage-Price Relationships in Regulated Industry: The Railways as a Case Study," 25 *J. of Bus.* 175–186 (1952).
[59] See, e.g., *I.C.C.* v. *New York, N.H. & H.R. Co.*, 272 U.S. 744 (1963).
[60] See Barriger, *op. cit.*, note 15 *supra*, and see comments in Nelson, *op. cit.*, note 2 *supra* at 392–397.

TABLE 6

AVERAGE TRAFFIC DENSITIES ON LARGE RAILROADS (1962)

Region	Freight Service				Passenger Service		
	Miles of road operated	Net ton-miles per train-mile	Net ton-miles per mile of road per day	Trains per mile of road per day	Mileage operated in passenger service	Passenger train-miles	Trains per mile of road per day
New England Region:							
Boston & Maine	1,536	1,096	5,019	4.58	614	2,486,678	11.1
Maine Central	936	863	2,409	2.78	251	256,829	2.8
New York, New Haven & Hartford	1,701	1,091	4,537	4.16	605	6,281,110	28.6
Great Lakes Region:							
Delaware & Hudson	763	1,740	11,274	6.48	334	387,853	3.2
Erie-Lackawanna	3,042	1,344	10,844	8.07	1,567	6,145,608	10.7
Grand Trunk Western	946	938	6,172	6.58	401	872,870	6.0
Lehigh Valley	1,106	1,471	7,343	4.99	0	0	0.0
New York Central	10,000	1,523	8,729	5.73	3,395	14,796,805	11.9
New York, Chicago & St. Louis	2,155	1,418	11,171	7.88	523	767,705	4.0
Pittsburgh & Lake Erie	219	2,921	14,836	5.08	66	142,601	5.9
Wabash	2,410	1,461	8,624	5.90	1,243	1,519,630	3.3
Central Eastern Region:							
Baltimore & Ohio	5,752	1,774	11,522	6.49	2,264	4,762,813	5.8
Bessemer & Lake Erie	203	2,561	13,409	5.24	0	0	0.0
Central R. R. of New Jersey	583	1,684	9,761	5.80	264	1,730,448	18.0
Chicago & Eastern Illinois	863	1,895	7,620	4.02	287	638,377	6.1
Elgin, Joliet & Eastern	205	1,743	13,316	7.64	0	0	0.0
Long Island	338	343	699	2.04	321	6,162,530	53.3
Pennsylvania System	9,750	1,605	12,866	8.02	4,076	18,577,679	12.5
Reading	1,285	1,706	11,846	6.94	392	2,698,534	18.8
Western Maryland	852	2,013	9,894	4.92	0	0	0.0
Pocahontas Region:							
Chesapeake & Ohio	5,083	2,225	16,128	7.25	2,047	2,779,117	3.7
Norfolk & Western	2,724	3,115	24,578	7.89	1,084	1,928,630	4.9
Richmond, Fredericksburg & Potomac	110	1,955	24,021	12.04	117	947,140	22.2

Southern Region:						
Atlantic Coast Line	5,536	1,446	5,728	3.96	2,727	4,745,191	4.8
Central of Georgia	1,711	1,545	5,267	3.41	723	732,673	2.8
Cincinnati, New Orleans & T. P.	334	1,794	21,907	12.21	336	505,775	4.1
Florida East Coast	572	1,126	5,438	4.83	395	1,043,028	7.2
Gulf, Mobile & Ohio	2,715	2,053	6,426	3.13	282	864,929	8.4
Illinois Central	6,463	1,748	8,343	4.77	2,586	6,682,651	7.1
Louisville & Nashville	5,639	1,604	8,980	5.40	2,748	4,598,018	4.6
Seaboard Air Line	4,118	1,537	7,269	4.73	2,082	5,202,694	6.8
Southern	6,250	1,630	7,171	4.40	2,665	6,049,110	6.2
Northwestern Region:						
Chicago & North Western	10,544	1,294	3,278	2.53	1,759	4,019,446	6.3
Chicago Great Western	1,430	1,797	5,238	2.91	470	367,381	2.1
Chicago, Milwaukee, St. Paul & P.	10,544	1,540	3,718	2.41	2,796	5,253,183	5.1
Duluth, Mesabe & Iron Range	535	3,206	9,547	2.98	0	0	0.0
Great Northern	8,256	1,537	5,467	3.56	3,197	4,651,707	4.0
Soo Line	4,670	1,213	3,308	2.73	1,506	1,102,434	2.0
Northern Pacific	6,494	1,377	5,052	3.67	3,110	4,092,872	3.6
Spokane, Portland & Seattle	935	1,503	6,939	4.62	380	550,921	4.0
Central Western Region:						
Atchison, Topeka & Santa Fe	12,967	1,319	7,907	5.99	6,342	14,862,948	6.4
Chicago, Burlington & Quincy	8,520	1,474	5,645	3.83	3,672	8,464,255	6.3
Chicago, Rock Island & Pacific	7,825	1,339	4,637	3.46	4,355	7,138,566	4.5
Denver & Rio Grande Western	2,128	1,675	7,013	4.19	1,027	1,450,862	3.9
Southern Pacific	11,686	1,459	11,528	7.90	5,013	9,069,679	5.0
Union Pacific	9,705	1,449	9,711	6.70	4,708	10,010,388	5.8
Western Pacific	1,187	1,413	9,151	6.48	933	683,838	2.0
Southwestern Region:						
Kansas City Southern	889	2,453	10,156	4.13	786	991,170	3.5
Louisiana & Arkansas	746	2,092	6,402	3.06	452	485,098	2.9
Missouri-Kansas-Texas	2,876	1,574	3,753	2.38	804	1,183,158	4.0
Missouri Pacific	9,355	1,720	6,535	3.80	3,485	5,032,438	4.0
St. Louis-San Francisco	4,503	1,284	5,456	4.25	2,366	2,294,454	2.7
St. Louis-San Francisco & Texas	141	1,168	4,274	3.66	0	0	0.0
St. Louis Southwestern	1,554	1,447	10,805	7.47	0	0	0.0
Texas & Pacific	1,809	1,466	7,132	4.86	1,220	2,124,932	4.8

SOURCE: Computed from U.S. Interstate Commerce Commission, *Transport Statistics in the United States* (1962).

will require much more intensive investment in about 20 per cent of present main lines by minimizing grades and curvatures, elimination of all level grade-crossings and installation of double-track, bidirectional centralized traffic control. These high-capacity railroads will carry 100-car freight trains between industrial centers at speeds of up to 130 miles per hour. Intensive investment in 40,000 miles of rail line will be profitable only if through traffic of all railroads is concentrated on these super-lines. All through freight traffic between Chicago and Omaha, for example, will have to be concentrated on one such line in order to pay its cost. The six railroad lines now operating between Chicago and Omaha will have to merge or combine trackage rights in order to make investment in one such line profitable. As a consequence of this general coördination, excess capacity would increase sharply on secondary main lines, and the need for disinvestment in unprofitable lines would be aggravated.

II

The Myth of Interrailroad Competition

The persistence of long-run excess capacity in an industry is inconsistent with effective competition, and in railroads is at least partly a result of the existence of cartel organization. Under cartel control of an industry, a firm must usually continue its investment in a market in order to claim a share in industry income, even if aggregate profits would be increased by some firms leaving the market.[1] In the railroad industry, this motive to continue maintenance of excess capacity is augmented by the regulatory constraints on mergers and abandonments.

Public policy designed to foster efficient allocation of resources must be aimed either at enforcing competition or, if this is not possible in a particular industry, at direct regulation of resource allocation. Yet Congressional policy toward railroads has been ambiguous. Rate cartels are approved while competition is still a standard, though a limited one, in administration of the Interstate Commerce Act.[2] As shown in detail in Chapter III, railroad mergers approved by the Interstate Commerce Commission are exempt from antitrust prosecution, but the effect on interrailroad competition must be given weight as one element of public interest.[3] The validity of this standard is examined in this chapter, in

---

[1] Hutt, *The Theory of Idle Resources* 104–107 (1939).

[2] Maintenance of interrailroad competition is presently a specified standard of only the pooling and division-of-traffic section of the Interstate Commerce Act. Such agreements are approved if they "will not unduly restrain competition." 24 Stat. 379 (1887), 49 U.S.C. §5(1) (1959). See Chapter V for applications of this statute.

[3] 41 Stat. 480 (1920), 49 U.S.C. §5(11) (1958). See especially, *Minneapolis & St. L. R. Co.* v. *United States,* 361 U.S. 173, 187 (1959).

which the tools of the economics of industrial organization are used. Market structure, conduct, and performanse tests will be used to estimate the extent to which interrailroad competition exists and to evaluate its effectiveness as a social control.

STRUCTURAL OLIGOPOLY

The so-called public-utility industries are those in which economies of scale in relation to size of market are such that least long-run average costs of production will result if there is only one firm, or at most a very few firms, in the market. Indivisibilities of one or more elements in production put a technical limit on the minimum optimum-sized firm. The distribution system of urban electric, gas, and water utilities, for example, results in most cities in one firm's supplying each of these services to the entire city. As noted in Chapter I, indivisibilities in the railroad industry are found mainly in lines and yards. The fixed roadbed and tracks of railroad lines and yards are analogous to the fixed system of poles and wires in electric distribution and the fixed system of pipes in gas and water distribution. The optimum number of railroad lines between metropolitan centers is likely to be one, although the scatter of intermediate towns with substantial industrial production may make the optimum number two or three (if parallel lines are at least 100 miles apart).

In the railroad industry, even with the present large overinvestment in railroad lines, there are very few through carriers between any two metropolitan areas.[4] The greatest number of one-line freight carriers between two cities are the six railroads between Chicago and St. Louis and the six between Chicago and Omaha. Between Chicago and the Pacific Northwest there are only five main routes, all of which are composed of two or three connecting carriers, except the Milwaukee Road. There are only three major rail lines serving each of the two major market areas of California. The fact that a carload of freight shipped across the United States could be routed over segments of twenty or more carriers does not indicate competitive structure. Since the connecting carriers must coöperate in routing, interchange, and pricing for such shipments, they are not independent decision units of a competitive market.

As significant as the small numbers of carriers is the fact that

[4] Meyer, Peck, Stenason and Zwick, *The Economics of Competition in the Transportation Industries* 205–211 (1959); Borts, "Production Relations in the Railway Industry" 20 *Econometrica* 71 (1952).

hundreds of intermediate towns between metropolitan areas are served by only one railroad. Such concentrated oligopoly (even without collusion of the firms) has the greatest likelihood of uncompetitive market results in the performance of the firms.[5] As Stigler states, "An industry which does not have a competitive structure will not have competitive behavior." [6] Indeed, the absence in the railroad industry of the automatic forces of the competitive market impelled the enactment of legislation resulting in the extensive rate and service regulation we have today.[7]

Price leadership by the largest firm in highly oligopolistic markets is typical. No differential advantage can be gained by cutting prices because price cuts will be immediately followed by the other firms. One would expect product or service rivalry to be very limited also (absent patent monopolies), since this too would result in immediate following by the other firms.

Monopoly profits are presumably sufficient motivation for oligopolists to avoid price or service competition. However, a high fixed-capital-output ratio resulting in high constant costs at the usual levels of operation is another structural element of railroads, said to make competitive pricing unlikely.[8] Short-run marginal costs which are substantially less than long-run marginal costs could induce each of the railroads in an area to cut rates below full costs for particular commodities. Under this condition, the carriers must be concerned in avoiding widespread intense price rivalry which might cause all of them to operate at losses for a long time.[9]

[5] Bain, *Industrial Organization* 33 (1959); Chamberlin, *Theory of Monopolistic Competition* 46–53 (1952).

[6] Stigler, "The Case Against Big Business," *Fortune*, May 1952, pp. 123, 167.

[7] The motor carrier industry, in contrast, has a structure of many small firms, which could be close to the competitive model. However, joint pricing in rate bureaus pursuant to federal statute makes the industry a well-organized cartel. Federal regulation of motor carriers resulted from attempts to avoid the market results of intense competition. U.S. Cong., Senate, Select Committee on Small Business, *ICC Administration of the Motor Carrier Act*, 164–165, 236–237, 246–250 (84th Cong. 1st Sess. 1955); U.S. Cong., Senate, Select Committee on Small Business, *Trucking Mergers and Concentration*, 124–126 (85th Cong. 1st Sess. 1957); Pegrum, "The Economic Basis of Public Policy for Motor Transport," 28 *Land Economics* 244, 249–258 (1952); Schwartz, "Legal Restriction of Competition in the Regulated Industries," 67 *Harv. L. Rev.* 436, 456–60 (1954). See generally, Hale and Hale, "Competition or Control III: Motor Carriers," 108 *U. of Pa. L. Rev.* 775 (1960).

[8] Heflebower, "Stability in Oligopoly," 29 *The Manchester School* 79, 81 (1961). See Marshall, *Industry and Trade* 455–458 (1919); Borts, "Increasing Returns in the Railway Industry," 62 *J. Pol. Econ.* 316 (1954) and authorities cited therein.

[9] Locklin, *Economics of Transportation* 289–291 (1960); Fellner, *Competition Among the Few* 177–183 (1949).

The changing structure of the entire transport industry also has worked to diminish the likelihood of interrailroad rivalry. The new and sometimes intense price and service rivalry of trucks, buses, automobiles, and airplanes has left the railroads with a much smaller proportion of total transport in which they have substantial monopoly power.[10] This expanded intermodal transport competition has shifted demand away from the railroads and made them a relatively declining industry.[11] In a declining industry, with both overinvestment and unneeded excess capacity, there are likely to be concerted industry efforts to prevent interfirm rivalry that could easily put all firms in bankruptcy.

Barriers to Entry.—Next to the economies of scale which determine optimum production size, the most significant long-run structural determinant of competition is freedom of entry.[12] In the railroad industry, however, the size barrier to new entry is augmented by a statutory limit to entry. Under the Transportation Act of 1920, all new construction and extensions of railroad lines other than spur, industrial, and team tracks, can be built only after issuance of a certificate of public convenience and necessity by the Interstate Commerce Commission.[13] Although 8,441 miles of new line were built under ICC authorization from 1920 to 1961,[14] most of these lines have been only a few miles long for the purpose of extending railroad service to new factories and mines. In some of these cases, the construction of short connecting lines to another carrier was authorized in conjunction with a permit to abandon a much longer segment of line parallel to the other carrier.[15]

In requiring the certification of new construction and the

[10] For detailed studies of intermodal competition, see Nelson, *Railroad Transportation and Public Policy* 40–66 (1959); Williams, *The Regulation of Rail-Motor Rate Competition* (1958); Oppenheim, *The National Transportation Policy and Inter-Carrier Competitive Rates* (1945); U.S. Cong., Senate, Committee on Interstate and Foreign Commerce, *Ratemaking Rule—ICC Act* (85th Cong. 2d Sess. 1958).

[11] See Chap. I, note 1, *supra.*

[12] Bain, "Conditions of Entry and the Emergence of Monopoly," in Chamberlin, ed., *Monopoly and Competition and Their Regulation* 215–40 (1954); Bain, *Barriers to New Competition* 1–41 (1956); Hines, "Effectiveness of 'Entry' by Already Established Firms," 71 *Q. J. Econ.* 132 (1957).

[13] 41 Stat. 477 (1920), as amended, 49 U.S.C. §1(18) (1958). For early interpretations of this statute, see 3A Sharfman, *The Interstate Commerce Commission* 348–367 (1935); Hypps, *Federal Regulation of Railroad Construction and Abandonment Under the Transportation Act of 1920* 40–57 (1929); Marshall, "Railroad Certificates of Convenience and Necessity Issued Under the Interstate Commerce Act," 22 *Ore. L. Rev.* 215, 248–257 (1943).

[14] U.S. Interstate Commerce Commission, *75th Annual Report* 209 (1961).

[15] See, e.g., *Chicago, R. I. & P. R. Co. Construction,* 295 I.C.C. 262 (1956).

extensions of railroad lines, the Congress recognized the growing excess capacity of the railroads. If a single railroad in an area, easily capable of handling all traffic, was making high profits, this was no ground to permit construction of another railroad eager to share the monopoly profits. In such a situation, high profits are a clear indication that the regulatory commission is failing in its duty to lower rates in the public interest whenever consistent with adequate railroad service. As noted by the Supreme Court, the purpose of the 1920 act was to develop and maintain an adequate railroad system; hence, "the building of unnecessary lines involves a waste of resources," and "the burden of this waste may fall on the public." [16] Accordingly, where adequate, efficient, and economic service exists the Commission will deny a permit for extension of another railroad into an area, even though industries desire the service of as many railroads as possible.[17] The one significant case which was an exception to this rule and allowed construction of a line solely to promote interrailroad competition is now only of historical value. The *Chesapeake & Ohio* case,[18] in which the court affirmed such action by the Commission, was decided before the Transportation Act of 1940 repealed the provisions for consolidation plans under the criterion, *inter alia,* of preserving competition among carriers. Efficient allocation of resources in railroad organization is now the overwhelming consideration in granting certificates for construction and extension of lines. Therefore a court will enjoin attempts to build new lines without a certificate of convenience and necessity under the guise that they are exempt industrial tracks.[19]

The mere presence of one railroad in an area, however, does not give it a legal right to bar the entry of other carriers which can establish clear economic grounds for their extension.[20] In one

---

[16] *Texas & Pacific Ry.* v. *Gulf C. & S. F. Ry. Co.,* 270 U.S. 266, 277 (1926).

[17] *Nashville, C. & St. L. Ry. Construction,* 295 I.C.C. 363, 378–379 (1956), *complaint dismissed sub nom. Georgia* v. *United States,* 156 F. Supp. 711 (N.D. Ga. 1957), *aff'd per curiam* 356 U.S. 273 (1958); *Northern Pac. Ry. Co. Construction,* 295 I.C.C. 281 (1956); *Alabama G. S. R. Co. Construction,* 295 I.C.C. 237 (1956); *Chicago B. & Q. R. Co. Construction,* 282 I.C.C. 725 (1953).

[18] *Chesapeake & O. Ry. Co.* v. *United States,* 283 U.S. 35 (1931), *aff'g* 35 F. 2d 769 (S. D. W. Va. 1929), *aff'g Construction by Virginian & Western Ry.,* 145 I.C.C. 167 (1928).

[19] *Union Pac. R. Co.* v. *Denver & Rio Grande W. R. Co.,* 198 F. 2d 854 (C.A. 10 1952); *Chicago, Milwaukee, St. P. & P. R. Co.* v. *Northern Pac. R. Co.,* 120 F. Supp. 710 (W. D. Wash. 1954), *aff'd* 225 F. 2d 840 (C.A. 9 1955).

[20] *Indian Valley R. R.* v. *United States,* 52 F. 2d 485, 487 (N. D. Calif. 1931), *aff'd per curiam* 292 U.S. 608 (1934). See *St. Mary's R. Co. Construction,* 295 I.C.C. 677 (1958), *aff'd* 312 I.C.C. 178 (1960).

recent example, a new industrial park in Peoria, Illinois was served only by the Rock Island Railroad, which offered through service to the north (Chicago) but could offer only connecting service with carriers to the south (St. Louis).[21] The Chicago & North Western was permitted to build a 1.91 mile extension into the area, costing $231,000 and creating competing service to Chicago, because it could offer through service to the St. Louis area.

With the few exceptions for certificates permitting extensions to be built, the railroad industry is essentially one of blockaded entry. Highly concentrated oligopoly with blockaded entry creates a maximum likelihood of monopolistic output restrictions.[22] In this structural environment, one should expect uncompetitive market conduct and performance.

Market Conduct

Given the structural oligopoly of the railroad industry, is there nevertheless interrailroad conduct that could be described as effective competition? [23] The extent to which price and output decisions are independently made by each firm is crucial to this question. Under imperfect but effective competition, interfirm rivalry usually centers on price. Price is the only component of marketing policy with the short-run flexibility to allow immediate reaction to shifts in demand and costs. The relationships among rail carriers in determining policies of sales promotion and other tactics of long-run market controls are also important. Under each category of market conduct, the degree of interrail rivalry will be evaluated.

Prices.—The outstanding aspect of railroad rate-making is the collusion of the carriers; that is, the absence of competition. The history of railroad-industry pricing is one of cartels. It can be recorded in pools and traffic associations set up to control rates.[24] The profit pools of the nineteenth century were designed to reinforce rate-fixing agreements by making it unprofitable to cut

---

[21] *Chicago & N. W. Ry. Co. Construction,* 312 I.C.C. 639 (1961), *aff'd sub nom. Chicago, Rock Island & P. R. Co.* v. *United States,* 205 F. Supp. 378 (N. D. Ill. 1962). See *Oregon Short Line R. Co. Construction and Operation,* 282 I.C.C. 741 (1953).

[22] Bain, *Industrial Organization* 35 (1959).

[23] For a summary of the tests of market conduct, see Bain, *Industrial Organization* 266–339 (1959); Clark, "Toward a Concept of Workable Competition," 30 *Am. Econ. Rev.* 241–256 (1940).

[24] See 1 Sharfman, *The Interstate Commerce Commission* 79–81 (1931); Troxel, *Economics of Transportation* 428–432 (1955).

rates.[25] When pooling agreements were outlawed in the Interstate Commerce Act,[26] rate-fixing was continued in traffic associations and rate bureaus. The enactment of maximum rate regulation in the Hepburn Act of 1906, while almost ineffective in lowering rates, gave the railroads an administrative peg for their system of price controls. The minimum-rate regulation, added by the Transportation Act of 1920, reinforced collusive rate-fixing by giving statutory approval to floors on price rivalry.[27] In spite of antitrust prosecution, control of rates by rate bureaus continued unhampered through the first four decades of this century.[28] When the rate bureaus came under renewed attack under the Sherman Act,[29] Congress created an antitrust exemption for them in the Reed-Bulwinkle Act of 1948.[30] The statute legalized rate bureaus when and if their procedures for setting rates were approved by the Interstate Commerce Commission. In addition, the Department of Justice charged that the Association of American Railroads participated in rate-making even though this was not exempt from antitrust prosecution.[31] The effect of the legalized joint rate-making has been to assure monopoly pricing for rail services within the constraints of ICC regulations and the competition of trucks and barges for certain commodities.[32]

[25] Ripley, *Railroads Finance and Organization* 575–607 (1915); Grodinsky, *The Iowa Pool* 163–167 (1950); Hudson, "The Southern Railway and Steamship Association," 5 *Q. J. Econ.* 70 (1890).

[26] Ch. 104, 24 Stat. 380 (1887).

[27] 41 Stat. 475, 49 U.S.C. §15(1) (1958). See note, "Minimum Rate Regulation by the Interstate Commerce Commission," 73 *Harv. L. Rev.* 762 (1960); Mansfield, "The Minimum Rate Power and the Control of Carrier Competition," 45 *Yale L. J.* 1406 (1936).

[28] See *United States* v. *Joint Traffic Ass'n.*, 171 U.S. 505 (1898); *United States* v. *Trans-Missouri Freight Ass'n.*, 166 U.S. 290 (1897).

[29] *United States* v. *Association of Am. Railroads,* 4 F.R.D. 510 (Neb. 1945); *Georgia* v. *Pennsylvania R. R.*, 324 U.S. 439 (1945). See Drayton, *Transportation Under Two Masters* (1946); Shott, *The Railroad Monopoly* (1950); Wiprud, *Justice in Transportation* (1945); Hale and Hale, "Competition or Control I: The Chaos of the Cases," 106 *U. of Pa. L. Rev.* 633–648 (1958).

[30] 62 Stat. 472 (1948), 49 U.S.C. §56 (1958). See Dennis, "Immunity of Rate Association Agreements from the Antitrust Laws," 17 *Ohio St. L. J.* 260 (1957); Bridgeman, "The Relief from the Operation of the Antitrust Laws Provided by Section 5a of the Interstate Commerce Act., 29 *ICC Prac. J.* 3 (1961); Daggett, "Railroad Traffic Associations and Antitrust Legislation," 37 *Am. Econ. Rev.* (Papers) 452 (1948).

[31] *Railway Age,* May 28, 1949, at 1095.

[32] Hilton, "Experience Under the Reed-Bulwinkle Act," 28 *ICC Prac. J.* 1207, 1217–1218 (1961). See generally Renshaw, "Utility Regulation: A Re-examination," 31 *J. of Bus.* 335 (1958).

The one significant exception to cartel rate-making is the market competition between groups of railroads in different parts of the country. The group of railroads serving California, for example, may agree to cut the carload rate for transporting oranges to eastern markets in order to meet the rate charged by the group of railroads serving Florida.

It should not be inferred that antitrust enforcement of railroad rate competition between major cities is feasible. Some form of coöperation for making joint and through rates by connecting roads is required.[33] One segment of a railroad is likely to be part of a through route with other connecting roads, while another main line of that railroad may cover the entire through route. When all connecting carriers in an area assemble in a rate bureau to set through routes they cannot avoid the joint setting of rates for their main lines also. The cost of setting rates for thousands of commodities to thousands of cities and towns is substantial and has been minimized by the use of regional rate bureaus. Although the 1948 Act protects individual carriers' rights to deviate from the traffic-bureau rates, the costs of reviewing the work of the bureau makes this rare. Thus, cartel pricing, the key element of railroad market conduct, results necessarily from the structure of the railroad industry.

Service.—The absence of price competition between railroads could conceivably be offset in part by service rivalries. Professor Sorrell has listed the elements of possible service rivalry. They include:

(a) despatch, or time required for getting goods to destination; (b) safety of goods in transit; (c) promptness in settlement of claims, when lost or damaged, and absence of narrow technicalities in the process of adjusting claims; (d) frequency and reliability of the train service; (e) carrier's special equipment for handling such commodities as livestock and perishable articles; (f) carrier's special attention to certain types of traffic; (g) carrier's willingness to trace shipments or keep shipper informed of the movement of important shipments; (h) carrier's willingness to support shipper's desire for change in rates, rules, or classification; (i) situation of the carrier's line, to avoid congested districts, or to constitute an alternative route in times of traffic embargoes.[34]

---

[33] See *In re Trans-Continental Freight Bur.,* 77 I.C.C. 252 (1923).

[34] Sorrell, "Railroad Consolidation—Discussion," 14 *Am. Econ. Rev.* 102, 104 (1924). See Ashton, "Some Aspects of Rail Transport Service," 4 *Transport and Comm. Rev.* 14–23 (1951).

It can be shown, however, that railroad-industry structure and collusion put severe limits on interrailroad service rivalry. With the decline of passenger service and of less-than-carload freight, the major service of railroads is carload freight.

Except for those few commodities whose transit time is purposely extended in order to save warehousing costs or while the owner negotiates their sale, the key aspect of possible rivalry in carload rail freight is speed. The fact that transport service is a homogeneous product centers rivalry on speed. President McGinnis of the Boston and Maine pointed out, however, that speed rivalry is minimal because the multiplicity of railroads means that the responsibility for transport of most shipments is divided by a number of roads.[35] The initial carrier is unable to guarantee the performance of the connecting roads that subsequently carry any shipment. Shippers charge that there is a general lack of coördination and coöperation among railroads. The size of railroads in the United States and the large distances a shipment may cover over a number of railroads make it difficult to place responsibility on one particular person for delays in transit. This has led one shipper to charge that "nobody seems to know what it is all about or perhaps they don't care." [36] This factor has been especially important in the diversion of less-than-carload freight to through truck lines. Rivalry in speed is further limited by the fact that most switching is done at fixed hours in the day or night. Usually, a carrier would have to offer service that was a full 24 hours faster than rivals in order to compete in speed by meeting day-earlier switching schedules.

The fixed roadbed and structural indivisibilities also impede service rivalry. A railroad can seldom run an entire train for the convenience of one customer. A long-haul train of 100 or more cars, hauling goods of many customers on a prescribed schedule is the only economic method of operation. A rail traffic solicitor can offer a potential customer the shortest route only if the fixed line of his railroad goes in the direction in which the customer wants to ship his goods and does go the shortest way. Optimum-size plants for railroad terminal facilities also put severe limits on effective rivalry. Where railroads have attempted service compe-

[35] McGinnis, "Radical Cures for Railroad Ills," *Commercial and Financial Chronicle* 2013, 2030 (Nov. 7, 1957). For a theoretical analysis of time as a product dimension in railroads, see Beckmann, McGuire and Winsten, *Studies in the Economics of Transportation* 113–126 (1956).

[36] *Railway Age*, Oct. 8, 1949, at 649.

tition by investment in duplicate terminals, the results have often been to cause losses for both carriers and increased costs to shippers because the wasteful capital expenditures increase the rate base.[37]

Such minimal service rivalries as could exist are further limited by collusion. In 1947, for example, Robert R. Young, then president of the Chesapeake and Ohio, published advertisements calling for the elimination of aggreements on freight-service schedules. In a controversy with William T. Faricy, president of the Association of American Railroads, Mr. Young charged:

> Mr. Faricy argues that if the roads did not practice deliberate slow-downs so that each road has the same schedule they might have to run shorter trains and more of them. . . . Mr. Faricy would deplore having what he calls freight "speed wars" (on trains now averaging 20 miles per hour)—just as a little while ago some of the roads deplored "quality wars" when they voted to suppress air conditioning. What is wrong with "quality wars" or "service wars"? [38]

The cartel in railroad industry is incomplete in that it does not divide output among railroads in the same market by assigning quotas of the total traffic.[39] Since rate rivalry does not exist among railroads, the question arises of how freight traffic is divided among them. A shipper will deliver loaded cars to that carrier or carriers which serve his sidings. For a large part of freight traffic, the shipper routes the cars to their final destination. He will most likely choose those routes which are most direct and which require the least number of interchanges, in order to avoid delays. For this reason, railroads with long, through routes control a large proportion of railroad traffic.

If the shipper does not control the entire routing of shipment, the initial carrier will be free to choose which connecting carriers will transport the shipment to its final destination. At major connecting points, such as Chicago, St. Louis, Kansas City, and Omaha, an initiating carrier must choose which of a number of connecting lines should receive shipments bound for major cities

---

[37] *Duplication of Produce Terminals*, 188 I.C.C. 323, 324, 333–334 (1932). See comments of Locklin, *Economics of Transportation* 306–307 (5th ed., 1960).

[38] *Railway Age*, Aug. 23, 1947, p. 335; see also, *ibid.*, Sept. 13, 1947, p. 454; *ibid.*, Sept. 20, 1954, p. 491.

[39] On the economic theory of cartels, see Hutt, *op. cit.*, note 1 *supra;* Machlup, *The Economics of Sellers' Competition* 480–490 (1952); Brems, "Cartels and Competition," 66 *Weltwirtschaftliches Archiv* 51 (1951); Patinkin, "Multiplant Firms, Cartels, and Imperfect Competition," 61 *Q. J. Econ.* 173, 192–200 (1947).

on two or more routes. In the absence of price competition, the choice is usually made on the principle of reciprocity.[40] A railroad transfers to connecting carriers as many cars as it receives from them, or, if traffic is not balanced in both directions, a railroad transfers cars to connecting carriers in some proportion to cars received.

But the reciprocity of interchange of connecting railroads is not short-term. A railroad will develop long-run interchange preference patterns to protect its own longest hauls by favoring connecting carriers that are not its rivals for any segment of traffic. Thus, the Chicago and North Western, which has a main line from Chicago to Omaha, has established wide interchange with the complementary Union Pacific which extends from Omaha west to Denver, Ogden, and Portland. Neither the North Western nor the Union Pacific has substantial interchange at Omaha with the Rock Island or the Burlington, both of whose lines run from Chicago to Denver and thus rival the North Western and part of the Union Pacific.

Rivalry between railroads is reported to exist for two types of service. The first is in the speed of local switching service in some areas. The second is in the supply of freight cars during periods of car shortages. The low per-diem rate for the use of another railroad's cars makes it cheaper to use any other railroad's cars than to build them.[41] The effect has been to discourage the building of railroad cars and to cause underinvestment in cars. As a result, during periods of business boom, insufficient cars are available to carry the output of American industry and farms. At these times railroads will vie with each other to supply large shippers with such cars as they can obtain in the hope of establishing long-run preference for their railroads.

One must conclude, however, that interrailroad service rivalry is minimal and is clearly insufficient to create effective competition between railroads. The function of the freight solicitor in dealing with shippers of carload freight is merely informative, to explain the routes and time schedules of trains. His function in dealing with shippers of less-than-carload freight is to

---

[40] See Grodinsky, *Railroad Consolidation: Its Economics and Controlling Principles* 30 (1930). On reciprocity in dealing between railroads and industrial firms, see *Railway Age*, Nov. 17, 1952, at 55.

[41] The per-diem rate cannot be changed without consent of the large majority of American railroads. See Grunfeld, "The Effect of the Per Diem Rate on the Efficiency and Size of the American Railroad Freight-Car Fleet," 32 *J. of Bus.* 52 (1959).

persuade them to ship by rail, meeting the intermodal competition to highway transport. Such minimal service rivalry as does exist between railroads could hardly be expected by itself to enforce the reallocation of resources to adjust to shifting demand and cost conditions.

MARKET PERFORMANCE

The reasoning of industrial-organization economics is that market structure and market conduct are determinants of the quality of market performance. Hence, evidence about market performance in an industry by itself is not sufficient for developing policies of social control. Evidence of market performance in an industry which substantially deviates from the competitive ideal is significant, however, if it confirms the conclusion that the industry's structure and conduct are not effectively competitive. The economic performance of the railroad industry will be evaluated in the light of these premises.

Efficiency.—Efficiency can be viewed as a combination of two main components: (1) internal efficiency of individual firms, and (2) efficiency of the organization of the industry or market. In the first aspect many railroads have responded well to changing market conditions. The drive for profit maximization has tended to promote efficient combination of resources within these firms even under imperfect competition.[42] In the railroad industry relatively increasing labor costs[43] have encouraged the substitution of capital for labor, thereby increasing the physical productivity of labor.[44] But this is the only large aspect in which there has been a reallocation of resources in response to market forces.

As to the industry or market, the second aspect of efficiency, "ideal performance would involve all output being produced by plants and firms of optimal scale, with an optimal degree of integration and without any chronic excess capacity." [45] Under competition, firms failing to minimize costs should eventually be driven from the industry. But railroad industry structure has failed com-

[42] See Dewey, "Imperfect Competition No Bar to Efficient Production," 66 *J. Pol. Econ.* 24 (1958); Rothschild, "The Wastes of Competition," in *Monopoly and Competition and Their Regulation* 303–304 (Chamberlin ed. 1954).

[43] Healy, "The Problem—Rational and Effective Allocation of Resources," 345 *The Annals* 39, 43 (1963).

[44] Barger, *The Transportation Industries 1889–1946: A Study of Output, Employment, and Productivity* 93–98 (1951); Nelson, *Railroad Transportation and Public Policy* 233–283 (1959).

[45] Bain, *Industrial Organization* 362 (1959).

pletely to adjust the size of firms to changing cost and demand conditions. Absence of rate competition has resulted in carriers with the most indirect routes and worst grades and curves remaining in business even though more efficient parallel carriers could adequately handle all business. Reorganization provisions of the bankruptcy statute have enabled least efficient railroads to continue when they should have been dismembered and only minor segments sold to adjacent carriers for continued operation. Railroad managements have generally failed to negotiate trackage and joint-operating agreements to enable abandonment of particular parallel sections of line or discontinuance of parallel, duplicate passenger services operated at a loss.[46] Statutory controls on pooling agreements, consolidations, and abandonments have also impeded adjustments in sizes of firms.[47] Even the estimated economies of consolidation resulting from the elimination of duplicate facilities, which would create no economies of scale, are hard to effect. Alleged diminution of competition and protection of other weak railroads are important in Interstate Commerce Commission reviews of mainline-railroad merger proposals. Obtaining agreeable merger terms in the light of complex financial structures and statutory protections for labor are also obstacles to unification.[48]

Chronic excess capacity and overinvestment in the railroad industry as a whole have existed for at least forty years, and interrailroad competition has not been effective in forcing firms to remedy this misallocation of resources. One of the earliest studies pointed out that the degree of interrailroad competition was too ineffective to eliminate this and therefore recommended pooling agreements under government control as a superior regulator of railroad resource allocation.[49] Other studies have demonstrated the need for consolidation to eliminate unneeded excess capacity in railroads.[50] President Greenough of the Pennsylvania charges that lax management must take at least part of the blame for this

[46] Dewey, "Problems of Transport Organization" in U.S. National Resources Planning Board, *Transportation and National Policy* 148 (1942).

[47] See Chaps. III, V, and VI.

[48] Sampson, *Obstacles to Railroad Unification* 18 (1960).

[49] Newcomb, "Railway Competition: A Problem in Statistics," 5 *J. Am. Stat. Ass'n.* 65 (1896).

[50] Splawn, *Consolidation of Railroads* (1925); Grodinsky, *Railroad Consolidation: Its Economics and Controlling Principles* (1930); Leonard, *Railroad Consolidation Under the Transportation Act of 1920* (1946); Behling, *Railroad Coordination and Consolidation: A Review of Economies* (ICC Bureau of Statistics 1940); Bruck, "A Plan to Save the Railroads," *Fortune*, Aug., 1958, at 82.

failure.[51] The government planning of railroad consolidations to protect weak carriers under the 1920 statute was eliminated in the Transportation Act of 1940. In the twenty years since 1940, market forces still have not had the strength to cause management to initiate any substantial move toward economic rationalization.

Progressiveness in Techniques.—The progressiveness of an industry is measured by the degree with which it exploits the available opportunities for invention and innovation.[52] Under imperfect but effective competition, invention and the innovation of new methods are ways in which existing firms may gain short-run differential advantage and new firms may gain an entry into imperfect markets. But the fixed roadbed structure and barred entry in the railroad industry greatly reduce the advantage over other railroads to be gained from innovation and eliminate the pressures from possible innovation by potential competitors. Consequently, railroad management had been concerned almost exclusively with current operations and neglected the pursuit of new methods until the recent great increase in intermodal competition. President McGinnis described this as a failure to recognize the need for effective managers, a lack of vision and imagination in the industry. Using hotboxes and outmoded, labor-consuming couplers as examples, he commented: "In the freight end of it, our greatest weakness is service. We haven't improved the service enough in the last 40 years to stick in your eye." [53]

Professor Lang, a former railroad officer, has pointed to some of the obstacles to technological change in railroads.[54] Not only is there an inherent inertia of large proportions, but the need for industry-wide standardization means that radical changes must await the concurrence of all major roads. Furthermore, significant innovations do not evolve as a matter of course. Automatic trains and complete new designs for freight cars require long-run industry planning of large-scale research. But this also requires long-range capital planning. And the weak financial condition of the railroads sharply limits the large capital expenditures that can be made to overcome the technological lag.[55]

---

[51] Greenough, "Taking a Critical Look at Railroad Management," *Commercial and Financial Chronicle,* April 21, 1960, at 1742.

[52] Bain, *Industrial Organization* 395 (1959).

[53] McGinnis, note 35 *supra,* at 2013.

[54] Lang, "New Goals for R. R. Research," *Railway Age,* Aug. 22, 1960, at 27.

[55] See Nelson, "Technological Change and the Railway's Need for Capital," in *Technological Change and the Future of the Railways* 63–80 (Nelson & Johnson,

Progressive pursuit and adoption of technological change is likely to exist within an industry characterized by product rivalry which will orient management to plan for change.[56] Railroad freight and passenger service has not been characterized by such interfirm rivalry. On the contrary, the available evidence indicates a general failure of the railroads to exploit the available opportunities for invention and innovation until the intermodal competition of highway and air carriers forced such changes upon them.[57] The three-level auto rack freight car, for example, was not developed until 1959 when a great part of auto transport had already moved to highway carriers.[58] The mechanical structure of such specialized freight cars indicates that research and development on them twenty years earlier would have enabled the railroads to prevent the loss of so much transport to trucks. Similar allegations have been made regarding trailer on flat-car service. The introduction of more powerful engines just before World War II, which made for faster freight trains, and the design of some new specialized types of freight cars were admitted to be in response to motor-truck rivalry.[59] Likewise, in passenger service, the introduction of the light-weight, streamlined trains was attributed to airline and bus rivalry and did not arise from interrailroad competition.[60]

In the area of research, as in prices and service, trade-association dominance further limits the possibility of interrail competition. Such research as is being done by railroads is centered in trade associations, especially the Association of American Railroads.[61] The results of these investigations become the property of all members, not the competitive advantage of any one.

Profits.—The absence of effective price or service competition among railroads, taken by itself, would lead one to expect con-

---

eds. 1961); Behling, "The Causes and Cure of Railroads' Ills," *Commercial and Financial Chronicle*, Aug. 18, 1960, at 651, 678.

[56] See Healy, "Management and Technological Change," in *Technological Change and the Future of the Railways* 126 (Nelson & Johnson, eds. 1961).

[57] See U.S. Board of Investigation and Research, *Technological Trends in Transportation* 2–4 (S. Doc. 76, 79th Cong. 1st Sess. 1945).

[58] *Railway Age*, May 1, 1961, at 12.

[59] Barriger, "Super Railroads to Meet Post-War Rivalry," *Railway Age*, Oct. 18, 1941, at 610. See, *ibid.*, May 25, 1940, at 885, 910; *ibid.*, Feb. 25, 1950, at 392.

[60] Statement of George A. Kelly, vice-president of Pullman Co. in *Railway Age*, Feb. 17, 1940, at 330. See *Business Week*, Oct. 19, 1946, at 46.

[61] Wall, "Customers' Needs Being Intently Studied," *Railway Age*, May 18, 1946, at 994. See Association of American Railroads, *Annual Report* 45–48 (1960).

tinuously high monopoly profits in railroads. Chronic excess capacity in lines and intense intermodal competition, however, makes the railroad industry one of relatively low profits.[62] State regulatory commissions have required most major lines to continue unprofitable passenger services.[63] The competition of highway and water carrier has also diverted freight revenues from railroads.[64] For these reasons, low profits cannot be indicative of interrailroad competition.

CONCLUSIONS

The structure of the railroad industry and the necessary statutory controls preclude effective interrailroad competition.[65] Like the electric utilities,[66] maximum railroad rates and service (except for commodities for which active intermodal competition exists) can be made to conform to welfare criteria only by commission regulation.[67] The railroads can minimize costs and, for services where intermodal competition of water, highway, and air carriers exists, meet this competition only if they are able to reallocate investment in fixed plant to accommodate for long-run shifts in demand. For this reason, railroad consolidations should be encouraged by statute.[68] The preservation of interrailroad compe-

[62] U.S. Cong., Senate, Committee on Interstate and Foreign Commerce, *National Transportation Policy* (87th Cong. 1st Sess. 1961), pp. 66, 75.

[63] *Ibid.*, 273–343. The railroad passenger deficit on the basis of fully distributed costs was $485.2 million in 1960, $408.2 million in 1961 and $394.0 million in 1962. U.S. Interstate Commerce Commission, *Transport Economics,* May 1961, p. 1, and May 1963, p. 2.

[64] U.S. Cong., House, Committee on Interstate and Foreign Commerce, *Transportation Diversification,* Hearings (86th Cong. 2d Sess. 1960).

[65] For a similar conclusion, see Melton, "Transport Coordination and Regulatory Philosophy," 24 *Law and Contemp. Prob.* 623 (1959).

[66] The structural similarities of railroads to electric utilities, where the preservation of competition is now never urged as a regulatory criterion, is stressed by the Special Study Group on Transportation Policies in the United States. U.S. Cong., Senate, Committee on Interstate and Foreign Commerce, Report on *National Transportation Policy* 260–261 (87th Cong. 1st Sess. 1961). See Whitlow, "The Failure of Competition in Public Utility Regulation," 39 *Public Util. Fort.* 597 (1947).

[67] For economic arguments supporting greater intermodal competition, see Nelson, "New Concepts in Transportation Regulation," in U.S. National Resources Planning Board, *Transportation and National Policy* 204–205 (1942); Adams and Gray, *Monopoly in America* 58–62 (1955); Roberts, "The Regulation of Transport Price Competition," 24 *Law and Contemp. Prob.* 557 (1959). None of these arguments has force when applied to railroads alone.

[68] See comments of Commissioner K. H. Tuggle, "Outlook for Railroad Consolidation and Mergers," in National Association of Railroad and Utilities Commissioners, *Proceedings,* 1960 Convention (1961) at 245; J. W. Barriger, "Why Consolidation?" in *Revolution in Transportation* (Ruppenthal ed. 1960) at 12–42.

tition should not be a criterion in the regulation of consolidations, since in effect it does not exist. Commission and judicial interpretations of public interest should not create the delusion that interrailroad competition is an operative social control when such delusion can only hinder the enactment of effective regulatory statutes and thereby impede the economic allocation of resources.

III

Railroad Consolidations and the Antitrust Laws

The application of the economics of industrial organization to railroads, as developed in the first two chapters, can be used to evaluate the history of the antitrust constraint on railroad consolidations.* Prosecution of railroad mergers and consolidations under the antitrust laws have had a profound effect in limiting such combinations. The preservation of competition as a public-interest standard in Commission approval of consolidations remains in effect during the railroad-merger movement of the 1960's. An economic critique of the court and Commission decisions will determine the scope and impact of this standard.

The Sherman Act of 1890 [1] did not contain an exemption for railroads or other regulated industries. Since the Interstate Commerce Act[2] of 1887 had not given the Commission power to set maximum rates or to control consolidations, it must be inferred that Congress expected the antitrust laws to be applied to railroads. Two early Supreme Court decisions confirmed this inference.[3] And even when maximum-rate regulation was enacted in the Hepburn Act of 1906,[4] Congress created no antitrust exemption for railroads.

* This chapter is a revised version of an article with the same title which appeared in 14 *Stanford Law Review* 489 (1962).

[1] 26 Stat. 209, 15 U.S.C. §§1–7 (1958).

[2] 24 Stat. 379, 49 U.S.C. §1 (1958).

[3] *United States* v. *Joint Traffic Ass'n.*, 171 U.S. 505, 560 (1898); *United States* v. *Trans-Missouri Freight Ass'n.*, 166 U.S. 290, 341 (1897).

[4] Act of June 29, 1906, ch. 3591, 34 Stat. 584 (codified in scattered sections of 49 U.S.C.).

Since the Transportation Act of 1920, railroad consolidations approved by the Commission are exempt from antitrust prosecution.[5] But the effect on competition as measured by antitrust standards is one major factor in ICC determination of whether any particular consolidation is in the public interest.[6] For this reason the whole body of Supreme Court decisions on railroad consolidations under the antitrust laws must be surveyed in order to assess the significance of the antitrust factor in such cases before the ICC today. The 1912 *Union Pacific* case,[7] for example, was quoted as binding authority in the brief of the United States Department of Justice in the Seaboard-Atlantic Coast Line[8] merger, approved by the ICC in 1963.

SHERMAN ACT PROSECUTIONS TO 1920

The first application of the Sherman Act to a railroad consolidation occurred in *Northern Sec. Co. v. United States*.[9] Northern Securities Company, incorporated to acquire control of the shares of the Great Northern and Northern Pacific railroads, was found to be an illegal combination in restraint of trade and an attempt to monopolize in violation of sections 1 and 2 of the Sherman Act.[10] The two railroads were parallel and were the only railroads between their common terminal points in St. Paul and Seattle. More than one-half of their lines were farther apart than 100 miles, however, and more than 70 per cent of the interstate traffic moving between two stations on one of the railroads was between towns not served by the other road.[11] The alleged competition, which the trial court found would be illegally restrained by the consolidation, was minimal, if it existed at all. Professor Meyer, a leading transportation economist who later was a member of the

---

[5] Transportation Act of 1920, ch. 91, §407, 41 Stat. 482 (now Interstate Commerce Act §5b(9), added by ch. 491, 62 Stat. 472 (1948), 49 U.S.C. §5b(9) (1958).

[6] *Minneapolis & St. L. Ry. v. United States*, 361 U.S. 173, 187 (1959).

[7] *United States v. Union Pacific R.R.*, 226 U.S. 61 (1912).

[8] Brief for U.S. Department of Justice, pp. 31–33, Seaboard Air Line R.R., Finance No. 21215, ICC, Oct. 30, 1961.

[9] 193 U.S. 197 (1904), *affirming* 120 Fed. 721 (D. Minn. 1903). An earlier attempt to consolidate these roads was held to violate a Minnesota statute prohibiting combinations of railroads with parallel or competing lines. *Pearsall v. Great No. R.R.*, 161 U.S. 646 (1896). A later action by the State of Minnesota against Northern Securities Company under both state and federal antitrust statutes was dismissed for lack of federal jurisdiction. *Minnesota v. Northern Sec. Co.*, 194 U.S. 48 (1904).

[10] 26 Stat. 209 (1890), 15 U.S.C. §§1, 2 (1958).

[11] Meyer, "A History of the Northern Securities Case," *University of Wis. Bull.* No. 142, at 247 (1906).

Interstate Commerce Commission, concluded his study of this case with findings exactly opposite to those made by the courts:

Whatever may be said for or against the Securities Company, it can scarcely be maintained that it affected the competitive relations of the two companies in any substantial manner. . . . They [Great Northern and Northern Pacific] are not, and have not been, competitive with respect to any but an inappreciable part of their total traffic.[12]

For twenty years before the organization of Northern Securities the two railroads had a community of interest that prevented competitive rivalry.[13] In 1901 Great Northern and Northern Pacific each bought one-half of the stock of the Chicago, Burlington & Quincy Railroad, giving them joint ownership of a line from St. Paul to Chicago. Joint rates from points on the Burlington, or from eastern cities to towns served by both Great Northern and Northern Pacific, were necessarily made in conference with the Burlington and other carriers. In fact, 97 per cent of the total interstate traffic of the two companies was carried under joint tariffs made in conference with more than a hundred other railroads.[14] In spite of these facts of market structure, the court ordered the holding company dissolved. However, this was accomplished by distributing the Northern Pacific and Great Northern shares pro rata to the Northern Securities shareholders.[15] The effect was to continue the same community of interest in control of the two roads,[16] while preventing the economies that would have resulted from consolidated operation.

In *United States* v. *Union Pac. R.R.*,[17] the stringent application of the Sherman Act to railroads was continued. In 1901 Union

[12] *Id.* at 254.

[13] *Id.* at 227 (citing testimony of James J. Hill).

[14] *Id.* at 246.

[15] An action by Union Pacific interests to enjoin this perpetuation of control by the Hill-Morgan group and recover the entire block of Northern Pacific shares they had sold to Northern Securities was dismissed. *Harriman* v. *Northern Sec. Co.,* 197 U.S. 244 (1905).

[16] Ripley, *Railroads—Finance and Organization* 498 (1915), notes that no outward change resulted from dissolution. "Harmony in rate policy has been unbroken; and in all subsequent changes in rates, the roads have acted practically as a unit." In 1926, for example, a tabulation showed the majority of stock of Great Northern and Northern Pacific to be owned by the same persons. *Great No. Pac. Co.,* 162 I.C.C. 37, 44 (1930); see U.S. Cong. House, Committee on Interstate and Foreign Commerce *Hearings on Regulation of Stock Ownership in Railroads,* 71st Cong., 2d Sess., pt. 1, at 382–395 (1931).

[17] 226 U.S. 61 (1912); see Daggett, "The Decision on the Union Pacific Merger," 27 *Q. J. Econ.* 295 (1913).

Pacific acquired control of Southern Pacific by purchase of 46 per cent of the latter's outstanding stock. The Southern Pacific line was a sea route from New York to New Orleans, and then a rail route from New Orleans to Los Angeles, San Francisco, and Portland.[18] The Union Pacific line extended from Omaha and Kansas City west to Ogden and thence northwest to Portland. But in the fiscal year preceding the acquisition of Southern Pacific, only .46 per cent of Union Pacific total tonnage was shipped from the eastern states to Portland. For the rest of the transcontinental traffic, Union Pacific was merely a bridge carrier, receiving freight from eastern railroads and carrying it west to Ogden. There, the cars had to be turned over to the Southern Pacific for movement to San Francisco, since, before 1908, the Central Pacific branch of Southern Pacific was the only route from Ogden to San Francisco. The necessary continuous coöperation of the two roads in planning rates and service over their joint route precluded competition between them.

The Justice Department alleged that competition for transcontinental traffic had been restrained by the combination. The trial court dismissed the action after finding that no substantial competition existed between the two railroads.[19] The Supreme Court reversed the lower court and made a finding that competition between the Union Pacific and Southern Pacific was substantial.[20] The finding was based primarily on testimony of railroad witnesses and shippers that both roads maintained soliciting offices in eastern cities. Since before the merger there was collusive fixing of rates, and since the transport time of the Union Pacific joint route by land was less than the Southern Pacific route by sea and rail because of a shorter route and the speed of trains, rivalry could only center on the handling of goods and the adjustment of claims. But goods handled by the Union Pacific on transcontinental runs also had to be handled by the Southern Pacific for the western 800 miles. It would be hard for shippers to determine which one of the four to seven railroads on a transcontinental carriage mishandled goods. In sum, the Supreme Court's reversal of the extensive findings of the trial court that there was no substantial competition rested more on a general condemnation of the aggregated economic power of the Harriman interests than on conviction that

[18] *United States* v. *Union Pac. R.R.*, 188 Fed. 102, 110 (D. Utah 1911).
[19] *Id.* at 102.
[20] 226 U.S. at 86–90.

the two railroads had been or could be made into competitors.[21] In carrying out the remedy in this case attempts to continue common control of the stock of the two roads were frustrated,[22] and complete divestiture was effected.[23]

United States v. *Southern Pac. Co.*[24] was another action in which the Supreme Court reversed a district-court dismissal of an antitrust attack on a railroad consolidation. Southern Pacific and Central Pacific had been under common control from the beginning of construction of the Southern Pacific in 1870. In 1885 Southern Pacific, having become dominant, leased all lines of Central Pacific. In 1899, as a result of settlement of the Central Pacific debt to the United States, the stock of Central Pacific was acquired by Southern Pacific. The Justice Department charged that this acquisition violated the antitrust laws. The district court found that the railroads were a single interdependent system and had never competed, and that the government had conceded that their joint operation was legal.[25] The Supreme Court reversal treated the Central Pacific line from San Francisco to Ogden as a separate link in another transcontinental route that should have competed with the Southern Pacific route via New Orleans and sea connection to New York. The Court thus used the argument that was the basis for decision in the *Union Pacific* case. And, as in the *Union Pacific* case, the Supreme Court refused to recognize that each route had a natural economic advantage in its own area of the West, and that

---

[21] This followed the conclusions of an earlier independent investigation by the Interstate Commerce Commission. 12 I.C.C. 277 (1907).

[22] A Union Pacific proposal to distribute its Southern Pacific shares to the Union Pacific stockholders, the remedy approved in the *Northern Securities* case, was in this instance vetoed by the Supreme Court. *United States* v. *Union Pac. R.R.* 226 U.S. 470 (1913).

[23] The decision of the Supreme Court, ordering the Union Pacific to sell its Southern Parific shares, stated that nothing in the Court's instructions was to be construed as preventing the Union Pacific from retaining the Central Pacific properties from Ogden to San Francisco. 226 U.S. at 97. At this time, the Attorney General was attempting to persuade the Southern Pacific to sell the Central Pacific in order to avoid further litigation in the government's attack on the Harriman interests. Daggett, "Later Developments in Union Pacific Merger Case," 28 *Q. J. Econ.* 772, 773 (1914). A subsequent plan to sell the Central Pacific to the Union Pacific was opposed by the California Railroad Commission on the ground that the local lines of the Central Pacific in California had become integral parts of the Southern Pacific and dissolution would impair the efficiency of rail service in that area. 2 OPS. CAL. R.R. COMM'N 233 (1913). Union Pacific finally divested itself of the Southern Pacific stock by exchanging most of it with the Pennsylvania for Baltimore & Ohio shares.

[24] 259 U.S. 214 (1922).

[25] *United States* v. *Southern Pac. Co.* 239 Fed. 998 (D. Utah 1917).

the potential competition was minimal where the routes were hundreds of miles apart and one was all rail whereas the other was half by sea. The divestiture decreed in this case was never carried out because of relief granted under the Transportation Act of 1920.

United States v. *Lehigh Valley R.R.*[26] was a third case in which a district court dismissal was reversed by the Supreme Court. This case, which primarily concerned exclusive dealing agreements between coal producing and selling subsidiaries of a railroad, also involved Lehigh control of the Delaware, Susquehanna & Schuylkill Railroad. The 45-mile, disconnected Delaware line owned no equipment and merely leased its roadbed to the Lehigh, since it was too small to operate efficiently by itself. Nevertheless, as part of the antitrust decree against the control of the coal subsidiaries, the Lehigh was ordered to divest itself of the Delaware line. This decree, like the one in the Southern Pacific case, was not carried out because special relief was granted under the Transportation Act of 1920.

The second *Reading Railroad* case,[27] also primarily a combination of coal companies, incidentally involved holding company control of the Philadelphia & Reading Railroad and the Central Railroad of New Jersey. In the carriage of coal the two roads were not competitive since their lines reached different mines.[28] Yet, as part of the dissolution demanded in the case, the common control of these carriers was ordered severed.

One consent decree was issued in dissolving a railroad unification. The New York, New Haven & Hartford consented in 1914 to divest itself of its controlling interest in the Boston and Maine.[29] This brought to an end the New Haven plans for control of the New England railroad system.[30] Although no other antitrust actions against railroad mergers took place before 1920, there were

[26] 254 U.S. 255 (1920).

[27] *United States* v. *Reading Co.*, 253 U.S. 26 (1920). The first *Reading* case, *United States* v. *Reading Co.*, 226 U.S. 324 (1912), involved a loose-knit combination of six railroads to control coal companies and the transportation of coal. See Jones, *The Anthracite Coal Combinations in the United States* (1914).

[28] *United States* v. *Reading Co.*, 226 Fed. 229, 271 (E.D. Pa. 1915).

[29] U.S. Department of Justice, *Decrees and Judgments in Federal Anti-trust Cases* 529 (1918).

[30] Ripley, *op. cit.*, note 16 *supra*, at 462–473, 571–573; see *New York, N.H. & H.R.R.*, 31 I.C.C. 32 (1914); *New Eng. Investigation*, 27 I.C.C. 560, 592 (1913). For state actions see *Attorney General* v. *New York, N.H. & H.R.R.*, 201 Mass. 370, 87 N.E. 621 (1909), and *Attorney General* v. *New York, N.H. & H.R.R.*, 198 Mass. 413, 84 N.E. 737 (1908).

a number of instances where stock control was dissolved under pressure from the Justice Department. Among these were the sale by the Pennsylvania of its Baltimore & Ohio shares and disposal by the New York Central of its controlling interest in the Nickel Plate.[31]

The pertinent question in these pre-1920 cases is why there was such a severe and strict application of the Sherman Act to railroad consolidations. In this period most divestiture actions by the government in manufacturing industries were unsuccessful.[32] Logically one would expect even more lenient application of the antitrust laws to railroads because their structural characteristics creating monopoly power led to governmental regulation to prevent abuse of that power.[33] The passage of the Interstate Commerce Act and the Hepburn Act was public recognition that competition could not be expected to operate in its usual automatic way in the railroad industry. Yet the railroad antitrust cases were all won by the government without any proof of abuse of monopoly power and, in most cases, without substantial evidence that the merging railroads ever had been or could be made competitive.

Dean Levi suggests that the stricter application of the Sherman Act to railroads was based on the Court's view that firms which have received a governmental grant of monopoly in a franchise should be barred from any actions that would extend the grant.[34] But the political environment was an additional factor. Agriculture and small-business groups had centered their antimonopoly sentiments on the railroads. And the *Northern Securities* case,[35] decided before the enactment of maximum-rate regulation and before the Court adopted the rule of reason in cases of nonancillary restraints, was a strong precedent for strict application of the Sherman Act to railroad consolidations. For these reasons the Attorney General in the Roosevelt trust-busting era could make railroad consolidations his prime target and receive the publicity of

[31] Senate Rep. No. 1182, 76th Cong., 3d Sess., 61–107 (1940).

[32] Adams, "Dissolution, Divorcement, Divestiture: The Pyrrhic Victories of Antitrust," 27 *Ind. L. J.* 1 (1951). The government lost the leading industrial merger prosecution of this period, the Supreme Court ruling that "the law does not make mere size an offence or the existence of unexerted power an offence." *United States* v. *United States Steel Corp.*, 251 U.S. 417, 451 (1920). See generally Handler, "Industrial Mergers and the Anti-Trust Laws," 32 *Colum. L. Rev.* 179 (1932).

[33] Note, "Application of the Sherman and Clayton Acts to Holding Companies Organized by Parent Railroad Corporations," 78 *U. Pa. L. Rev.* 652, 654 (1930).

[34] Levi, "The Antitrust Laws and Monopoly," 14 *U. Chi. L. Rev.* 153, 157 (1947) (citing *Northern Sec. Co.* v. *United States,* 193 U.S. 197, 363 (1904) (Brewer, J., concurring).

[35] *Northern Sec. Co.* v. *United States,* 193 U.S. 197 (1904).

victory in every case, whereas he was generally unsuccessful in trying to dissolve industrial mergers. The Supreme Court seemed to have succumbed to the antirailroad policies of the Attorney General, even though the trial courts in at least three cases had found no substantial competition between consolidating carriers.

TRANSPORTATION ACT OF 1920

The Transportation Act of 1920 [36] gave the Interstate Commerce Commission its first jurisdiction over railroad unifications with respect to two methods of combination: Consolidations, which were covered by sections 5(4) to 5(6); and acquisitions of control not involving consolidation, covered in section 5(2). Section 5(8) relieved the carriers from the operation of the antitrust laws when a unification under any paragraph of section 5 was approved by the Commission.

Only four complete consolidations were approved by the Commission,[37] so that the consolidation provisions of the 1920 act were deemed a failure.[38] Section 5(4) required the Commission to draw a comprehensive plan for consolidation of railroads in the United States and also required it to take into account as fully as possible the following factors: Preservation of competition; maintenance of existing routes and channels of trade; and arrangement of carriers so that systems could earn substantially the same rate of return under a uniform system of rates. Under section 5(6), no consolidation proposed by carriers could be approved that did not conform to the final plan. The comprehensive consolidation plan failed primarily because it was designed to save weak railroads by causing strong railroads to absorb them,[39] and this the strong railroads, already burdened with excess capacity, refused to do. In addition, the criteria of preserving competition and maintaining existing routes were inconsistent with any policy of consolidation that would eliminate the excess capacity in duplicate facilities. Furthermore, the final plan was not completed until 1929,[40] and

[36] Chap. 91, 41 Stat. 456.

[37] Leonard, *Railroad Consolidation under the Transportation Act of 1920*, at 259 (1946).

[38] *Id.* at 256–286.

[39] See Herring, *The Problem of Weak Railroads* 99–124 (1929); Leonard, *op. cit.*, note 38 *supra*, at 281; Splawn, *The Consolidation of Railroads* 7–29 (1925); Moore, *Our Lagging Railway Mergers*, 15 *Va. L. Rev.* 743 (1929).

[40] *Consolidation of R.Rs.*, 159 I.C.C. 522 (1929), *modified*, 183 I.C.C. 663 (1932). The tentative plan is found in *Consolidation of R.Rs.*, 63 I.C.C. 455 (1921). See Bledsoe, "Consolidation and Coordination Problems," 17 *Acad. Pol. Sci. Proc.* 250, 252 (1937).

soon thereafter railroad bankruptcies created insurmountable financial barriers to consolidations.

Acquisitions of control under lease, by purchase of stock or other means not involving complete consolidation, as provided in section 5(2), became the primary method of railroad combination between 1920 and 1940. This section tested the acquisition only against the criterion of "public interest," and did not demand conformity to the general plan of consolidation. But the whole regulatory scheme was rather peculiar. Although the specific "preservation of competition" criterion of the consolidations section was not repeated in section 5(2), the effect on competition was one factor of public interest considered in the cases. As noted in detail later, the most common definition of competition in the Commission decisions was that two railroads served common points. Competition was thus defined as the possibility of competition, regardless of the scope of the cartels preventing interfirm rivalry.

Many acquisitions of control were achieved by virtually complete stock ownership and long-term leases of lines, which produced the same economic effects as a complete consolidation.[41] Consolidations carried out under state law were also held by the Commission not to require approval under federal law.[42] Furthermore, until passage of the Emergency Railroad Transportation Act of 1933, stock control of two or more railroads by a nonoperating holding company was held not to be regulated by section 5(2).[43] Consequently, before 1933, indirect unification of carriers was unregulated, while consolidations and acquisitions of control —the methods that could effect real operating economies—required Commission approval.

The cases decided under section 5(2) illustrate the view of the Commission and of Congress in passing the 1920 act that interrailroad competition was much less important since rates and service had become subject to extensive regulation.[44] This is illustrated

[41] *Alabama & V. Ry.*, 111 I.C.C. 161, 179–180 (1926) (Eastman, Comm'r, dissenting); *El Paso & Southwestern Sys.*, 90 I.C.C. 732, 739 (1924) (same).

[42] *New York, C. & St. L.R.R.*, 79 I.C.C. 581, 586 (1923). For effects of the Transportation Act of 1920 on state laws which restricted the consolidation of parallel or competing railroads see *People* v. *Illinois Cent. R.R.*, 324 Ill. 591, 155 N.E. 841, 51 A.L.R. 1236 (1927); Quarles, "Consolidation of Interstate Railroads," 20 *Va. L. Rev.* 200 (1933); Note, "Railroad Consolidation and State Corporations," 31 *Colum. L. Rev.* 651 (1931).

[43] *Denver & R.G.W.R.R.*, 70 I.C.C. 102, 105 (1921); see Ansnes, "Federal Regulation of Railroad Holding Companies," 32 *Colum. L. Rev.* 999 (1932). For a key example see Senate Rep. No. 714, 77th Cong., 1st Sess. (1942).

[44] See Daniels, "The Changing Attitude of Public Policy Toward Railroad Consolidation," 13 *Acad. Pol. Sci. Proc.* 433 (1929)

first by three Commission decisions approving acquisitions which, before 1920, had been held to violate the Sherman Act. Southern Pacific was allowed to retain control of Central Pacific, reversing the dissolution order of the Supreme Court in the *Southern Pacific* case.[45] The Commission found that the lines of the carriers in California and Oregon were one integrated unit, that dissolution would "disrupt existing routes and service" and result in "increased cost of operation and duplication of capital investment in railroad facilities and increased cost of transportation" to shippers.[46] The new investment required to operate Central Pacific independently would create unneeded excess capacity in rail lines and terminals, and the Commission doubted that Central Pacific had the financial ability to sustain the heavy burden of fixed charges necessary to make this investment. The Commission also approved retention by the Lehigh Valley of its stock in the Delaware, Susquehanna & Schuylkill.[47] This nullified the divestiture order in the Lehigh Valley case,[48] the Commission noting that operation of the Delaware as a separate road was not economically feasible. In a third decision the Commission approved the merger of Great Northern and Northern Pacific, thus permitting the consolidation that was dissolved in the *Northern Securities* case.[49] The Commission found that no material loss of competition would result, since the west-coast cities and the eastern termini were also served by the Milwaukee or the Union Pacific.[50] The carriers chose not to carry out this merger, since the Commission conditioned approval on their divesting themselves of control of the Burlington. The condition was occasioned by the Burlington's placement in another system under the Commission's comprehensive plan for railroad consolidation.

In almost all cases where lessening of competition was urged as an objection to acquisitions of control, the Commission found it offset by other factors in the public interest. The leading case was

[45] Control of Cent. Pac. by So. Pac., 76 I.C.C. 508 (1923). In a subsequent suit by the Department of Justice, Southern Pacific was relieved from the operation of the Sherman Act so far as necessary to carry out the Commission's plan. *United States v. Southern Pac. Co.*, 290 Fed. 443 (D. Utah 1923). The approval was conditioned on Southern Pacific joining Union Pacific in maintaining continuous through routes and schedules from Chicago to west coast cities. See Blair, "Process and Results of Railroad Unification," 13 *Acad. Pol. Sci. Proc.* 339, 342–344 (1929).

[46] 76 I.C.C. at 518–519.

[47] *Delaware, S. & S.R.R.*, 86 I.C.C. 567 (1924).

[48] *United States v. Lehigh Valley R.R.*, 254 U.S. 255 (1920).

[49] *Great No. Pac. Ry.*, 162 I.C.C. 37 (1930); see note 9 *supra*.

[50] 162 I.C.C. at 69. Only 1.8 per cent of the tons of traffic, equal to 2.7 per cent of freight revenues, were from towns served only by the two carriers. *Id.* at 55.

New York Cent. S. Corp. v. *United States.*[51] Applicant was authorized to lease the lines of the Big Four and the Michigan Central,
two roads it had previously controlled by stock ownership. Although the Commission had made no detailed findings on competition, the issue was treated by the courts on appeal. The Supreme Court stated:

> . . . the fact that the carriers' lines are parallel and competing cannot
> be deemed to affect the validity of the authority conferred upon the
> Commission. . . . The question whether the acquisition of control in
> the case of competing carriers will aid in preventing an injurious
> waste and in securing more efficient transportation service is thus com-
> mitted to the judgment of the administrative agency upon the facts
> developed in the particular case.[52]

The Commission has stated that "competition between carriers,
within the purpose of section 5 of the act, exists wherever there is
such possibility of election of routes as may have an influence upon
service or rates." [53] Since rates were fixed by rate bureaus and
service determined primarily by the route of the lines and the state
of technology in operating equipment, this definition was rather
chimerical. In most cases where there were parallel lines, competition was presumed to exist between common points served by two
or more carriers.[54] But mere parallel lines meeting at only one
terminal were not presumed to create competition since the lines
would serve different communities and industrial sections.[55] In
the large group of cases where intervenors alleged that the acquisition of control would lessen competition, the issue appears more
contrived than real. Whether the acquired lines were parallel or
complementary to the acquiring line, the intervenors were ob-
viously apprehensive that new and more efficient through routes
would be created that would rival intervenors' through routes[56] or

---

[51] 287 U.S. 12 (1932), *affirming* 54 F.2d 122 (S.D.N.Y. 1931), *affirming New York Cent. Unification*, 150 I.C.C. 278 (1929); see 154 I.C.C. 489 (1929) (subsequent proceedings); 158 I.C.C. 317 (1929) (same).

[52] 287 U.S. at 25–26.

[53] *Wheeling & L.E. Ry.*, 138 I.C.C. 643, 649 (1928).

[54] See, e.g., *Alabama & V. Ry.*, 111 I.C.C. 161, 169 (1926); *International-Great No. R.R.*, 90 I.C.C. 262, 267 (1924).

[55] *El Paso & Southwestern Sys.*, 90 I.C.C. 732, 737 (1924).

[56] See, e.g., *St. Louis So. Ry.*, 180 I.C.C. 175, 206 (1932), *aff'd sub nom. Missouri Pac. R.R.* v. *United States*, 4 F. Supp. 449 (E.D. Ky. 1933), *aff'd per curiam*, 293
U.S. 524 (1934); *Buffalo, R. & P. Ry.*, 158 I.C.C. 779, 784–785 (1930), *modified*, 193
I.C.C. 557 (1933); *Columbia, N. & L.R.R.*, 117 I.C.C. 219, 224 (1926); *Clinchfield Ry.*,
90 I.C.C. 113, 128 (1924).

bypass intervenors operating as connecting lines.[57] Thus inter-venors' charges of possible injury to the public by lessened com-petition were usually shams which attempted to prevent the pro-motion of consolidations that effected more efficient allocation of resources and more genuine competition.

The parallel nature of two rail lines has not been a controlling criterion in consolidation proceedings. Both may be light-traffic, weak lines; combining the most direct and level segments of both could create one strong, efficient line with sufficient earnings to carry on continuous quality maintenance.[58] In view of this, the usual policy was to approve such mergers. If a weaker road was acquired by a stronger one, other connecting roads were given protection by the Commission's conditioning approval of the ac-quisition on the maintaining of all previously existing through routes and gateways.[59] Although this condition was enforced in later proceedings,[60] it was considered by intervenors as offering little protection from the diversion of traffic which resulted from the creation of new through routes. Another solution for protec-tion of connecting roads was to condition approval of the pro-posed acquisition on applicant's allowing those roads to become coöwners by paying a proportionate share of the purchase price.[61]

In cases where the Commission denied approval of control, com-petition was treated rarely, although it was occasionally given weight.[62] In the *Nickel Plate Unification* case, denial of proposed acquisition of control was based primarily on the unreasonable-ness of financial terms.[63] The Commission noted that the possible

[57] See, e.g., *Alabama & V. Ry.*, 111 I.C.C. 161, 170–173 (1926); *Gulf & S.I.R.R.*, 99 I.C.C. 169, 171–172 (1925).

[58] See the arguments presented by applicant and intervenor in *Louisiana & Ark. Ry.*, 150 I.C.C. 477, 484, 487 (1929).

[59] *Buffalo, R. & P. Ry.*, 158 I.C.C. 779, 788 (1930), *modified*, 193 I.C.C. 557 (1933); *Alabama & V. Ry.*, 111 I.C.C. 161, 178–179 (1926); *Clinchfield Ry.*, 90 I.C.C. 113, 133 (1924). A specious argument of protesting carriers in the *Buffalo* case was that, even though Baltimore & Ohio and the Buffalo road it was acquiring served differ-ent areas and had no possibility of direct competition, there was "substantial mar-ket competition" between them because they carried goods to the same industrial market. The Commission accepted this argument but held that it was overcome by the economies to result from permitting the acquisition. 158 I.C.C. at 785, 788.

[60] See, e.g., *Atlantic Coast Line R.R. v. United States*, 284 U.S. 288 (1932).

[61] *Central Cal. Traction Co.*, 131 I.C.C. 125, 139 (1927).

[62] For instances in which competition apparently played a part in the approval or denial of applications see Frederick, Hypps & Herring, *Regulation of Railroad Finance* 77–81 (1930); 3A Sharfman, *The Interstate Commerce Commission* 458–459 nn. 274–276 (1935).

[63] 105 I.C.C. 435, 444 (1926). In a later proceeding, the Chesapeake & Ohio was authorized to control the Pere Marquette, but application to control the Erie was

lessened competition among the Nickel Plate, Erie, and Chesapeake and Ohio railroads would be offset by the creation of a fourth strong eastern trunk line.[64] The proposed acquisition of the Virginian by the Norfolk & Western was denied primarily because it would upset existing routes, and because the Virginian had been allotted to the Chesapeake and Ohio in the Commission's comprehensive plan of consolidation.[65] Elimination of alleged competition was, however, one ground for denial, in spite of a showing that the two coal roads served different mining areas and that they had common customers only for a small amount of merchandise traffic.[66] The proposed acquisition by the Kansas City Southern of the Missouri-Kansas-Texas and the Cotton Belt was denied because the prices set for the stock transactions were too high and because there was inadequate protection for minority stockholders of the latter railroads.[67] The Commission noted that the three carriers were parallel only to a limited extent and that competition in local or short-distance traffic was minimal. The Commission did find an indeterminable amount of indirect competition between the M-K-T and Cotton Belt for traffic from North Texas to St. Louis. It cited the *Nickel Plate Unification* case, however, in noting that the combination could result in increased competition with other carriers after economies of the combine were realized.[68]

The only cases in which the allegation of competition or antitrust violations played a significant part under the Transportation Act of 1920 were Commission actions for Clayton Act violations against three combinations.[69] Section 11 of the Clayton Act gave the Commission exclusive jurisdiction to enforce section 7 of the act where it was applicable to carriers subject to the Interstate Commerce Act.[70] One such action was filed against the Kansas City

---

again denied on the ground that it would disturb existing channels of traffic. *Erie R.R.*, 138 I.C.C. 517, 530, 537 (1928). A final proceeding authorized the Chesapeake & Ohio to acquire control of the Nickel Plate and the Erie. *New York, C. & St. L.R.R.*, 224 I.C.C. 259 (1937).

[64] 105 I.C.C. at 434–435; see Swaine, "Reorganization of Corporations: Certain Developments of the Last Decade," 28 *Colum. L. Rev.* 29, 55–56 (1928).

[65] *Virginian Ry.*, 117 I.C.C. 67 (1926).

[66] *Id.* at 73. In 1959 the Commission changed its view and concluded that there was no direct competition between the two carriers. *Norfolk & W. Ry.*, 307 I.C.C. 401, 440 (1959).

[67] See *Proposed Unification of Southwestern Lines*, 124 I.C.C. 401, 431–439 (1927).

[68] *Id.* at 415–417.

[69] See Senate Rep. No. 1182, 76th Cong., 3d Sess., 2057–2072 (1940).

[70] 38 Stat. 734 (1914), 15 U.S.C. §21 (1958). Section 7 prohibited one corporation from acquiring the stock of another "where the effect of such acquisition may be

Southern for its acquisition of large interests in the M-K-T and Cotton Belt, which, as noted above, was not approved by the Commission. No order was issued, however, because the facts showed that the defendant had divested itself of the shares in question.[71]

Another action was brought against the Baltimore & Ohio, New York Central, and Nickel Plate for acquiring the capital stock of the Wheeling & Lake Erie in violation of section 7 of the Clayton Act.[72] In a previous case denying the same defendants permission to have interlocking directors with the Wheeling, testimony was given that 73.4 per cent of Wheeling's traffic was competitive with at least one of the eastern trunk lines.[73] Competition in this sense was the total proportion of revenue carload traffic handled by the Wheeling which could have been moved by other railroads between the same points over one-line routes.[74] On this basis, the Commission found that the effects of the acquisition may have been substantially to lessen competition between the Wheeling and defendants,[75] and held that the defendants must divest themselves of their Wheeling stock.[76] A supplemental proceeding allowed the Nickel Plate to acquite the Wheeling shares sold by the B. & O. and New York Central, and deposit these shares, together with its own Wheeling shares, with a trustee.[77] In 1946 the Commission reviewed the relationship of the Nickel Plate and the Wheeling and reversed its position. It found that "comparatively little mileage of the two systems can be regarded to be parallel. . . . The two systems are not competitive to any considerable degree, and essentially they are supplementary and complementary to each other." [78] Consequently, unification of these two carriers was authorized. A similar action was brought against the B. & O. for having acquired control of the Western Maryland without ICC authorization.[79] Using the same tests applied in the *Wheeling* case,

---

to substantially lessen competition" between the corporations, "or to restrain such commerce in any section or community, or tend to create a monopoly of any line of commerce." 38 Stat. 731 (1914), 15 U.S.C. §18 (1958).

[71] *Kansas City So. Ry.*, 156 I.C.C. 359 (1929).

[72] *Baltimore & O.R.R.*, 152 I.C.C. 721 (1929).

[73] *Wheeling & L.E. Ry.*, 138 I.C.C. 643, 646 (1928).

[74] 152 I.C.C. at 723.

[75] "Competition between carriers, within the purposes of section 5 of the act, exists whenever there is such possibility of election of routes as may have an influence upon service or rates." 138 I.C.C. at 649; see 152 I.C.C. at 731.

[76] *Id.* at 737.

[77] *Baltimore & O.R.R.*, 156 I.C.C. 607 (1929).

[78] *Wheeling & L.E. Ry.*, 267 I.C.C. 163, 174 (1946), *supplemented*, 267 I.C.C. 203 (1947).

[79] *Baltimore & O.R.R.*, 160 I.C.C. 785 (1930).

the Commission apparently found 43.5 per cent of Western Maryland traffic competitive with the B. & O.[80] As a result it ordered B. & O. to transfer its Western Maryland stock to a trustee.[81]

The most important Clayton Act proceeding brought by the Commission was against the Pennsylvania for having acquired stock control of the Lehigh Valley and the Wabash without ICC approval.[82] Using the same "possibility of competition" tests as in the *Wheeling* case, the Commission found the acquisitions were in violation of section 7 of the Clayton Act, in that their effect may have been substantially to reduce competition or restrain commerce.[83] The court of appeals reversed the divestiture order, stating that a mere possibility of substantial lessening of competition does not violate the Clayton Act.[84] There was no material evidence of a probable lessening of competition. The court stated that the evidence showed increased competition between the Pennsylvania and the acquired roads, though it did not define the sense in which it used the term. By 1941 the Commission had changed its position on the materiality of competition between the Pennsylvania and the Wabash, and allowed the former to take control of the latter.[85] The Commission then concluded that the "lines of the Wabash are naturally complementary to those of the Pennsylvania and together form a direct route from Kansas City to the eastern seaboard." [86] The only mention of competition in the decision was a summary of applicant's allegation that the combined roads would create new competitive routes and intervenor's claim that approval would decrease competition.[87]

[80] It is not entirely clear that the Commission may not have found 29.2 per cent of the traffic competitive, utilizing a different definition of competition. See *id.* at 788–789.

[81] *Baltimore & O.R.R.*, 183 I.C.C. 165 (1932).

[82] *Pennsylvania R.R.*, 169 I.C.C. 618 (1930).

[83] *Id.* at 627. Lehigh Valley traffic was found to be 49 per cent competitive with the Pennsylvania, and Wabash traffic east of the Mississippi was found to be 75 per cent competitive with the Pennsylvania. *Id.* at 625. The Commission also included "market competition" (the situation in which the shippers compete, although the railroads serve different shippers of the commodity) in its discussion of competition. *Id.* at 627.

[84] *Pennsylvania R.R.* v. *I.C.C.*, 66 F.2d 37, 38 (3d Cir. 1933), *aff'd by an equally divided Court*, 291 U.S. 651 (1934).

[85] *Wabash R.R.*, 247 I.C.C. 365 (1941), *supplemented*, 252 I.C.C. 319 (1942). Both roads were required to place their Lehigh Valley stock in the hands of a trustee as a condition of the authorization of control. In 1962 the Commission repealed this condition and allowed the Pennsylvania to exercise operating control of the Lehigh Valley. *Pennsylvania R. Co.*, 317 I.C.C. 139 (1962).

[86] 247 I.C.C. 376.

[87] *Id.* at 371–372.

The amendments of the Emergency Railroad Transportation Act of 1933 [88] were the final chapter in the two decades of regulation under the Transportation Act of 1920. The changes in the law relating to unification of carriers operated more than anything else as impediments to combinations. Consolidations and acquisitions of control were united in a new section 5(4), which established two tests for Commission approval: harmony with the ICC general plan of consolidation; and promotion of the public interest. Requiring mere acquisitions of control to conform to the plan of consolidation—the innovation of this statute—established another barrier to such acquisitions.[89] In addition, holding-company control of railroads was for the first time brought under control of the Commission, and section 7 of the 1933 act gave such guarantees to railroad labor against any loss of jobs resulting from consolidation or coördination programs that many of the potential savings from such programs were eliminated.

TRANSPORTATION ACT OF 1940

The Transportation Act of 1940 repealed all provisions directing the Commission to formulate or adhere to a comprehensive plan of consolidation.[90] Congress thus finally adopted the recommendations of the Commission that such planning to combine strong and weak railroads was not feasible.[91] The 1940 act also combined consolidation laws for both railroads and motor carriers into one section. Section 5(2) continued the policy of the Emergency Railroad Transportation Act of 1933 in regulating both complete consolidations and looser acquisitions of control under a single set of standards. These new considerations to which the Commission was directed to give weight were: the effect of the proposed transaction upon adequate transportation service to the public; the effect upon the public interest of the inclusion or noninclusion of other railroads in the territory involved in the proposed transaction; the total fixed charges resulting from the proposed transaction; and

[88] Chapter 91, 48 Stat. 217. See generally Latham, *The Politics of Railroad Coordination 1933–1936* (1959).

[89] The Coördinator of Transportation, an officer appointed under the 1933 act, recommended that the statutory requirement of conformance to the ICC's over-all plan of consolidation be dropped as impractical. U.S., ICC Federal Coordinator of Transportation, *Report on Transportation Legislation* 62–64 (1934). This was not done by Congress until 1940.

[90] 54 Stat. 898, 905 (1940), 49 U.S.C. §5 (1958).

[91] See 39 ICC Annual Rep. 13 (1925) (containing the recommendations of the Commission); Payne, "History of the Consolidation Provisions of the Interstate Commerce Act," 19 *ICC Prac. J.* 453, 461 (1952).

the interest of the carrier employees affected. This attempt to afford unified treatment to the two types of carriers reflected a highly questionable policy, in the light of the radically different economic structures of the two industries.[92]

Although the 1920 act's specific consolidation criterion of preserving competition was dropped, the Commission has continued to consider this standard as one element of public interest.[93] Congress anticipated this by continuing, in section 5(11) of the 1940 act, the 1920 act's exemption from antitrust prosecution of consolidation or acquisitions of control approved by the Commission.

The effects on competition have been an issue, but only a minor one, in a number of unifications under the 1940 act.[94] Where the roads to be acquired were complementary to the acquiring road, merger or control was usually approved. The Commission found in a number of these cases that the new through routes would strengthen competition with other carriers.[95] Since rates and many aspects of service were cartelized in the rate bureaus, this conclusion is questionable. The Commission seems to mean by strengthened competition that new through routes created by consolidating connecting lines may divert traffic from parallel railroads by becoming able to offer equally fast service. The only real question of monopoly power in such cases was whether other carriers which had previously exchanged traffic with the acquired road would now be excluded from such interchange. This exclusion was usually prohibited by the Commission's conditioning approval of the unification on the continued maintenance of all existing through routes and connections without discrimination.[96]

The confusion of the Commission on the meaning and existence of competition is illustrated by *Spokane Int'l R.R.*[97] The Commission approved acquisition of the Spokane International by the Union Pacific, a complementary, connecting route. It denied the

---

[92] See Chap. II note 7 *supra*. See generally Harbeson, "The Transportation Act of 1940," 17 *J. Land & P.U. Econ.* 291 (1941).

[93] See *Minneapolis & St. L. Ry.* v. *United States*, 361 U.S. 173, 187 (1959).

[94] See Huntington, "The Marasmus of the ICC: The Commission, the Railroads, and the Public Interest," 61 *Yale L.J.* 467, 491 (1952).

[95] E.g., *Pere Marquette Ry.*, 267 I.C.C. 207, 233 (1947); *Wheeling & L.E. Ry.*, 267 I.C.C. 163, 183 (1946).

[96] See, e.g., *Detroit, T. & I.R.R.*, 275 I.C.C. 455, 492 (1950). A suit by competitors to enjoin the ICC-approved plan of acquisition of control was dismissed. *New York, C. & St. L.R.R.* v. *United States*, 95 F. Supp. 811 (N.D. Ohio 1951).

[97] 295 I.C.C. 425 (1956), *aff'd sub nom. Canadian Pac. Ry.* v. *United States*, 158 F. Supp. 248 (D. Minn. 1958).

intervening petition of Northern Pacific and Great Northern (each of whose lines paralleled a section of Spokane International) to be included in the acquisition on an equal basis with Union Pacific. The facts showed substantial excess capacity in rail facilities in the Spokane International territory. Intervenors' evidence indicated that joint control of the Spokane by three or four roads would enable coördination of lines, allowing abandonment of segments of Spokane's 150-mile line, including a large bridge which needed replacement. In denying intervenors' petition, the Commission held that the ease by which intervenors' coördination plans could be effected convinced it of the "intense competition presently existing between the Spokane International" and intervenors.[98] Efficient coördination of carriers was thus sacrificed to the delusion that competition would function in an environment of a few carriers with substantial excess capacity.

The proposed acquisition of a complementary, connecting line was denied approval when it would have created a new through route to which so much traffic was likely to be diverted that it would endanger the solvency or impair the operation of other carriers. In *Chicago, B. & Q. R.R.*[99] the Burlington and the Santa Fe jointly proposed to acquire the entire capital stock of the Kansas City, Chicago and St. Louis Railroad Company. This 156-mile line from Mexico, Missouri, to Kansas City (Rock Creek Junction) together with a 112-mile segment of the Burlington, over which the Santa Fe applied for trackage rights, formed a short route from St. Louis to Kansas City. The transaction, in addition to giving the Burlington a much shorter line between St. Louis and Kansas City than it previously had, was intended to give the Santa Fe an entry into St. Louis. The other roads from the southwest intervened and protested that a direct Santa Fe route into St. Louis would divert so much traffic to it that intervenors' loss of revenues would cause them to curtail service and abandon some lines. Accepting this argument,[100] the majority of the Commission denied the acquisi-

[98] *Id.* at 437.

[99] 271 I.C.C. 63 (1948). Another minor proposal in this case, which was also denied, was to allow the Burlington trackage rights over a Missouri section of the Santa Fe line from Chicago to Kansas City.

[100] See *id.* at 162–163. See also *Chicago & E. Ill. R.R.*, 312 I.C.C. 564 (1961), where a main line carrier was denied permission to merge its wholly owned subsidiary terminal line, Chicago Heights Terminal Transfer Railroad (6.8 miles of main line and 22.5 miles of side tracks), because substantial traffic would be diverted from other carriers. The Commission thought that no compensating efficiency in rail transportation had been shown.

tion.[101] Commissioner Mahaffie dissented, pointing out that the majority rationale would prevent the operation of competition in resource allocation as a provider of the most direct and efficient rail routes. He stated:

Of course if the line is greatly improved and traffic can be handled over it more economically and efficiently than over existing lines there will be, and there should be, some diversion of traffic. . . . The reasoning of the report [which was approved by the majority], if applied generally, would pretty much freeze the railroad plant. If it had been applied to all transportation as of, say, 1920 it would have prevented the entry of motor carriers and perhaps of air carriers into the transportation field. It is not, as I see it, in accord with the principles of the act, which, as indicated above, are intended to promote adequacy and efficiency of transportation service for the benefit of the public.[102]

Chesapeake & O. Ry.[103] was the one significant denial of a petition under the 1940 act to control an allegedly competing parallel carrier. In 1947 the Chesapeake and Ohio had acquired 400,000 shares, or 6.2 per cent, of the common stock of the New York Central and had deposited the stock in a voting trust pursuant to a 1945 order of the Commission.[104] In 1947 the Chesapeake and Ohio and its holding company, Alleghany, petitioned for modification of the 1945 order, first, to permit Chesapeake and Ohio to acquire title to and exercise full voting rights in the 400,000 New York Central shares and, second, to permit interlocking directorates between the Chesapeake and Ohio and the New York Central.[105] The case was complicated procedurally because the Chesa-

---

[101] The Burlington aspect of this case, a second, shorter St. Louis-Kansas City route, was not a significant issue. Although joint acquisition of this new route, theoretically a competitor of Burlington's old, longer route, was denied in this case, the same acquisition by the Burlington alone was approved one year later. *Chicago, B. & Q.R.R.,* 271 I.C.C. 675 (1949).

[102] 271 I.C.C. at 166–167.

[103] 271 I.C.C. 5 (1948).

[104] In 1945 the Commission had approved continued control through stock ownership by the Alleghany Corporation of the Chesapeake & Ohio, Nickel Plate, and Pere Marquette Railroads subject to two conditions: To deposit with a named voting trustee all stock then owned or to be acquired in other carriers not then affiliated with the Chesapeake & Ohio system; and to enter no interlocking directorates or relationships between the Alleghany-C. & O. system and other companies whose stock was trusteed according to the first condition. *Chesapeake & O. Ry.,* 261 I.C.C. 239, 262 (1945).

[105] 271 I.C.C. at 6. In contrast to this case, the 1952 application of the Delaware, Lackawanna & Western to control the Nickel Plate, because it owned 14.8 per cent of Nickel Plate's common stock and had the power to elect two or three of Nickel Plate's fifteen directors, was dismissed on motion of applicant. No question of control within the regulatory scope of §§5(2) and 5(4) was found because the existing

peake and Ohio did not file a formal petition under section 5(2) to control the New York Central. It alleged that voting its 6.2 per cent of the New York Central stock and coördinating operations with the New York Central in itself did not constitute control. The Commission found, however, that modification of the voting trust in this case was intended to give and would give the Chesapeake and Ohio power to control the policies of the New York Central. Under the circumstances, the Commission concluded that granting the petition would sanction violation of section 5(4) of the 1940 act, which prohibits control of one carrier by another unless prior approval is granted under section 5(2).[106] The Commission further held that the requested voting power, which it had found to constitute control, had to be denied in this case because it might well have violated section 7 of the Clayton Act.[107] Because of the existence of roughly parallel routes between three pairs of industrial centers, the Commission found substantial competition between the two carriers, which would have been lessened by the proposed control.[108]

The second aspect of the petition in this case, to permit interlocking directors for the Chesapeake and Ohio and the New York Central, was also denied. Common officers or directors for carriers had been controlled under section 20a(12) of the Interstate Commerce Act since 1920.[109] This section makes interlocking directorates unlawful unless authorized by the Commission upon a showing by the applicant "that neither public nor private interests will be adversely affected thereby." Section 20a(12) had been broadly

---

management of the Nickel Plate opposed control by the Lackawanna and had solicited sufficient proxies to prevent Lackawanna from gaining control. In addition, Lackawanna deposited its Nickel Plate stock with a trustee, precluding any power to lessen competition, so that an investigation of whether there had been a violation of §7 of the Clayton Act was discontinued. *New York, C. & St. L.R.R.*, 295 I.C.C. 703, 714, 718 (1958), *supplementing* 295 I.C.C. 131 (1955).

[106] Section 5(4) makes it unlawful, except as provided in §5(2), to effectuate control or management in a common interest of two or more carriers "whether directly or indirectly, by use of common directors, officers, or stockholders, a holding or investment company or companies, a voting trust or trusts, or in any other manner whatsoever." 54 Stat. 907 (1940), 49 U.S.C. §5(4) (1958). For a case involving violation of this section by the St. Louis-San Francisco Railway Company, by acquiring control of the Central of Georgia, see *Central of Ga. Ry.*, 307 I.C.C. 39 (1958), *supplemented*, 312 I.C.C. 125 (1960), 312 I.C.C. 539 (1961), *reversing* 295 I.C.C. 563 (1957).

[107] 271 I.C.C. at 17, 43.

[108] Chesapeake & Ohio and New York Central were roughly parallel between Chicago and Cincinnati; Charleston and Toledo via Columbus; and the Niagara frontier and Chicago. *Id.* at 22–23, 38.

[109] Added by 41 Stat. 496 (1920), as amended, 49 U.S.C. 20a(12) (1958).

construed to prohibit a common director of two carriers even if there was no direct competition between them.[110] The mere fact that one of the two carriers in routing traffic at interchange points, no matter how far distant, can choose between the other of the two carriers and another road, indicates that public and private interests will be adversely affected by the interlocking directorate. In the present case, the Commission concluded that Chesapeake & Ohio had failed to show that the common directors would not adversely affect the private interests of the New York Central. It also concluded that the evidence of benefit to the public by coördination of the two carriers was not sufficient to overcome the evidence of possible adverse effects to the part of the public served by the Virginian Railway, New York Central's established connecting route in the Pocahontas region.[111]

The Commission's delusion about the existence of interrailroad competition reached its climax in a case approving the Louisville & Nashville's merger with the Nashville, Chattanooga & St. Louis.[112] The two roads had a number of parallel lines, both of them serving Nashville, Memphis, and Atlanta. The L. & N. had controlled the N. C. & St. L. since 1880 and owned 74.9 per cent of its common stock.[113] Although the two railroads were operated separately, decades of agreements on rates, routing, and solicitation precluded any competition between them.[114] After reviewing the facts of these agreements, the Commission did an about-face and found extensive competition between the two carriers. It held, however, that the competitive situation was different from a situation involving wholly independent carriers.[115] The Commission

[110] *In re Boatner,* 257 I.C.C. 369, 372–373 (1944). For an analysis of other cases under 20a(12) see 271 I.C.C. at 17–21.

[111] *Id.* at 39.

[112] *Louisville & N.R.R.,* 295 I.C.C. 457, aff'd sub nom. *City of Nashville* v. *United States,* 155 F. Supp. 98 (M.D. Tenn.), aff'd mem., 355 U.S. 63 (1957). A complaint of minority stockholders about the exchange ratio of the shares was dismissed in *Stott* v. *United States,* 166 F. Supp. 851 (S.D.N.Y. 1958). A complaint of employees was dismissed in *Arnold* v. *Louisville & N.R.R.,* 180 F. Supp. 429 (M.D. Tenn. 1960).

[113] 295 I.C.C. at 461.

[114] *Id.* at 482–485; see *Louisville & N.R.R.,* 33 I.C.C. 168 (1915); U.S. Cong., House, Comm. on the Judiciary, *Merger in a Regulated Industry* 30, 40–54 Comm. Print. (84th Cong. 2d Sess. 1956).

[115] "As pointed out in *Louisville & N. Co. Financial Relations,* 33 I.C.C. 168, and as shown by the expert testimony introduced through the traffic witnesses presented on behalf of the Nashville interests, the Kentucky Company and the Tennessee Company compete extensively with each other. . . . Under such circumstances, it cannot be said that an antagonistic competitive situation has existed between them." 295 I.C.C. at 485–486.

found that the loss in competition was outweighed by total savings from unified operations of parallel lines and elimination of interchange costs, estimated to be $3,243,000 per year.[116] Shippers and representatives of two other railroads testified in support of the merger, so that the only opposition was from the labor unions and the City of Nashville, which alleged adverse effects from loss of employment. The Commission concluded that the protestants' arguments for continuing inefficient railroad operations were clearly overcome by the economic effects of growing intermodal competition.[117] This increased competition of highway, water, and air carriers made it imperative for the railroads to do everything in their power to effect economies and promote efficient operations.

Toledo, P. & W. R.R.,[118] concerning a contest between opposing railroads to acquire this line, further illustrates the declining importance of the preservation of alleged interrailroad competition as a regulatory standard. The Pennsylvania and the Santa Fe jointly were allowed to acquire the entire stock of the T. P. & W. This bridge carrier across central Illinois connects with the Pennsylvania on the east and with the Santa Fe on the west, allowing transcontinental shipment without moving cars through the congested Chicago and St. Louis terminals. The T. P. & W. was a rival of the Pennsylvania in the sense that the Pennsylvania could get its longest haul on transcontinental traffic by carrying it into St. Louis or transferring it to the Wabash, which it controlled, for carriage into Kansas City. The T. P. & W. was a rival of the Santa Fe in the sense that the Santa Fe could get the longest haul on traffic from the west by hauling it across Illinois into Chicago. The Commission declared that "the important thing is not whether there is possibility of competition, but whether there is probability of existing or potential competition being diminished or strangled by the [T. P. & W.] under the control of the Santa Fe and the Pennsylvania." [119] The negative answer to this question was based on a finding that the two acquiring roads were "just about as well off financially when handling traffic via the T. P. & W. as they would be on the long haul" [120] through the congested terminals. The continuing of the T. P. & W. as an independent carrier and

---

[116] *Id.* at 488–493.
[117] *Id.* at 468; see *id.* at 475–476.
[118] 295 I.C.C. 523 (1957), *aff'd sub nom. Minneapolis & St. L. Ry.* v. *United States,* 165 F. Supp. 893 (D. Minn. 1958), *aff'd,* 361 U.S. 173 (1959).
[119] *Id.* at 536.
[120] *Ibid.*

the requiring of neutrality in its handling of traffic to and from all connecting lines would further prevent it from being strangled by the acquiring roads. The Commission thought that the Pennsylvania and the Santa Fe would act as checks on one another to ensure that the T. P. & W. service was not impaired, and thus protect other carriers interchanging traffic with the T. P. & W.[121]

The Minneapolis & St. Louis wished to end the independence of the T. P. & W. by complete merger, and filed an opposing petition to acquire the T. P. & W. This the Commission denied. The Pennsylvania and the Santa Fe had already contracted for acquisition of the T. P. & W. stock. The Commission's approval, based on findings that there would be no significant lessening of competition and that the contracted acquisition would be in the public interest, obviated the antitrust objections.[122] Furthermore, the alleged diversion of traffic from the M. & St. L. which would result from the Pennsylvania and the Santa Fe's taking control of the T. P. & W. was neither proved nor found to be against the public interest. As in the Louisville & Nashville merger, the Commission ruled that the acquisition here would ensure a strong and reliable carrier, adequate to meet the impact of intermodal competition.

Subsequent to the discussed case, the sale of the Minneapolis & St. Louis Railway to the Chicago and North Western Railway was also approved by the Commission.[123] The fact that the M. & St. L.'s main terminal cities, Minneapolis and Peoria, were served by both carriers was not even mentioned in the decision. Since the lines were not parallel, the Commission ignored the idea of potential competition to which it had given weight in so many cases. It noted, first, the expected annual savings of $3,000,000 and, second, the probability of strong competition by other rail, motor, and air carriers.[124]

The *Soo Line* case, *Duluth, So. S. & Atl. R.R.*,[125] was almost identical. The Commission approved the merger of the Minneapolis, St. Paul & Sault Ste. Marie and the Wisconsin Central into the Duluth, South Shore & Atlantic Railroad. As in the *Minneapolis & St. Louis* case, the carriers here had common terminals (at

[121] *Id.* at 545.
[122] *Minneapolis & St. L. Ry.* v. *United States,* 361 U.S. 173, 186 (1959).
[123] *Chicago & N.W. Ry.,* 312 I.C.C. 285 (1960).
[124] *Id.* at 291, 297.
[125] 312 I.C.C. 341 (1960). For a similar case, see *Pennsylvania R. Co.,* 317 I.C.C. 139 (1962). The Commission approved control of the Lehigh by the Pennsylvania without mentioning competition in its opinion even though both carriers hauled freight from Buffalo to New York City.

Duluth-Superior and Sault Ste. Marie), but their lines were not parallel. Here, also, no material effect upon competition was found. Approval was again conditioned on the maintenance of existing joint rates, through routes, and gateways in order to protect shippers and connecting carriers.

The lessened emphasis on preserving alleged interrailroad competition, and a greater recognition of intermodal competition, were most strikingly illustrated in *Norfolk & W. Ry.*[126] The Commission approved a merger of the parallel Virginian Railway into the Norfolk & Western, reversing a 1926 decision.[127] Contrary to its earlier decision, the Commission now concluded that the effects on competition would not be material. It held:

> The Norfolk & Western and the Virginian serve different areas of the Appalachian coalfields and, therefore, there is no direct competition between them for their principal traffic. Such competition as does exist for coal traffic is in the nature of market competition between mines, and this will not be affected by the merger. As to traffic other than coal, the record shows, that while the two lines do have competitive through routes from and to commonly served points, there is little direct competition between them. The Norfolk & Western considers the competition of motor carriers much more severe than that afforded by Virginian.
>
> While there may be some slight lessening of competition as a result of the proposed merger, we do not regard that fact as of controlling importance. The evidence establishes that, after the merger, strong competition will still be afforded by other forms of transportation. We conclude that the public interest would not be adversely affected by any lessening of competition which may result from the proposed merger.[128]

As in other recent merger cases, the Commission found that the efficiencies from combining the most level and direct segments of parallel lines and eliminating interchange costs overcame any possible detriment of allegedly lessened competition.

The second largest of the recent mergers of parallel railroads, affecting 3,200 miles of lines, was the Erie Railroad merger with the Delaware, Lackawanna & Western.[129] This merger, too, demon-

---

[126] 307 I.C.C. 401 (1959).

[127] See *Virginian Ry.,* 117 I.C.C. 67 (1926); text accompanying note 65 *supra.*

[128] 307 I.C.C. at 440. Similar stress on the economic effects of intermodal competition is found in the Atlantic Coast Line merger of the Charleston & Western Carolina. *Atlantic Coast Line R.R.,* 307 I.C.C. 614, 618 (1959).

[129] *Erie R.R.,* 312 I.C.C. 185 (1960). A complaint of employees under §5(2)(f) of the Transportation Act was dismissed in *Brotherhood of Maintenance of Way Em-*

strates the declining importance of preserving interrailroad competition as a merger criterion but also illustrates the continuing confusion of the Commission on the meaning of competition. The examiner's report, which was adopted as part of the Commission's decision, indicated that the both railroads had lines from New York to Buffalo, that many segments were parallel, and that the lines met at fifty-five common points. Upon recommending approval of the merger, the examiner made the following finding concerning competition:

> In the situation herein, the traffic affected by competition between the applicants is substantial; the railroads involved are weak financially; and the existing competition by other railroads and other forms of transportation would continue as strong, or stronger, than at present. Considering all the circumstances, the change in the competitive situation between the Erie and the Lackawanna would reflect to the benefit of the general public, and its elimination would have no adverse effect upon adequate transportation service.[130]

The Commission approved the merger and adopted the examiner's report without comment on his finding that competition was substantial because the carriers were parallel.

The largest merger of parallel railroads approved by the Commission to the end of 1963 was the Seaboard Air Line Railroad merger of the Atlantic Coast Line Railroad.[131] These combined lines of 9,719 miles extend south along the east coast from Richmond to Florida with sixty-seven common points. Alleged competition and the antitrust laws became a major issue in this case, since two commissioners dissented on the ground that the merger should have been disapproved in order to preserve competition.

In the area of their operations, the merged companies had 54 per cent of the route mileage and their largest rival, the Southern had about 34 per cent. Of the combined freight traffic of the merged companies in 1957, 33.4 per cent could have been carried by either of them. Since other railroads, primarily the Southern, could have carried 19.7 per cent of the combined tonnage of the merged lines, possible railroad rivalry was eliminated for only 13.7 per cent of their traffic.

---

ployees v. *United States,* 189 F. Supp. 942 (E.D. Mich. 1960), *aff'd,* 366 U.S. 169 (1961). A stockholder's complaint challenging the exchange ratio of shares was dismissed in *Fried* v. *United States,* 212 F. Supp. 886 (S.D.N.Y. 1963).

[130] 312 I.C.C. at 246.

[131] *Seaboard Air Line Railroad Merger,* ICC Finance No. 21215, Report of the Commission, Dec. 2, 1963.

The Commission found that there would be a significant reduc-tion of rail competition in Florida. This reduction was minimized by the Commission because it affects only smaller cities and because of the increasing importance of intermodal competition. In applying the statute, the Commission stated:

In resolving the conflicting considerations of section 5(2) of the act and the antitrust legislation, primary emphasis must be placed upon the public advantages that will accrue from the merger, including improved services, safer operations, lower costs and other potential benefits that further the objectives of the national transportation policy. . . . Moreover, as railroads have the basic economic characteristics of public utilities and are subject to regulation in the public interest at both the Federal and State levels, it is not realistic to insist that intramodal rail competition must be preserved in all places, at all times and under all circumstances.[132]

In conclusion, the Commission found that the net reduction of rail competition caused by the merger would not be substantial and would have no appreciably injurious effect upon shippers and communities.

The dissenting commissioners suggested that the merger would result in a substantial lessening of competition and that this was sufficient ground to deny approval to it. They emphasized the strong financial condition of the Seaboard and the Coast Line as an important issue. To the disinterested observer, the earnings of the two carriers together with the expected savings from merger would result in a rate of return high enough to suggest a failure of the Commission in its primary function of maximum rate regulation. The dissenters even stated that the major opinion "exaggerates the efficacy of regulation." In proclaiming their faith in competition, the dissenters did not mention the congressional policy of approval for rate cartels, the antithesis of competition. Numerous analogies were made to the banking and trucking industries, even though the basic structures and conditions of entry for new firms in those industries create a much greater potential for competition than in railroads.[133]

CONCLUSION

The Interstate Commerce Commission decisions in consolidation cases demonstrate inconsistency and vagueness concerning the

[132] *Ibid.* at 60–61.
[133] See Chap. II, note 7, *supra.*

definition of competition. Most cases treat the mere possibility of moving traffic between two cities by either of two railroads as constituting interrailroad competition. A few decisions state that the probable lessening of competition is the significant public-interest aspect of alleged interrailroad rivalry. In none of the cases does the Commission show an understanding that railroad-industry structure and technology, combined with government-sponsored cartels in rate-making, preclude the operation of interrailroad competition in any meaningful sense.

The antitrust exemption for railroad consolidations or acquisitions of control approved by the Commission, enacted in 1920, marked the turning point in governmental policy in the direction of favoring consolidations and lessening the barrier of the antitrust laws. The Emergency Railroad Transportation Act, 1933 and the Transportation Act, 1940, by eliminating preservation of competition as a specific statutory consolidation criterion, marked a further step in the same direction. But the preservation of competition as an element of the public-interest concept still looms as a weakened but possibly significant factor to block railroad consolidations. At this writing, a number of large railroad consolidation cases are pending before the Interstate Commerce Commission. In some of these, the Department of Justice has intervened in opposition and filed a brief alleging antitrust violation because the two roads "are in extensive and vigorous competition." [134] Except for competitive investment in duplicate lines and facilities, which raises transport costs to the public, this allegation is simply unfounded. The carriers in these cases are in the embarrassing position for privately owned firms in a free-enterprise economy of meeting this charge by demonstrating that the nature of railroad technology, augmented by a smoothly working cartel, makes rivalry between them minimal and precludes the operation of effective competition between them.

[134] See, e.g., Brief for U.S. Department of Justice, p. 6, *Seaboard Air Line R.R.*, Finance Docket No. 21215, ICC, Oct. 30, 1961; Brief for U.S. Department of Justice, pp. 26–63, *Great Northern Pacific & Burlington Lines*, Finance Docket No. 21478, ICC, Jan. 4, 1963.

IV

Economic Appraisal of
Recent Mergers

Railroads merge for many reasons. Most mergers are designed to achieve greater economies of scale or to eliminate duplicate facilities or both in an effort to lower costs and increase net income. Some are primarily designed to create longer through routes and divert traffic from parallel lines. Others are defensive and made to forestall another proposed merger that would divert traffic to rival parallel lines. Still others may have the purpose of exploiting financial gains from exchange of securities and result in no operational economies.

If an end-to-end merger of connecting lines is effected, saving will derive from reduced costs of interchange, car accounting, and general administration. In addition, the new and longer through route may offer faster service, thereby diverting traffic to it from other carriers. If parallel lines are merged, cost savings may derive from the elimination of duplicate facilities within the limits imposed by labor unions and the regulatory control of line abandonments.[1] Economies from more intensive use of smaller total fixed plant may, however, be offset by diseconomies of scale in administration. Professor Healy's study concludes that railroads with more than 10,000 workers suffer diseconomies of scale.[2] If such diecon-

---

[1] See Barriger, "Why Consolidation?" in Ruppenthal, ed., *Revolution in Transportation* 12, 33–36 (1960), for discussion of savings from consolidation.

[2] Healy, *The Effects of Scale in the Railroad Industry* 3 (1961). For critique of this study, see statement of Merrill J. Roberts in U.S. Cong., Senate, Committee on the Judiciary, *Hearings on Rail Merger Legislation* 333–334 (87th Cong. 2d Sess. 1962).

omies truly exist, new administrative structures will have to be developed for larger railroads to enjoy the full benefits of mergers in process in 1963.

The basic criterion of economics as applied to proposed consolidations is that aggregate transport costs be minimized.[3] A consolidation should be permitted if it can be estimated to result in long-run reductions in cost of transportation which would be greater than if some other possible consolidation with either of the affected carriers were to take place. Thus, priority should go to the consolidations of railroads with the most parallel, duplicate facilities and the greatest excess capacities in relation to historical peak-traffic data. Under this rule, specialized parallel carriers with many common terminals such as the Pocahontas coal roads, Norfolk & Western Railway and Chesapeake and Ohio Railway, should be consolidated before consideration of other possible mergers by either of them. Likewise, the Nickel Plate and New York Central, with their many parallel segments from Buffalo west to Chicago and St. Louis, should receive priority consideration in consolidation planning.

Under federal regulation in the United States, consolidation proposals are made by the railroads concerned, not by the Interstate Commerce Commission. Furthermore, the statutory criteria for approval of consolidations by the Commission do not coincide with the basic economic criterion of minimizing transport costs through a geographic region. For these reasons many railroad consolidations in the United States do not conform to the primary rule of priority in efficient organization of transport.

Since the consolidations before 1945 were reviewed in earlier studies,[4] this chapter will examine only those which occurred since that date. Under the Transportation Act of 1940, the Interstate Commerce Commission may approve a combination of carriers which it finds "will be consistent with the public interest."[5] In passing on a proposed transaction, the statute directs the Commission to give weight, *inter alia*, to the following considerations:

---

[3] Troxel, *Economics of Transport* 549–551 (1955).

[4] Leonard, *Railroad Consolidation Under the Transportation Act of 1920* (1946); Behling, *Railroad Coordination and Consolidation: A Review of Estimated Economies* (ICC Bureau of Statistics 1940); Chapman, *Railroad Mergers* (1934); Grodinsky, *Railroad Consolidation: Its Economics and Controlling Principles* (1930); Splawn, *Consolidation of Railroads* (1925).

[5] 54 Stat. 898, 905 (1940), 49 U.S.C. §5 (1958).

(1) the effect of the proposed transaction upon adequate transportation service to the public; (2) the effect upon the public interest of the inclusion, or failure to include, other railroads in the territory involved in the proposed transaction; (3) the total fixed charges resulting from the proposed transaction; and (4) the interest of the carrier employees involved.

The term "public interest" had been defined in a 1932 merger case to include adequacy of transportation service, essential conditions of economy and efficiency, and appropriate provision and best use of transportation facilities.[6] This definition has been adopted by the Commission in a number of recent cases.[7] The adequacy of service part of the definition is emphasized in the first specific standard of the 1940 act. But the idea of efficiency is not specifically mentioned in the 1940 statute. And the other three specific standards of the 1940 act, like the attempt to enforce inter-railroad competition, may actually work to impede the economic reorganization of the railroad industry through mergers.

A 1962 staff study by the Interstate Commerce Commission reviews the application of these standards of public interest.[8] This chapter will examine only a few recent, major consolidations of previously unaffiliated lines to test the statutory public-interest standards against the criteria for efficient allocation of resources.[9]

GULF, MOBILE AND OHIO MERGER OF THE ALTON

The Gulf, Mobile and Ohio Railroad Company merger of the Alton Railroad in 1947 is an example of a complementary, end-to-end merger. The 1941-mile G. M. & O. line extended from St. Louis south to Mobile and to New Orleans. The 959-mile Alton extended from Chicago south to St. Louis with a main branch west to Kansas City. The merger thus created a new 2,900-mile railroad with a through route from Chicago to Mobile and New Orleans to rival the parallel Illinois Central.

The Alton Railroad, which formerly was controlled by the Baltimore & Ohio Railroad, was in bankruptcy reorganization,

---

[6] *New York Central S. Corp.* v. *United States,* 287 U.S. 12, 25 (1932).

[7] See, e.g., *Louisville & Nashville Railroad Co. Merger,* 295 I.C.C. 457, 502–503 (1957); *Erie Railroad Co. Merger,* 312 I.C.C. 185, 246 (1960).

[8] U.S., Interstate Commerce Commission, *Railroad Consolidations and the Public Interest—A Preliminary Examination* (1962).

[9] Two recent mergers between previously affiliated railroads will not be discussed. See *Louisville & Nashville Railroad Co. Merger,* 295 I.C.C. 457 (1957); *Duluth, South Shore & Atlantic R. Co. Merger,* 312 I.C.C. 341 (1960).

and its properties had not been maintained.[10] The Commission approved the sale of the Alton to the G. M. & O. as being in the public interest.[11] The unified system was expected to increase combined revenues of the two railroads by at least $2.7 million per year through holding traffic on the system for longer hauls.[12] The combined carriers could offer improved and expedited service from Chicago to the Gulf, thus meeting the first of the specific criteria of the Transportation Act of 1940. Furthermore, this acquisition offered the lowest fixed charges as compared to the five alternate plans of reorganization for the Alton which had been proposed. Thus, the third of the specific criteria of the 1940 act was met. The Commission held that the Washington Job Protection Agreement of 1936 adequately protected the interests of employees and thus satisfied the fourth of the specific criteria of the 1940 act. Since no other carriers had petitioned to purchase the Alton, no questions were raised concerning the relative efficiency of G. M. & O. control as compared to that of lines paralleling the Alton.

The Alton Railroad was finally absorbed by the G. M. & O. on June 1, 1947. In 1948 President Tigrett asserted that the benefits derived from the Alton acquisition were in line with the previous estimates of approximately 5 per cent increase over 1945 gross revenues.[13] The revenue statistics tend to support his conclusion, but general freight-rate increases make any definite statements on the effect of the merger impossible. Table 7 is a freight revenue and freight ton-mile comparison of the combined G. M. & O. and Alton with the parallel Illinois Central. Before the 1947 merger of the Alton the G. M. & O.'s growth in freight revenues was proportionately behind the Illinois Central. After the 1947 merger, G. M. & O.'s growth in freight revenues was about proportionately equal to that of the Illinois Central. The freight ton-mile statistics do not show G. M. & O. growth equal to the Illinois Central after 1947. These statistics indicate that the growth was probably due to the general expansion of economic activity and tend to refute the argument that some portion of the G. M. & O. revenue growth was the result of the merger.

[10] See Lemly, *Gulf, Mobile and Ohio: A Railroad That Had to Expand or Expire* 183 (1953).

[11] *Gulf, M. & O. R. Co. Purchase, Securities,* 261 I.C.C. 405, 435 (1945); *Alton R. Co. Reorganization,* 261 I.C.C. 343, 361 (1945). For supplementary decisions, see 261 I.C.C. 817 (1945), 267 I.C.C. 145 (1947), 267 I.C.C. 201 (1947), 267 I.C.C. 265 (1947), 267 I.C.C. 830 (1947).

[12] See Gulf, Mobile and Ohio Railroad Company, *Sixth Annual Report* 5 (1946).

[13] Gulf, Mobile and Ohio Railroad Company, *Eighth Annual Report* 6 (1948).

TABLE 7

FREIGHT REVENUE AND FREIGHT TON-MILE COMPARISONS

GULF, MOBILE & OHIO AND ALTON RAILROADS WITH ILLINOIS CENTRAL RAILROAD

(1943–1952)

Year	Gulf, Mobile & Ohio and Alton Railroads				Illinois Central Railroad			
	Freight revenues (000 omitted)	Index of freight revenues (1947 = 100)	Ton-miles of revenue freight (000 omitted)	Index of ton-miles (1947 = 100)	Freight revenues (000 omitted)	Index of freight revenues (1947 = 100)	Ton-miles of revenue freight (000 omitted)	Index of ton-miles (1947 = 100)
1943	$58,765[a]	96.3	7,036,603	112.6	$195,346	101.9	24,641,062	127.5
1944	58,544[a]	95.9	6,392,466	102.3	200,810	104.7	23,823,779	123.2
1945	56,496[a]	92.6	6,294,983	100.7	184,772	96.4	20,871,618	108.0
1946	49,763[a]	81.5	5,612,492	89.8	165,361	86.2	18,297,365	94.7
1947	61,034[a]	100.0	6,250,008	100.0	191,740	100.0	19,330,383	100.0
1948	69,131	113.3	5,965,597	95.4	213,973	111.6	19,061,114	98.6
1949	62,675	102.7	5,088,025	81.4	203,743	106.3	16,885,990	87.4
1950	67,074	109.9	5,373,595	86.0	224,418	117.0	19,214,134	99.4
1951	76,845	125.9	5,967,622	95.5	243,126	126.8	20,314,765	105.1
1952	81,782	134.0	6,099,800	97.6	252,220	131.5	19,873,157	102.8

SOURCES: Annual Reports of the Gulf, Mobile & Ohio Railroad, Alton Railroad, and Illinois Central Railroad, 1943–1953.
[a] Combined revenues of G. M. & O. and Alton Railroads. Merger was effective June 1, 1947.

NORFOLK & WESTERN MERGER OF THE VIRGINIAN

The 1959 merger by the Norfolk & Western Railway Company of the Virginian Railway Company was the first merger of two Class I independent, parallel railroads in this century.[14] The 2,138-mile Norfolk & Western extended from Norfolk west to Columbus and Cincinnati and into the West Virginia coal fields. The 608-mile Virginian also extended west from Norfolk, parallel to and south of the Norfolk & Western. But the Virginian served different coal fields from the Norfolk & Western. In 1958, 67.1 per cent of Norfolk & Western's $190.3 million freight revenues were attributable to coal and coke traffic whereas 86.1 per cent of the Virginian's $47.6 million freight revenues were derived from coal and coke traffic. In spite of this dependence on coal traffic, both carriers were profitably operated and were in good financial condition.

The economies to be derived from the N. & W.-Virginian merger were to arise not primarily from abandonment of duplicate facilities but from the joint operation of the two lines as a single firm. The greatest cost savings were to arise from using the lowest-grade tracks for eastbound loaded coal trains over three mountain ranges. Over the most westerly range the Norfolk & Western had the lowest grade. Over the other two, the Virginian had the lowest grade. The Virginian's eastbound grade over the Blue Ridge Mountains, for example, was .2 per cent, while the Norfolk & Western's was 1.2 per cent. Consequently, with the same amount of power the merged lines can handle four times the tonnage over the Virginian line than over the Norfolk & Western line. Further economies were to be derived from concentrating coal loading of ships at Norfolk & Western's piers, merging freight yards and stations in a few key cities, and combining supervisory and office work.

After five years the estimated savings from the merger were to be $12 million per year. The $3,009,000 estimated savings in transportation expense included $798,559 in Norfolk & Western train operations and $878,500 in labor.[15] The $2,173,931 estimated savings on maintenance of way and structures included $950,000 in labor cost.[16] Total estimated savings on maintenance of equipment was $3,403,300.[17]

[14] The facts summarized here are from *Norfolk & Western Railway Co. Merger,* 307 I.C.C. 401 (1959).
[15] *Ibid.,* Exhibit H-50.
[16] *Ibid.,* Exhibit H-51.
[17] *Ibid.,* Exhibit H-54.

In approving the merger, effective December 1, 1959, the Commission held that "the evidence shows without doubt that the merger will have a favorable effect on transportation service. It will result in more adequate, efficient, and economical transportation service to the public." [18] The merger thus met the first standard of the Transportation Act; since no other railroad had requested inclusion and since no increase in fixed charges was contemplated, the second and third standards of the Transportation Act was met; the fourth standard, interest of the employees, was met by section 5(2)(f) of the act and supplementary stipulations.

Norfolk & Western executives reported that the result of the Virginian merger exceeded the predicted economies.[19] Not only were savings expected to exceed by 20 per cent the predicted $12 million per year at the end of five years, but many savings were realized much sooner. In the first eight months, the merged railroads saved $300,000 in maintenance costs by closing the Virginian's tidewater coal pier near Norfolk and diverting the trains to the Norfolk & Western piers whose excess capacity could easily absorb the extra shipments. Because of the lower grades of the Virginian lines over the Blue Ridge and Allegheny mountains the carriers were able to operate with 22 fewer locomotives and 1800 fewer cars. This resulted in a maintenance and interest saving and had the immediate effect of cutting the rate of spending on new equipment. This was offset, however, by capital expenditures to bring the Virginian line up to the high running standards of the Norfolk & Western. This included buttressing the roadbed and installing centralized traffic control on a 138-mile line.[20]

The financial reports of the Norfolk & Western illustrate the economic success of the merger.[21] Maintenance of way and structures per mile of road in the ten years before the merger averaged $12,542 on the Norfolk & Western and about $9,000 on the more poorly maintained Virginian. In 1961, with a high level of maintenance on the combined lines, the maintenance per mile of road was $8,651. Maintenance of equipment per mile of road was similar. For the ten years before the merger, Norfolk & Western averaged $18,664 and the Virginian averaged about $13,940. In 1961, the combined carrier's maintenance of equipment per mile of

[18] 307 I.C.C. at 440.
[19] See report in *Wall Street Journal*, Aug. 9, 1960, p. 1.
[20] Norfolk & Western Railroad, *Annual Report* 3–6 (1959).
[21] *Ibid.*, 1950–1962; Virginian Railway, *Annual Reports*, 1950–1959.

road was $13,929. The freight operating ratios of the Norfolk & Western in nine years before the merger averaged 63 and the Virginian 55.9. In 1961 the operating ratio of the combined roads was 54.7.

ERIE MERGER OF THE DELAWARE, LACKAWANNA & WESTERN

The Erie Railroad Company merger of the Delaware, Lackawanna & Western Railroad Company became effective in 1961.[22] The 2,313-mile Erie extended from New York to Buffalo and to Chicago. The 918-mile Lackawanna extended from New York to Buffalo. For a distance of about 125 miles the two lines were adjacent to each other, and for another 75 both railroads used the same tracks. Between New York and Buffalo the carriers served fifty-five common cities, and financial pressures favored merger of facilities. A long-run decline in anthracite-coal traffic, rising labor costs, and unprofitable commuter service caused both railroads to take financial downturns. In fact, they both showed net losses in 1958, 1959, and 1960.

The major economies to be derived from the Erie-Lackawanna merger were to come from combination of lines, terminals, and trains and from abandonment of duplicate facilities. The expected annual savings after five years were $13,540,000. Of this amount, $4,529,000 was to result from the unifications of freight-yard operations and facilities in thirteen common cities. Among the four largest of these were Buffalo, Binghamton, Scranton-Avoca, and Hoboken-Jersey City. Annual savings from the abandonment of 73 miles of duplicate lines were estimated at $555,700, or $7,612 per mile of line abandoned. Further savings were to result from combining scheduled freight trains on one through route utilizing the most advantageous portions of the two lines and from pooling of less-than-carload freight traffic and of freight and passenger equipment. Estimated annual savings from unification of general expense items were $1,849,000; from unification of traffic departments, $1,592,000; from unification of supervisory forces, $1,092,000; and from reduced maintenance of way costs (other than yards), $1,317,000.

In approving the merger, the Commission held that it would

---

[22] *Erie Railroad Company Merger*, 312 I.C.C. 185 (1960), injunction dismissed in *Brotherhood of Maintenance of Way Employees* v. *United States*, 189 F. Supp. 942 (E. D. Mich. 1960), *aff'd* 366 U.S. 169 (1961).

enhance the adequacy of service available to the public.[23] The factors listed were expected to result in faster trains and expedited movement through modernized yards. Savings to the carriers were also to be derived from reduced unit costs of traffic, from centralized accounting, and from other departments. It was found that the savings would result in continuing benefits to the shipping public and to the owners of securities of the applicants. Since no other railroads petitioned to be included and since fixed charges were not increased, the criteria of section 5(2) pertaining to these issues were also met. Labor was held to be adequately protected by the statute and supplementary conditions to which the carriers consented.

In spite of generally declining traffic and continued net losses, the Erie-Lackawanna maintained that the financial results of the merger in the first two years were better than the premerger estimate. At the end of two years, annual savings in wages, rental payments, and material costs approximated $6.6 million, as opposed to an expected savings rate of $6.2 million.[24] The average cost of maintenance of way and structures per mile of road in 1961 was $7,249 as compared with a five-year average before the year of merger of $8,466 on the Erie and $10,151 on the Lackawanna. The average maintenance of equipment per mile of road in 1961 was $13,081 as compared with a five-year average before the year of merger of $11,565 on the Erie and $13,393 on the Lackawanna.

The problems of effecting a railroad merger are well illustrated by that of the Erie-Lackawanna.[25] The greatest and most costly difficulties arose from the seniority rights of workers, contained in twenty-five different labor contracts. The carrier planned to eliminate 1,600 jobs and transfer 1,700 workers into other jobs during a five-year period. The policy was to eliminate jobs by attrition. During the first year, approximately 750 workers left employment; but those were not necessarily the ones whose jobs the railroad wished to terminate. In centralizing major locomotive repairs at Erie's Hornell, New York, shop, the railroad wanted to transfer 75 Lackawanna men from Scranton. But half of these men quit, causing a shortage of mechanics. A worse situation arose from the decision to centralize Erie-Lackawanna revenue accounting in Cleveland and disbursement accounting in Scranton. Under union

[23] 312 I.C.C. at 247.
[24] Erie-Lackawanna Railroad Company, *1962 Annual Report* 4 (1963).
[25] See *Wall Street Journal*, Feb. 12, 1962, p. 1.

rules Lackawanna's revenue clerks in Scranton had the right to refuse to move to Cleveland and by seniority to displace experienced disbursement clerks. As a result, 70 per cent of the disbursement accounting positions at Scranton had to be filled by revenue clerks who did not know the work. Similar but less serious problems arose in the program to standardize equipment on the two roads.

CHESAPEAKE AND OHIO CONTROL OF THE BALTIMORE AND OHIO

The control by the Chesapeake and Ohio Railway Company of the Baltimore and Ohio Railroad Company, although not a merger case, is significant as an intermediate step toward a contemplated merger and for the economies of coördination which resulted. The control was approved by the Interstate Commerce Commission to become effective on February 4, 1963.[26] The 5,091-mile C. & O. extended from Newport News, Virginia, on the east to Cincinnati and then to Chicago on the west. Another C. & O. division extended from Chicago into Michigan and to Buffalo. The 5,910-mile B. & O. line was north of the C. & O. main line, extending from New York to Washington on the east and then to St. Louis and Chicago. Thus, for the most part the two roads were complementary, the main C. & O. line serving the Pocahontas coal mines and the B. & O. serving northern industrial cities. The strong financial position of the C. & O. and the weak financial condition of the B. & O. were factors, favoring ties between the roads. Not only could C. & O. help to finance the rehabilitation of B. & O., but longer hauls of C. & O. coal over B. & O. lines would make for continued strength of the coördinated lines. These longer hauls would for the most part result from diverting traffic from other carriers, a transfer of resource use and not a net increase.

Even though the C. & O. and B. & O. had only 25.5 miles of parallel lines, the annual savings from coördination following acquisition of control and completion of capital improvements were estimated at $13 million.[27] Of this, annual savings of $7 million were to result from consolidation of stations and terminals in nine cities where the roads met. Among these were Chicago, Cincinnati, and Toledo. About $2 million in annual savings were to

---

[26] *Chesapeake & Ohio Railway Co. Control*, 317 I.C.C. 261 (1962), *aff'd sub nom. Broth. of Maint. of Way Employees* v. *United States*, 221 F. Supp. 19 (E.D. Mich. 1963), *aff'd per curiam* 375 U.S. 216 (1963).

[27] 317 I.C.C. at 275.

result from consolidation of offices, principally through joint use of a C. & O. computer. Pooling of equipment was estimated to result in $3.7 million of annual savings. Savings from abandonment of 25.5 miles of duplicate lines were estimated at $84,000 annually, or $3,294 per mile of line. Annual savings from combining duplicate passenger trains were estimated at $566,275, part of which would result from B. & O.'s using C. & O. tracks into Detroit and abandoning trackage rights over the New York Central.

In approving the acquisition of control, the Commission found that C. & O. financial support would enable B. & O. to provide more adequate transportation service in its area.[28] Both the roadbed and equipment of the B. & O. were deteriorated, and C. & O. financing would allow rehabilitation. Failure to include the New York Central in joint control of B. & O. was found not greatly injurious to that carrier. New York Central estimates of large traffic which would be diverted from it were rejected by the Commission. No increase in fixed charges was to result from the exchange of shares. Labor protections in addition to those in section 5(2)(f) of the Interstate Commerce Act were specified as in previous cases.

SEABOARD AIR LINE MERGER OF ATLANTIC COAST LINE

The merger by the Seaboard Air Line Railroad of the Atlantic Coast Line Railroad was approved by the Interstate Commerce Commission on December 2, 1963.[29] This merger would join two large Class I, parallel railroads. The 4,146-mile Seaboard and the 5,573-mile Atlantic Coast Line both extend from Washington, D.C., south through the states of the Atlantic coast and into Florida. The two carriers have facilities and provide service at 121 common points, and at 64 of these points facilities for interchange of traffic between the two carriers are available. Both roads were in strong financial condition so that the arguments based on financial distress, like that of the B. & O. in the C. & O.-B. & O. merger case, were not applicable.

The annual savings resulting from the merger after five years were estimated in 1963 at $38,732,624. Consolidation of stations and terminals at 67 of the common cities were expected to result

---

[28] See Chesapeake & Ohio Railway Co., *1962 Annual Report* 13 (1963).

[29] *Seaboard Air Line Railroad Company Merger*, I.C.C. Finance Docket 21215, Report of The Commission (Dec. 2, 1963).

in annual savings of $4,485,990. The carriers contemplated abandonment of 1,139 miles of duplicate, parallel lines, or 11.7 per cent of their combined lines. Specific application for abandonment was not made in this proceeding but was to follow completion of the merger. This was to result in an annual savings of $7,465,784 or $7,371 per mile of line abandoned. Annual savings from consolidation of retained lines was to be $5,126,236. By consolidation of offices, the total number of employees was to be reduced from 3,954 to 2,850, with annual savings of $10,226,559. Annual savings from use of shorter or more economical routes were estimated at $2,553,135; from pooling of equipment, $2,164,-960; and from consolidation of heavy repair facilities, $2,228,665. Increased income from longer hauls of freight, partially by diversion from other railroads, was estimated at $4,910,000 annually.

Further savings were to result from new investment made profitable by the increased traffic density on a single line, enabling the combined line to realize greater economies of scale. Thus the merged lines were to build a new modern hump retarder railroad yard at Jacksonville, Florida, at a net annual saving of $2,545,991. This was equivalent to a 17.7 per cent return on the net investment of $14,411,395. Such a yard was to expedite the assembly and handling of through movement of solid trains between Jacksonville and Richmond with no terminal handling enroute. Because of the lower rates and better service to result from new through routes, many industrial firms voiced favor of the merger.

A significant aspect of this case was the petition of intervening railroads that as a condition of approval the Commission require the Seaboard and Atlantic Coast Line to transfer specific sections of their lines to intervenors. Florida East Coast Railway Company requested transfer to it of Seaboard's line on the southeast coast of Florida. Southern Railway System requested transfer to it of a line from Hardeeville, South Carolina, to Jacksonville, Florida. The Central of Georgia Railway requested trackage rights over Atlantic Coast lines from Albany, Georgia, to Jacksonville, Florida, and use of yards of the merged railroads. All these requests for conditions to the merger were based on the argument that the merged line would divert so much traffic from intervenors that their solvency would be endangered. In following the hearing examiner's recommendation of denial of these requests for conditions the Commission found that they would frustrate the over-all objective of the merger of creating new and more efficient through routes.[30] The Commission likewise denied a request that the Atlantic Coast Line be required to divest itself of its 33.69 per cent interest in the Louisville & Nashville Railroad. In the light of other trackage conditions imposed, it found that the existing reciprocity between carriers would prevent traffic diversions large enough to injure significantly the intervening railroads. The Illinois Central and Gulf, Mobile & Ohio would both be able to retaliate against diversions of their northbound traffic to the L. & N. by diverting their southbound traffic to the Southern and Florida East Coast railroads.

In approving the merger the Commission held that it would achieve the twin objectives of eliminating wasteful transport and the fuller utilization of the merging railroads' potential for rendering efficient and economic service. To protect the Southern Railway and its affiliated Central of Georgia, the Commission attached conditions to the merger approval guaranteeing these carriers trackage rights over the merged lines into Jacksonville and removing restrictions on existing agreements for routing north of Jacksonville. Joint rates with the Southern no higher than those over the merged lines were ordered, provided the Southern would grant similar joint rates to the merged lines. New connecting routes with new joint rates for the Norfolk-Southern Railway were also ordered. The new routes and rates were designed to assure rival carriers equal opportunity to carry shipments terminating on the merged lines.

CASES PENDING IN 1964

A large number of railroad mergers was in the planning stages in early 1964. Many of them will probably fail to secure sufficient stockholder approval for execution. This section will review only four major pending mergers which have secured stockholder approval and were before the Interstate Commerce Commission at the beginning of 1964. Two of these had received favorable recommendations from hearing examiners.

Great Northern—Northern Pacific-Burlington consolidation.— The two main parties to this consolidation are the 8,279-mile Great Northern Railway Company and the 6,800-mile Northern Pacific Railway Company.[31] Both carriers operate between Min-

---

[30] *Ibid.,* 79–90 and Appendix XI.

[31] *Great Northern Pacific & Burlington Lines, Inc. Merger,* I.C.C. Finance Docket Nos. 21478–21480, Brief on Behalf of Applicants (1963).

neapolis and Seattle, but the Great Northern, running near the Canadian border, is much further north. Also included in the consolidation are two subsidiaries of the two main carriers, the 8,648-mile Chicago, Burlington & Quincy Railroad and the 600-mile Spokane, Portland and Seattle. The Burlington main lines run from Minneapolis to Chicago and from Billings and Denver through Omaha to Chicago. Together with minor subsidiaries the combined lines would be the longest U.S. railroad, 24,728 miles.

The estimated annual savings from this consolidation are $49,-385,414, reduced by an allowance for contingencies of 12½ per cent to $43,212,237. Savings from consolidation of stations and yards at thirty-nine of one hundred common points would be $15,846,690 annually. Of these savings, 85 per cent is concentrated in five principal cities: Minneapolis, Seattle, Duluth, Spokane, and Portland. The second largest annual savings of $10,586,135 would arise from reduced general office, traffic, and superintendence expense. Savings from internal rerouting of traffic on the shorter and most economical routes of the unified company would be $6,118,936 annually. Annual savings from pooling of equipment would be $3,352,737. Abandonment of about 480 miles of line, or 1.94 per cent of the merged lines, would result in annual savings of $3,059,838—equal to $6,375 per mile of line abandoned. Annual savings from consolidation of those lines retained in service would be $2,488,026; from consolidation of repair facilities, $2,194,535; and from combining duplicate trains, $2,195,885.

The applicants argued that the consolidation met the prime standard of the Transportation Act of 1940 in its provision of more adequate service to shippers. The carriers maintained that much faster through-freight schedules could be adopted, whereby shipping time on perishable fruit and vegetables from the Northwest to Chicago would be cut by as much as thirteen hours. The pooling of freight cars would give shippers a better supply of cars and the new routes would give processors additional advantages for transit and routing privileges. Rising labor costs had aggravated the problem of maintaining adequate service in the sparsely settled areas west of Minnesota and east of Washington. The new consolidated trains and reorganized service would help keep the previous service standards. The better balance of traffic resulting from the unified system would also reduce total transportation costs and add to the stability of the carrier.

The overwhelming majority of shippers along the Great Northern and Northern Pacific favored the consolidation. Two railroads strongly opposed the consolidation and asked for conditions to be attached. The Chicago, Milwaukee, St. Paul and Pacific, which parallels much of the Northern Pacific from Minneapolis to Seattle, asked that eleven new gateways be opened by the merged company. In this way, freight originating in a town served only by the merged company in cars supplied by the merged company could be diverted to the Milwaukee at the nearest gateway on direction of the shipper. The Milwaukee also requested conditions giving it trackage rights into Portland, Oregon, and Bellingham, Washington. All requested Milwaukee conditions are designed to divert new traffic to it, traffic which it never received previously because of its route location. Similar conditions were proposed by the Chicago and North Western. Since these conditions would force the merged company to short-haul itself on many routes, they are strongly opposed by the company. Such severe conditions for merger are not usually granted by the Commission.

Norfolk & Western merger of Nickel Plate and lease of Wabash. —The two primary parties to this merger, the Norfolk & Western Railway Company and the New York, Chicago, & St. Louis Railroad Company (Nickel Plate) are carriers with no direct connections.[32] The 2,747-mile Norfolk & Western extends from Norfolk, Virginia, west to Cincinnati and Columbus. The 2,170-mile Nickel Plate extends from Buffalo west to Chicago and St. Louis. In order to connect the two lines, the plan includes purchase by the merged road of the 108-mile Sandusky line from the Pennsylvania Railroad. This line extends north from Columbus to Sandusky, Ohio. The 2,424-mile Wabash extends from Buffalo west to Chicago, St. Louis, and Kansas City. Many Wabash lines parallel those of the Nickel Plate.

The economies to be derived from this merger would not result from abandonment of duplicate lines or from the reduction of local service. Most economies would result from combining the parallel operations and yards in common cities of the Nickel Plate and Wabash. The Nickel Plate line from Buffalo to Chicago and the Wabash line from Detroit to St. Louis would become the main through freight lines for the merged roads. Parallel lines could then be reduced to lower maintenance levels for local, slow freights only. Combining of yards and services of the Nickel Plate

[32] *Norfolk and Western Railway Company and New York, Chicago and St. Louis Railroad Company—Merger,* I.C.C. Finance Docket 21510–21514 & 21567, Report and Order of Hearing Examiner (April 17, 1963).

and Wabash could take place at thirteen common points, including Buffalo, Chicago and St. Louis. Further economies would result from combining motive-power maintenance, retirement of equipment, and the combining of maintenance of way, traffic, and executive departments.

The total estimated annual economies after five years would be $27 million.[33] Of this, $9,950,000 would be from changed operating organization of trains, yards, switching, and trackage. Although no breakdown of figures is reported, most of this must result from the Nickel Plate-Wabash part of the unification. More than $6,650,000 annually would result from combining maintenance of motive power, purchases, and stores departments of the three lines. About $5,190,000 annually would result from combining executive, finance accounting, and other offices of the lines and $3,330,000 from combining traffic and industrial departments.

The ICC hearing examiner, in reporting favorably on the proposed merger, found benefits to the Norfolk & Western in more diversified traffic and longer hauls. Improved service to the public is expected in reduced shipping time from the Midwest to the East, primarily on the Wabash-Nickel Plate combined lines. For goods originating on the Norfolk & Western for the Midwest, there still would have to be one switching of cars at Bellevue, Ohio. Public benefit is also expected from the combination of Nickel Plate and Wabash yards, especially in the handling of trailers on flat cars. Pooling of equipment, a larger joint traffic department, and electronic processing of car-movement data are also expected to increase the quality of service to the public.

Pennsylvania-New York Central consolidation.—The proposed consolidation of the Pennsylvania Railroad Company and the New York Central Railroad Company would create the largest railroad in the country in terms of total traffic. The 12,037-mile Pennsylvania system and the 10,306-mile New York Central system both extend from New York west to Chicago and St. Louis. Most New York Central lines lie north of the Pennsylvania. Together they account for 44 per cent of the miles of railroad in the Eastern District.

Savings from the Pennsylvania-New York Central proposal, in its original form, are not derived primarily from line abandonments, but from more economic use of existing facilities. The total estimated annual savings at the end of five years are $81,550,-

[33] *Ibid.*, Appendix "R."

000.[34] Of this, $42,200,000 annual savings are expected from consolidation of freight terminals in the one hundred common points served by the two roads. These include most major cities in the northeastern United States. The next largest annual savings component is $14.5 million on road freight service. This includes, for example, routing all through freight from Chicago or St. Louis to New York on the more level New York Central lines. This northern route from St. Louis to New York is 49 miles longer than the Pennsylvania route but is faster and more economical because of the lower grades. Total annual savings in traffic and general office expense would be $11,650,000; savings from reorganized passenger service would be $6,800,000, and from reduced maintenance of equipment, $6,400,000.

Missouri Pacific control of the Chicago & Eastern Illinois.— The ICC hearing examiner recommended approval of this control petition connecting the two railroads end-to-end.[35] The 11,000-mile Missouri Pacific lines extend from St. Louis west to Colorado and south to Louisiana and Texas. The 862-mile Chicago & Eastern Illinois main lines extend south from Chicago to Evansville and to St. Louis. The two carriers have their main interconnections at East St. Louis and at Thebes, Illinois. The weak financial condition of the C. & E. I. appears to be a major factor in its search for affiliation with a longer, through carrier. Specific dollar savings expected from effecting this control were not listed by Missouri Pacific and were not found by the examiner. Some undetermined savings would result from decrease in terminal switching absorptions wherever direct interchange would replace intermediate switching service, and from joint use of cars, locomotives, and roadway machinery. Missouri Pacific estimated added aggregate freight revenues of $10.9 million by diversion of traffic from other carriers.

Rival petitions of the Illinois Central and the Louisville & Nashville were recommended by the hearing examiner to be denied. The 6,500-mile Illinois Central has lines paralleling most of the C. & E. I. and in addition has through routes from Chicago to New Orleans and to Birmingham. Estimated annual cost savings from control of C. & E. I. by Illinois Central, without abandon-

[34] *Pennsylvania Railroad—New York Central Railroad—Merger*, I.C.C. Finance Docket Nos. 21989–21990, Exhibit H 313 (1963).
[35] *Missouri Pacific R. Co.—Control—Chicago & Eastern Illinois R. Co.*, I.C.C., Finance Docket No. 21755, Report and Recommended Order by Hearing Examiner Hyman J. Blond, Sept. 19, 1963.

ment of any lines, would be $4,422,395. Of this total, $1,446,450 would be from unification of freight and passenger terminals, $1,337,800 from unifying mechanical departments, and $1,200,000 from combining administrative, corporate, treasury, and accounting expenses. The control proposal by Illinois Central did not include increases in traffic by diversion from other railroads. The examiner recommended against Illinois Central control because C. & E. I. would be eliminated as an effective competing railroad and Illinois Central would be able to favor its own lines in derogation of C. & E. I. lines. The closing of C. & E. I. yards and offices would make it unable to resume later its independent existence.

Louisville & Nashville Railroad, a 5,683-mile line extending south from Evansville and Cincinnati to Atlanta and New Orleans, did not petition for complete control of C. & E. I. It asked that any railroad acquiring control be required to sell to L. & N. the 205-mile C. & E. I. line from Evansville north to Woodland and half-interest in the 82-mile C. & E. I. line from Woodland north to Chicago. The effect would be to extend L. & N.'s northern terminus, Evansville, to Chicago, giving it a through route from the Great Lakes to the Gulf of Mexico to rival Illinois Central. L. & N. estimated cost savings to the two carriers resulting from this acquisition to be $2.7 million annually and increased annual revenues by diversion of traffic from other carriers to be $2.5 million. The examiner recommended dismissal of this petition to create a condition precedent to allowing control by the other petitioners as being impractical. Before being allowed to exercise control, Missouri Pacific or Illinois Central could not force C. & E. I. to sell part of its line. If terms of sale of the Evansville line to C. & E. I. could not be reached, the major control would be blocked. Any alternate petition of C. & E. I. to acquire only trackage rights on the Evansville line was held to be independent of the major control petitions here and not a basis to condition them.

ECONOMIC CONCLUSIONS

Presuming the continuance of adequate transportation service as required by the Interstate Commerce Act, the key economic criterion for railroad consolidations is efficiency or lowest attainable cost for a given output. The two main aspects of economic efficiency are the organization of the industry and the internal

efficiency of the individual firms.[36] Most proposed railroad mergers are estimated to result in increases in efficiency on both levels.
The first aspect concerns the absolute size or scale of firms and
the extent to which chronic excess capacity exists in the industry.
Although every merger increases the size of the firms, the carriers
deny the existence of diseconomies of scale. Rather, they argue that
consolidation of executive, accounting, and traffic departments
create real economies of scale. Further, they argue that to the
extent that some yards and piers can be dismantled and some
duplicate lines abandoned, the chronic excess capacity of the industry is reduced.

Mergers are also argued as contributing to the internal efficiency
of railroads. Rising labor costs relative to costs of capital equipment make more intensive investment profitable. But some types
of investment, such as the modern electronic hump-retarder yards,
require a scale of local operations much larger than many single
carriers can obtain. Thus, unification of the Atlantic Coast Line
and Seaboard Air Line railroads will make it practicable for the
merged carrier to build hump retarder yards in a few key cities,
whereas traffic on either of the two lines alone was insufficient to
justify such investment.[37] Similar economies in accounting and
car-control systems require electronic data processing equipment
on a scale too large to be profitable for many single lines. Furthermore, specialized managerial skills which are presently available
in only one of the merging railroads will, upon merger, become
available to the entire unified system.

Table 8, showing cost savings from mergers as a percentage of
combined operating expenses, confirms the theoretical assumption
that the railroads with the closest parallel lines and the greatest
number of duplicate yards and terminals will effect the largest
relative savings. Although every railroad cost structure is unique
and comparability is limited, Table 8 can be used as a general
estimate of the value of different consolidations. The Gulf, Mobile
& Ohio-Alton merger and the proposed Missouri Pacific-Chicago & Eastern Illinois merger are both end-to-end consolidations
of complementary lines. They were not expected to result in any
material cost savings but were proposed only to increase revenues
by diverting traffic from other lines. In contrast, the proposed

[36] See Bain, *Industrial Organization* 343 (1959).
[37] Rice, "Why Not Merge and Survive?" 345 *Annals of the American Academy of
Political and Social Science* 103, 106 (1963).

TABLE 8

COST SAVINGS FROM MERGERS IN RELATION TO OPERATING EXPENSE

Carriers	Year of merger or pending proposal	Expected annual cost savings or increased revenue[a]	Total operating expense	Cost saving as a percentage of operating expense
Gulf, Mobile & Ohio merger of Alton	1946	$ 2,700,000[a]	$ 55,241,240	0.00
Norfolk & Western merger of the Virginian	1959	12,000,000	150,989,847	7.95
Erie merger of Delaware, Lackawanna & Western	1961	13,540,000	192,164,820	7.05
Chesapeake & Ohio control of the Baltimore & Ohio	1963	13,380,000	556,370,261	2.34
Seaboard Air Line merger of Atlantic Coast Line	1962	38,732,624	259,783,905	14.91
Great Northern-Northern Pacific-Burlington merger	1962	49,385,414	565,064,130	8.74
Norfolk & Western merger of Nickel Plate and lease of Wabash	1962	27,000,000	333,059,655	8.11
Pennsylvania-New York Central consolidation	1962	81,550,000	1,214,967,841	6.71
Missouri Pacific control of Chicago & Eastern Illinois	1962	10,900,000[a]	251,365,289	0.00

SOURCE: See footnotes in this chapter pertaining to particular unifications.

[a] In Gulf Mobile & Ohio-Alton and Missouri Pacific-Chicago & Eastern Illinois cases, carriers note no exact cost saving. Amount listed is expected increased revenue from diverting traffic from other carriers.

merger showing the greatest estimated relative cost saving is that of the Seaboard Air Line and Atlantic Coast Line with 14.9 per cent. Of all proposed mergers, these two carriers have the most closely parallel lines. Data from individual proposals also demonstrate that the largest single elements of estimated savings arise from consolidation of terminals and yards and from rescheduling of trains to the shortest, most level routes. Thus the New York Central-Pennsylvania merger proposal with total estimated annual savings after the fifth year of $81.5 million would realize $56.7 million or 69.5 per cent from terminal and road freight changes. Even in the Chesapeake and Ohio control of the Baltimore and Ohio, primarily an end-to-end unification of complementary lines, $7 million of the total estimated annual savings of $13 million were to result from consolidation of stations and terminals in the nine cities where the roads met.

From the viewpoint of promoting economic efficiency, the present regulatory statutes for railroad mergers are clearly deficient. As noted in the Doyle Report,[38] the first step in promoting reorganization of railroad investment toward greater efficiency is to amend the consolidation section of the Transportation Act of 1940 so that it fosters, rather than hinders mergers. The specific economic criteria should become the prime standards of whether a merger is approved. The primary statutory requirement should be the economic rule that the proposed consolidation is estimated to result in long-run savings in costs which are greater than if some other possible consolidation were to be effected. The detailed economic criteria should amplify this rule.

The failure of two railroads to include some third railroad in their merger proposal should not be a ground to deny Commission approval. Mere financial weakness of railroads is not a rational economic criterion for approval or disapproval of a merger.[39] If, for example, the Pennsylvania and the New York Central can demonstrate that their proposed consolidation will result in greater savings than any other merger by either of them, failure to include the financially unstable Erie-Lackawanna in their proposal should not carry weight. Likewise, any consolidation standard that requires traffic to move over previously existing routes should be eliminated.[40] The diversion of traffic from some of the existing routes to more efficient routes is one key economic purpose of mergers and is clearly inconsistent with the maintenance of traffic levels on existing routes.

Both the railroads and the Interstate Commerce Commission must realize that merger regulation based on the premise that the existing amount of railroad lines and yards is optimum is erroneous. Protection of weak carriers by allowing them to block mergers of stronger carriers and protection of existing traffic routes as against more efficient ones are both based on this erroneous premise. The facts of the railroad industry are that chronic excess capacity exists in lines and yards in many areas and that this proliferation of fixed plant is not consistent with our present technology and competitive conditions. Mergers of parallel rail-

---

[38] U.S. Congress, Senate, Committee on Interstate and Foreign Commerce, *National Transportation Policy* (Doyle Report) 268–272 (87th Cong. 1st Sess. 1961).

[39] But see *Missouri Pacific R. Co.* v. *United States*, 4 F. Supp. 449, 458 (E.D.Ky. 1933).

[40] See dissent of Commissioner Mahaffie in *Chicago, B. & Q. R. Co. Control*, 271 I.C.C. 63, 166–167 (1948), quoted above at page 60.

road lines and abandonment of duplicate facilities are in order. Intensive investment in fewer miles of road, in centralized traffic control and in more cars, must replace existing extensive investment. As a result of such mergers and abandonments, the most direct and efficient railroads can become financially strong and able to adapt changing technology toward ever greater cost reductions. Weak and inefficient carriers may end up at bankruptcy sales. This should be recognized as one of the methods by which a free economy stops the wasting of its resources. Sections of such roads which can be rehabilitated and made viable operations will be acquired at bankruptcy sale by more efficient, connecting railroads and incorporated into them. The remaining sections will be abandoned. The economic facts must be faced. The majority of railroads can be revitalized by radical changes in the structure of the industry. As in all other sectors of the economy, least efficient rivals may be driven from business. Only this kind of reallocation of resources in the railroad industry can save its firms, both strong and weak, from bankruptcy.

V

Functional Mergers: Pooling and Trackage Agreements

Part of the answer to the problem of excess capacity in railroad fixed plant is found in the consolidation of carriers and the abandonment of some lines and yards.* But there are limits to railroad mergers. Some railroads may serve different territories and then converge and become parallel over only 20 to 200 miles of line. Diseconomies may arise from consolidating the main, unrelated sections of two such carriers.[1] The financial problems of negotiating mergers and the costs of effecting mergers may also impede any general consolidation movement. In these cases, alternative means of railway coördination may be adopted as part of a program of reducing excess capacity in fixed plant.[2] This can be accomplished through functional mergers of particular duplicate facilities or services, followed by abandonment of redundant fixed plant or discontinuance of certain services. Functional mergers can be accomplished by pooling agreements, trackage agreements, joint ownership of facilities, or a combination of these. The economic advantages of each of these methods of partial combination will be examined and compared. The applicable regulatory statutes will be reviewed critically, and new statutes designed to effect economic reallocation of resources will be suggested.

---

* This chapter is a revised version of an article with the same title which appeared in 47 *Minnesota Law Review* 769 (1963).

[1] See Healy, *The Effects of Scale in the Railroad Industry* (1961).

[2] See Baker, "Possibilities of Economies by Railroad Consolidation and Co-ordination," 30 *Am. Econ. Rev.*, Supp. 140, 150 (1940); Landon, "Regional Transportation Coordination," 5 *Sou. Econ. J.* 1 (1938).

POOLING AGREEMENTS

Railway pooling agreements are of two main types: pooling of profits by an agreement to divide traffic or revenues in order to reinforce rate-fixing agreements and prevent rate rivalry,[3] and pooling of services by an agreement to control the number of trains or services that each carrier will operate, which may incidentally result in the sharing of traffic and revenues.[4] The first type has only long-run effects on the amount of resources in the industry. The second type, however, is concerned explicitly with limiting the resources used, thereby reducing aggregate costs of operations of the carriers.

The pooling agreements of the nineteenth century were of the first type and were designed to eliminate the rate rivalry of that period.[5] Since these agreements were in restraint of trade and therefore were unenforceable at common law,[6] they were highly unstable, and secret concessions to some shippers were accentuated when drops in aggregate demand increased excess capacity. Complaints of shippers led to the complete prohibition of pooling agreements in section 5 of the Interstate Commerce Act.[7] They were later also held illegal under section 1 of the Sherman Act.[8]

The absolute prohibition on pooling agreements was not relaxed until 1920. Parallel, duplicate services of two railroads, both operated at net losses because of severe excess capacity, required a remedy based on agreement if one was to continue to serve shippers on both lines. The request of the carriers and the recommendations of the ICC, based in part on the experience under unified operations during World War I, resulted in an amendment of the Interstate Commerce Act.[9] Section 5(1), which is still the effective law, enables the Commission to approve and author-

[3] See Troxel, *Economics of Transport* 428 (1955).

[4] See *In re* Pooling Freights, 115 Fed. 588, 589 (W. D. Tenn. 1902); *Boston & Me. R.R.*, 298 I.C.C. 703, 708–709 (1956).

[5] See Grodinsky, *The Iowa Pool* 163–67 (1950); Ripley, *Railroads Finance & Organization* 575–607 (1915); Newcomb, *Railway Economics* 125–137 (1898); Hudson, "The Southern Railway & Steamship Association," 5 *Q.J. Econ.* 70 (1890).

[6] See *Chicago M. & St. P. Ry. v. Wabash, St. L. & R. Ry.*, 61 Fed. 993, 997 (8th Cir. 1894) and cases cited therein; Locklin, *Economics of Transportation* 292–96 (5th ed. 1960).

[7] 24 Stat. 380 (1887), as amended, 49 U.S.C. §5(1) (1958).

[8] See *United States v. Trans-Missouri Freight Ass'n*, 166 U.S. 290 (1897). For an illegal rate-fixing agreement that also contained a clause for the sharing of traffic, see *United States v. Joint Traffic Ass'n*, 171 U.S. 505 (1898).

[9] See 3A Sharfman, *The Interstate Commerce Commission* 404 (1935).

ize pooling-of-service agreements between carriers if it finds that the agreements "will be in the interest of better service to the public, or economy in operation, and will not unduly restrain competition." [10]

The comprehensive scope of section 5(1) is indicated by the decision in *Chicago & N. W. Ry. Co.* v. *Peoria & P. U. Ry. Co.*[11] In that case, plaintiff line-haul railroad, which passed near Peoria, Illinois, agreed in 1911 with the defendant local-transfer railroad to allow defendant to handle the transfer and switching of all cars of plaintiff coming into, going out of, or through the city. In 1957, plaintiff completed outside Peoria a direct interchange with the Toledo, Peoria & Western, a line-haul carrier which also traversed the city of Peoria. Plaintiff filed a declaratory judgment action, alleging that its 1911 contract with defendant was in part a pooling agreement, extended after 1920 without ICC approval. Decision was rendered for plaintiff, the court holding that even though the carriers did not serve the same specific customers, their agreement was a division of traffic between potential competitors. When plaintiff made a direct connection with T. P. & W., actual competition was found to exist between plaintiff and defendant for transfer of plaintiff's cars to T. P. & W. at Peoria.

The complete elimination of the competition that might exist between particular services of parallel carriers is a necessary concomitant of the pooling-of-service agreement. If duplicate trains or facilities are abolished, this elimination of competition is seen even more clearly. The statute failed to meet this issue. Recognizing that restraint of competition is a necessary part of pooling agreements, the statute created confusion by failing to recognize that the restraint is necessarily total; instead, it required some amount of competition. In one case, the Commission sidestepped the issue by a noncommittal interpretation. In speaking of the restraint on competition, it said that "whether [it] . . . is undue depends not on its scope but on whether it is improper or inappropriate." [12] It is not surprising that such an ambiguous statute was little used, especially since the same type of constraint was not part of the consolidation section of the 1920 act.[13]

Numerous situations exist where rivalry of two parallel rail-

[10] 41 Stat. 481 (1920), 49 U.S.C. §5(1) (1958).
[11] 201 F. Supp. 241 (S.D. Ill. 1962), *aff'd* 319 F. 2d 117 (1963), *cert. denied* 375 U.S. 969 (1964).
[12] *Express Contract, 1929*, 275 I.C.C. 739, 744 (1951).
[13] 41 Stat. 481 (1920), 49 U.S.C. §5(2) (1958).

roads with great excess capacity results in losses in particular services for both carriers. In such a situation, improvements in technology are not made, for both carriers would also show losses on
this new investment. Yet neither carrier may find it wise to discontinue the service as long as revenues exceed out-of-pocket costs,
and regulatory commissions may even require continuance of
those services that do not earn enough to cover out-of-pocket costs.
There have been a number of cases involving passenger services
where pooling agreements have been approved as a solution to
this problem.[14] Thus, pooling of passenger service by three carriers between Portland and Seattle resulted in the reduction of
the total number of trains operated and made investment in a
new, faster train economically feasible.[15] Since not all trains were
pooled, the Commission found that competition would not be
unduly restrained. In a similar passenger pool between the Minneapolis and Duluth areas,[16] the Duluth Chamber of Commerce
petitioned the Commission to end the pool on the ground that it
had destroyed competition and resulted in poor service.[17] The
petition was denied; the Commission held that competition was
not unduly restrained since competition included buses and private automobiles. In a later proceeding to reduce the number of
trains on this run, it was held that competition was not unduly
restrained and that any restraint of competition that did result
was necessary to insure the continued operation of passenger service by the three lines.[18] Declining patronage caused by highway
competition resulted in approval of a similar passenger pooling
agreement for carriers between Chicago and Duluth.[19]

The superior door-to-door service of trucks has resulted in a
sharp decline in railroad less-than-carload freight (LCL). To
minimize losses on LCL service while still offering daily service,
parallel railroads have entered pooling-of-service agreements. Each
carrier hauls an LCL car over the route on alternate days or weeks

[14] For discussion of excess capacity in passenger service, see U.S. Federal Coordinator of Transportation, *Passenger Traffic Report* (1935).

[15] *Puget Sound–Portland Joint Passenger-Train Serv.*, 96 I.C.C. 116 (1925), *modified*, 128 I.C.C. 149 (1927), 167 I.C.C. 308 (1930), 169 I.C.C. 244 (1930), 194 I.C.C.
426 (1933), 218 I.C.C. 239 (1936).

[16] *Twin Cities & Head of Lakes Joint Passenger Train Serv.*, 107 I.C.C. 493 (1926),
modified, 112 I.C.C. 403 (1926), 132 I.C.C. 413 (1927), 161 I.C.C. 1 (1930).

[17] *Twin Cities & Head of Lakes Joint Passenger Train Serv.*, 237 I.C.C. 381 (1940).

[18] *Joint Passenger Train Serv.*, 302 I.C.C. 355, 362 (1957).

[19] *Pooling Passenger Train Revenues & Serv.*, 194 I.C.C. 430 (1933), *modified*, 220
I.C.C. 659 (1937), 223 I.C.C. 343 (1937), 243 I.C.C.. 765 (1941), 269 I.C.C. 590 (1948);
see Note, "Regulation of Railroad Service Competition," 48 *Yale L. J.* 143 (1938).

for all LCL freight of both roads without regard to routing instructions by the shipper. Although rates and service are fixed by pooling agreements, the ICC has held that LCL pools will not unduly restrain competition as long as each road continues to solicit traffic.[20] In the *New York-Miami Pool* case, the Commission held that competition would not be unduly restrained since neither the other railroad in the area nor rival types of transport appeared to protest the approval.[21] In the *New York-Macon Pool* case, the Commission stated that the record established that the arrangement did not unduly restrain competition; it did not state which facts in the record proved this, however.[22] These cases indicate that expedited service, savings in costs, and rivalry of highway transport will result in approval of LCL pooling agreements.

A number of pooling agreements have related to the use of the iron-ore docks on Lake Superior and the access tracks to them.[23] There was substantial excess capacity in ore docks in Northern Michigan, and some of them had not been maintained. Rather than make the large investments necessary to restore deteriorated docks, the carriers pooled the use of the newer, maintained docks. Such combination pooling-and-trackage agreements resulted in more intense use of some docks and tracks, which in turn resulted in savings. The leading ore-pooling agreement, between the Chicago and North Western Railway and the Chicago, Milwaukee, St. Paul and Pacific Railroad, has been summarized in litigation over nonpooled traffic on the same lines. The essential facts were as follows:

The pooling agreement contemplated that the Milwaukee would discontinue its operations under trackage rights over the line of the Escanaba and Lake Superior Railroad (E. & L. S.) from a connection at Channing to Escanaba, and would abandon its ore docks at Escanaba; that the North Western would abandon its line from Amasa to Crystal Falls, approximately paralleling a line of the Milwaukee; and that the

[20] *Pooling of Merchandise Traffic, St. Louis to Los Angeles,* 276 I.C.C. 424, 426 (1949).

[21] *Pooling, L.C.L. Freight Serv., New York to Miami,* 283 I.C.C. 171, 174 (1951).

[22] *Pooling, L.C.L. Freight Serv., New York and Philadelphia to Macon,* 283 I.C.C. 158, 162 (1951); see *Pooling, L.C.L. Traffic, Nashville to Memphis,* 291 I.C.C. 79 (1953).

[23] *Pooling of Ore Traffic in Wis. & Mich.,* 219 I.C.C. 285 (1936), *aff'd in part sub. nom, Escanaba & L.S.R.R. v. United States,* 21 F. Supp. 151 (1937), *aff'd,* 303 U.S. 315 (1938); *Pooling Ore Traffic in Wis. & Mich.,* 201 I.C.C. 13 (1934), *modified,* 302 I.C.C. 65 (1957); *Northern Pac. Ry.,* 154 I.C.C. 279 (1929); see *Chicago & N.W. Ry. v. United States,* 195 F. Supp. 708 (N.D. Ill. 1961).

pooled ore consigned over either railroad from the mines to Escanaba would be carried by the North Western to its docks at Escanaba, the Escanaba ore moving from the mines over the lines of the Milwaukee being delivered to the North Western at Iron Mountain.[24]

In all ore-pooling cases, the Commission found that competition would not be unduly restrained, but in none of them did the Commission analyze the factual elements of the alleged competition.

There are some railroad services in which erratic shifts in demand for equipment make a single firm or association the most efficient operating unit for the entire country. The freight cars of the United States are the prime example of a pool in which all railroads use each other's equipment at a fixed fee.[25] Pooling of refrigeration cars has indicated that operation and leasing of specialized equipment by one firm is the lowest-cost operation. Leading firms supplying refrigerator cars are Pacific Fruit Express Company, which was organized by the Southern Pacific and Union Pacific railroads, and Fruit Growers Express Company, organized by nineteen eastern and southern railroads.[26] In approving the agreement of thirty-six railroads to pool revenues and share losses from furnishing ice, supervision and repair of refrigerator cars, the Commission held:

> The facts of the record indicate that the arrangement will promote the maintenance of the present excellent refrigeration service. It may be reasonably expected that, without some arrangement whereby the losses can be distributed in proportion to the service rendered, the carriers experiencing the disproportionate losses would seek means for curtailing the service to be rendered by them. . . . The employment of Fruit Growers Express Company for the furnishing of refrigeration service undoubtedly entails less aggregate expense than would be incurred if the several carriers undertook to furnish the service themselves. The arrangement will not in any wise restrain competition. On

----

[24] *Chicago & N.W. Ry. Co.* v. *United States*, 195 F. Supp. 708, 710 (N.D. Ill. 1961). See *Chicago & N.W. Ry. Co. Trustees Abandonment and Operation*, 224 I.C.C. 8 (1937).

[25] See generally U.S. Federal Coordinator of Transportation *Report on Freight Car Pooling* (1934); Symes, "The Great American Car Pool," 112 *Railway Age* 492 (1942). See also Grunfeld, "The Effect of the Per Diem Rate on the Efficiency and Size of the American Railroad Freight-Car Fleet," 32 *J. of Bus.* 52 (1959).

[26] E.g., *Charges for Protective Serv. to Perishable Freight*, 215 I.C.C. 684, 686 (1936). The mere ownership and furnishing of cars to the railroads does not make such owners "carriers by railroad" subject to regulation by the Interstate Commerce Act. *Ellis* v. *Interstate Commerce Comm.*, 237 U.S. 434, 443 (1915); *Chicago Refrigerator Co.* v. *I.C.C.*, 265 U.S. 292, 296 (1924).

the contrary, it is likely to promote competition, for with the charges the same by all routes, as they are and necessarily must remain, the more traffic handled by some of the carriers without the arrangement, the greater will be their loss.[27]

The supply of sleeping cars is another situation in which seasonal and geographic shifts in demand make one national company the most efficient operating unit. The Pullman Company, which had bought out its competitors between 1867 and 1900, was the sole supplier and operator of sleeping cars in the United States between 1900 and 1944.[28] As a result of an antitrust prosecution, Pullman was found to have monopolized sleeping-car service by exclusionary devices embodied in its exclusive dealing contracts with railroads,[29] and the Court ordered an end to the exclusive agreements and the separation of the Pullman manufacturing and service companies. In a later proceeding, the Court approved the sale of the Pullman operating subsidiary to a pool of fifty-six railroads in spite of objections by the Department of Justice. The Court held:

We see no danger of the perpetuation of monopoly in a railroad-owned sleeping car business. Here we must look rather closely at our concept of what constitutes an unlawful monopoly in this connection. The thing which got the Pullman Company into trouble was not that it was the only company furnishing sleeping car service, but that Pullman made it virtually impossible for anybody else to get into the business. This applied not only to a competing concessionaire, but even to a railroad which sought to run part of its own sleeping car service and let Pullman do the rest. We think we have got rid of all that by the careful limitations imposed upon Pullman Company by the original judgment in this case, and which will be imposed upon its successors by the order which we shall enter. A railroad may join with others and use exclusively the services of Pullman. It may do part of that service itself, or through some other concern of its own choosing, and ask Pullman to do the rest. It may own all of its own sleeping cars, or part of them, or none of them. All of this is provided for in our judgment. There is, then, no strangle hold on the sleeping car busi-

---

[27] *Pooling of Refrigeration Earnings,* 258 I.C.C. 24, 28 (1944), *modified,* 269 I.C.C. 490 (1948).

[28] Sleeping-car manufacture is not subject to regulation by the ICC, but companies providing sleeping-car service are common carriers. Interstate Commerce Act §1(3), 24 Stat. 379 (1887), as amended, 49 U.S.C. §1(3) (1958).

[29] *United States* v. *Pullman Co.,* 50 F. Supp. 123 (E.D. Pa. 1943), *hearing on form of judgment,* 53 F. Supp. 908 (E.D. Pa. 1944), *judgment approved per curiam,* 55 F. Supp. 985 (E.D. Pa. 1944).

ness by a railroad owned Pullman Company or anyone else. Therefore, there is no unlawful monopoly.[30]

Upon purchase of the Pullman operating subsidiary, the railroads applied to the ICC for permission to pool service and earnings, and this was approved.[31] Under this agreement, most sleeping
cars were sold to individual railroads, who then employed the
former Pullman subsidiary to operate them. The testimony indicated that unified operation was the most economical because it
minimized excess capacity and coördination costs, standardized
design enabling reduced cost of cars purchased in larger quanti-
ties, and reduced maintenance costs by using regional repair
centers and standard parts.[32] This is especially significant if one
recalls that sleeping-car and parlor-car operations together (combined data being the only data available) cause U.S. railroads to
lose more than $100 million per year.[33] The Commission felt that
railroad ownership of the operating company would give the carriers a direct interest in its efficiency and the quality of its service.
Thus it rejected the renewed contention of the Department of
Justice that dissolution of the Pullman operating functions or
operation by nonrailroad interests were economically feasible solutions to the monopoly problem.[34] The Commission also found
that the pooling agreement would not unduly restrain competition because fares would be fixed by Pullman under ICC regulation in the same way as before the acquisition by the railroads.
It held that competition for passenger traffic would be just as
"keen and dramatic" as it always had been.[35]

The pooling agreements of the Railway Express Agency exceeded the restrictions of the *Pullman* case, for the ICC expressly
approved exclusive agency agreements with the railroads. The
operation of express cars on trains has many of the economic
characteristics of railroading. An express company must offer na-
tionwide service, and the optimum number of express cars on a

[30] *United States* v. *Pullman Co.,* 64 F. Supp. 108, 112 (E.D. Pa. 1946), *aff'd mem.*
330 U.S. 806 (1947).
[31] *Pullman Co.,* 268 I.C.C. 473 (1947), *modified,* 276 I.C.C. 5 (1949), 294 I.C.C. 703
(1955), 306 I.C.C. 138 (1959). See *Pooling of Railroad Earnings and Service, Pullman
Co.,* 322 I.C.C. 100 (1964).
[32] 268 I.C.C. at 482–484.
[33] See estimates for 1955 in U.S. Cong., Senate, Committee on Interstate and
Foreign Commerce, *National Transportation Policy* (Doyle Report) 298 (87th Cong.
1st Sess. 1961).
[34] 268 I.C.C. at 489.
[35] *Id.* at 487–490.

single train is usually only one. The local collection and delivery of small parcels is most efficiently operated by one firm in order to minimize excess capacity.

American Railway Express Company was organized in 1918 under supervision of the Federal Director General of Railroads to take over operations of the four largest existing express companies. Under section 407 of the Transportation Act of 1920,[36] the ICC approved the permanent consolidation of these firms.[37] A pooling agreement between the express company and the railroads was also approved.[38] The Commission noted that even before consolidation, interlocking stock ownership had minimized competition among the predecessor companies. Although the potential competition between these companies was eliminated by the consolidation and pooling agreements, the Commission found that competition would not be unduly restrained.

In 1929, eighty-six railroads combined to organize Railway Express Agency, Inc., to purchase the assets of the former express company and to operate the service. The Commission approved uniform agreements of all the railroads appointing the express agency as their exclusive agent for transacting express business.[39] Pooling arrangements similar to those under the 1920 agreement were approved as not undue restraints on competition. When the exclusive-agency aspect of this agreement was attacked by the Department of Justice as an attempt to monopolize,[40] the Commission made a special finding that such clauses were essential to the approved pooling. After reviewing the economies in investment and coördination of the hundreds of local offices of a single national express company, the Commission ruled:

For obvious reasons avoidance of duplicate facilities and operations such as those above referred to is of particular importance in the present national emergency. . . . It is a well-known fact that for many years actual competition within the express business as it has been conducted in this country has been unimportant. To a considerable extent governmental policy has encouraged the diminution of this competition. . . . The Government argues that "it is perfectly obvious

[36] 41 Stat. 480; now 54 Stat. 905 (1940), as amended, 49 U.S.C. §5 (1958).
[37] *Consolidation of Express Cos.*, 59 I.C.C. 459 (1920).
[38] *Express Contract, 1920*, 59 I.C.C. 518 (1920).
[39] *Railway Express Agency, Inc.*, 150 I.C.C. 423, 429 (1929); see *Railway Express Agency, Inc.*, 227 I.C.C. 517 (1938).
[40] *United States* v. *Railway Express Agency, Inc.*, 89 F. Supp. 981 (D. Del. 1950), *motion to dismiss granted*, 101 F. Supp. 1008 (D. Del. 1951).

that the restraint here is 100 percent complete, and is certainly an undue restraint." In our opinion the question whether the restraint is
undue depends not on its scope but on whether it is improper or inappropriate.[41]

Under section 5(11) of the Interstate Commerce Act.[42] the pooling
agreement became exempt from antitrust prosecution.

The one recent pooling agreement to be denied approval by
the ICC concerned division of traffic, but the agreement was designed to end previous restraints on service rather than to create
new ones. The Boston & Maine Railroad and the New Haven
Railroad consented to terminate their 1934 routing combination
and joint solicitation agreement that had diverted traffic from the
New Haven's rival, the Delaware & Hudson Railroad.[43] The
Boston & Maine and the Delaware & Hudson also undertook,
as part of this agreement, not to engage in joint solicitation of
traffic, which would divert traffic from the New Haven. All three
carriers agreed not to change the existing division of revenues on
shipments along the lines of any two of the carriers, and each of
the three roads agreed to solicit traffic separately. The Commission
found that the agreement resulted in neither better service to the
public nor economy in operation. The carriers were thus left free
to engage in joint solicitation or to modify the existing division of
revenues.

TRACKAGE AGREEMENTS

Agreements of one railroad to use the tracks of another or of
several railroads for joint use of terminals are frequently adjuncts
to programs of parallel carriers for the abandonment of excess
capacity. Less often, they are designed to give a railroad entry
into an area that it has never before served. Like pooling agreements, trackage and joint-use agreements have been little used by
the railroads. Where portions of two railroads become parallel
in a particular area and both have substantial excess capacity,
trackage agreements over the straightest and most level segments
of the two lines could enable line abandonments and substantial
cost reductions. Yet such agreements are extremely difficult to

[41] *Express Contract, 1929,* 275 I.C.C. 739, 744 (1951). For renewals, see *Express
Contract, 1954,* 291 I.C.C. 11 (1953); *Express Contract,* 1959, 308 I.C.C. 545 (1959).
[42] 24 Stat. 380 (1887), as amended, 49 U.S.C. §5(11) (1958).
[43] *Boston & Me. R.R.,* 298 I.C.C. 703 (1956).

negotiate.[44] A railroad with a monopoly franchise on the most efficient route through an area is reluctant to share this route even though rentals would include a monopoly gain. A carrier is especially concerned not to lose its monopoly of the smaller towns solely on its route because, even with monopoly service, such stations incur great costs for excess capacity. The carrier acquiring trackage rights and abandoning its own less-efficient route, runs the risk that the owner will refuse to renew the trackage agreement after the initial term expires. There is also the possibility that in times of heavy traffic, the owning carrier will give the right of way to its own trains and make the leasing carrier suffer all delays. Such uncertainties, when added to the barriers to abandonment of less-efficient routes, make carriers reluctant even to start negotiations for trackage rights on parallel lines.

The total mileage of railroad lines operated under trackage rights in the United States at the end of 1962 was 12,567.[45] In addition, trackage rights were operated over 2,082 miles of way-switching tracks and over 6,007 miles of yard-switching tracks. The total mileage of road and switching tracks operated under trackage agreements has changed little over the last twenty years.

The number of trackage agreements negotiated in the United States in one year is usually less than twenty-five and the aggregate lines are usually less than 400 miles. From July 1, 1960, to June 30, 1961, for example, the ICC approved twenty-three trackage and joint-use agreements for a total of 401 miles.[46] Most agreements were for segments of less than 20 miles. One for 138 miles provided for joint use of Louisville terminal lines of the Kentucky and Indiana Terminal Railroad Company; the second longest, 77 miles, was the Central of Georgia trackage over its subsidiary, the Savannah & Atlanta.

Two sections of the Interstate Commerce Act give the ICC regulatory powers over railroad trackage agreements. Explicit power to approve the voluntary agreements of carriers is in section 5(2)(a):

It shall be lawful, with the approval and authorization of the Commission . . . (ii) for a carrier by railroad to acquire trackage rights

[44] For a discussion of trackage agreements before 1930, see Grodinsky, *Railroad Consolidation: Its Economics and Controlling Principles* 245–265 (1930).
[45] U.S., Interstate Commerce Commission, *Annual Report of Transport Statistics in the United States* 6 (1962).
[46] 75 I.C.C. *Annual Report* 212 (1961).

over, or joint ownership in or joint use of, any railroad line or lines owned or operated by any other such carrier, and terminals incidental thereto.[47]

In section 3(5), a more limited power is given the Commission to compel trackage agreements when incidental to required terminal unifications.[48] The general power under section 5(2) will be discussed first.

Trackage Agreements Generally.—The trackage agreements that are relatively easy to negotiate are those entirely within one railroad system, those between parent and subsidiary, or those between two subsidiaries of the same parent. In *St. Louis S. W. Ry. Abandonment*,[49] both the petitioner and the owner of the line were subsidiaries of the Southern Pacific. Petitioner asked to abandon 51.24 miles of line between Commerce and Sherman, Texas, and take trackage on 46.23 miles of the Texas & New Orleans Railroad at a rental of $1.58 per train-mile. Counting the revenue from bridge traffic and ignoring deferred maintenance of $881,-000, the line abandoned was a profitable operation. Nonetheless, substitution of the trackage route was approved since the bridge traffic could move more economically over it. Under this condition, forced rehabilitation of the abandoned line would have been an undue burden on petitioner and on interstate commerce.[50]

Most trackage agreements are between carriers which are not part of the same railroad system. In *Chicago & N. W. Ry. Co. Trackage Rights*,[51] for example, the petitioner had large losses on the 55 miles of a branch line nearest the main line, but the end of the branch served larger towns to which petitioner wished to continue service. It applied to abandon the 55-mile segment and

---

[47] 54 Stat. 905 (1940), 49 U.S.C. §5(2)(a) (1958). The ICC was originally given the power to regulate trackage agreements by §1(18) of the Transportation Act of 1920. 41 Stat. 477 (1920), as amended, 49 U.S.C. §1(18) (1958). See *Fresno Passenger Terminal Case* 290 I.C.C. 753, 757 (1955).

[48] Transportation Act of 1920 §3(4), 41 Stat. 479, as amended, 49 U.S.C. §3(5) (1958).

[49] 290 I.C.C. 53 (1953). For a similar recent case, see *Central of Georgia Ry.*, 317 I.C.C. 184 (1961), aff'd, *Burke County, Ga. v. United States*, 206 F. Supp. 586 (S.D. Ga. 1962).

[50] 290 I.C.C. at 76. For a similar trackage case of a Western Pacific subsidiary over its parent's line, see *Sacramento No. Ry.*, 295 I.C.C. 73 (1955). In this case, the necessary rehabilitation that was avoided by abandonment and trackage over the parent's line was about $2,800,000 on a 50-mile line. On the issue of including bridge traffic in revenue calculations for the profitability of lines, see *Chicago, B. & Q.R.R.*, 271 I.C.C. 261, 279 (1948), reversing in part 267 I.C.C. 38 (1946). The earlier decision included a denial of trackage rights.

[51] 317 I.C.C. 350 (1962).

take trackage over 29 miles of a Chicago, Burlington & Quincy line connecting the remaining segment of the branch with another North Western line. The Commission granted the abandonment and trackage rights, noting that 90 per cent of the revenues of the line were from bridge traffic to and from towns on the remaining segment of the branch. The effect was to turn a branch line with an annual deficit of more than $80,000 into a profitable operation.

Where the carriers are not part of the same system, the problems of one railroad's abandoning a segment of line and negotiating an agreement for trackage on a parallel line are numerous. The *Illinois Terminal Ry. Abandonment*[52] is an example. Petitioner applied to abandon 42 miles of line and acquire trackage on the Illinois Central, part of which paralleled petitioner's line. A rental of $1.48 per train-mile was agreed upon. While petitioner was able to bargain to keep exclusive service to those industries on the parallel portion of line served only by its spur tracks, it had to agree not to serve industries on the portion of trackage over the Illinois Central line that had not been parallel to its own. Petitioner further agreed not to allow other railroads to use any portion of its tracks or facilities on the line in question; the Illinois Central's purpose in bargaining for this clause was to prevent its rival, the Wabash Railway, from acquiring trackage over petitioner's line in Decatur to a major industrial firm served only by petitioner and the Illinois Central. In spite of the restrictive character of this clause as a barrier to market entry by other carriers over Illinois Terminal's tracks, the Commission overruled the protests of Wabash and other protestants. The restriction was held consistent with the public interest.

Delaware, L. & W. Ry. Trackage Rights[53] illustrates the magnitude of expenses saved by trackage rights over parallel main lines and abandonments of excess capacity. In this case, which preceded the Erie-Lackawanna merger, the Lackawanna acquired trackage over 75.8 miles of the parallel Erie Railroad from Binghamton to Gibson, New York, and the Erie acquired trackage over 20.2 miles of the Lackawanna. The Lackawanna was permitted to abandon 54.2 miles of its main line. The Erie main line was easily able to accommodate the thirty-one daily trains of the Erie and the twenty-four daily trains of the Lackawanna. The installation of reversible signaling doubled the capacity of the Erie's Elmira yards and made

[52] 312 I.C.C. 607 (1961).
[53] 295 I.C.C. 743 (1958); see *Central of Ga. Ry.*, 317 I.C.C. 184 (1961).

it more than able to handle the trains of both carriers. The estimated annual reduction of expenses was $481,000 for the Erie and $625,000 for the Lackawanna, or a total of $1,106,000 for the two carriers.

Another method of increasing railroad capacity through trackage agreements is for parallel single-track lines of two railroads to be operated jointly. In *Atchison T. & S. F. Ry. Operation*,[54] the Santa Fe and the Rio Grande each owned single track lines between Denver and Bragdon, Colorado, a distance of 105 miles. Each of them granted trackage rights to the other, and they operated the two lines jointly as a double-track operation. A third railroad, the Colorado & Southern, was also granted trackage rights over both of these lines. The Southern Pacific and the Western Pacific have a similar joint double-track operation of their parallel lines in Nevada.

Trackage rights may be negotiated to replace the previous transfer of cars to a local connecting road and thereby expedite service. The North Western and the Milwaukee road, when transferring freight cars in the Chicago area to some Eastern railroads, delivered them to the Indiana Harbor Belt Railroad which carried them less than 40 miles to the Eastern connections. By negotiating trackage rights over the Indiana Harbor Belt line, the North Western and Milwaukee were able to eliminate one switching and to reduce car accounting.[55] The estimated savings to all carriers was more than $1 million annually.

In situations where trackage agreements prove not to be the most economic operation for parallel lines, a joint-use agreement may be possible. This is common in terminal areas. In *Operation by Union Belt*,[56] the Pennsylvania, the Pere Marquette, and the Wabash had formerly used trackage over each other's lines in the Detroit terminal area. Finding this uneconomical, they organized the Union Belt as their agent to operate all Detroit tracks of the owners. This enabled merger of the owning carriers' trains in the terminal area, a significant cost-reduction factor. In *International-Great No. R. R. Trustee Trackage Rights*,[57] a similar joint-use agreement, allowing combined trains, switching, and supervision, was substituted for a trackage agreement over an international bridge at Laredo, Texas.

[54] 244 I.C.C. 32 (1940), *supplementing* 221 I.C.C. 145 (1937).
[55] *Chicago, M., St. P. & P. R. Co.*, 317 I.C.C. 14, 550 (1962).
[56] 131 I.C.C. 384 (1927). For a case involving terminal trackage rights and joint use of a passenger station, see *Erie R.R.*, 395 I.C.C. 303 (1956).
[57] 282 I.C.C. 30 (1951), *supplementing* 275 I.C.C. 27 (1949).

Where a trackage agreement is not over lines of a parallel carrier and, therefore, is not part of an abandonment proceeding, its purpose is usually to give the railroad acquiring trackage an entry into a territory it has not before served. Such a case is *Operation of Line by Gulf, M. & No. R. R.*[58] Petitioner's northern terminus had been Jackson, Tennessee; in this proceeding, it acquired trackage over the Louisville & Nashville from Jackson, 145 miles north to Paducah, Kentucky. It was not claimed that this extended operation would create new transport business. Nevertheless, the application was granted. The carrier demonstrated that eliminating the Jackson interchange and moving trains over a longer through route was a more economical operation, and no other carriers protested the agreement. It is clear that the Louisville & Nashville would not have entered the agreement if its rentals, which were set at one-half the interest and operating cost of the line, were not expected to exceed the previous revenues from interchange with petitioner.

If a trackage agreement merely creates duplicate facilities without more economical routes, application for Commission approval will be denied.[59] But one leading case indicates that approval of a trackage agreement that does create more economical routes will also be denied where so much traffic is likely to be diverted to it that it would endanger the solvency or impair the operation of rival carriers. In *Chicago, B. & Q. R. R.*,[60] the Burlington and the Santa Fe jointly proposed to acquire the entire stock of the Kansas City, Chicago & St. Louis Railroad Company, a 156-mile line from Mexico, Missouri, to Kansas City. The Santa Fe also applied to acquire trackage over a 112-mile segment of the Burlington from Mexico, Missouri, to St. Louis. The acquisition and trackage together would have given the Santa Fe an entry into St. Louis. The other railroads from the Southwest intervened and protested that a direct Santa Fe route into St. Louis would divert so much traffic that they would have to curtail service and abandon some lines. Accepting this argument, the Commission denied the acquisition and the trackage rights.[61] As pointed out in Commissioner Ma-

---

[58] 111 I.C.C. 583 (1926), *supplemented*, 124 I.C.C. 641 (1927). See discussion of economies in a similar case, *Fort Worth & D. C. Ry.*, 99 I.C.C. 73, 75 (1925).

[60] *Lehigh Valley R.R.*, 312 I.C.C. 389 (1961); *Northeast Okla. R.R.*, 252 I.C.C. 273, 285 (1942). The former case involved 179 miles of trackage over the Erie to enable the applicant to become a rival to carriers offering second-day service between the Midwest and New England.

[60] 271 I.C.C. 63 (1948).

[61] *Id.* at 162–163. Another trackage proposal in this case, which was also denied,

haffie's dissent, such a barrier to new, more efficient routes cannot be in the public interest.[62] Subsequently, the Burlington was allowed to acquire trackage over the Kansas City, Chicago & St. Louis Railroad from Mexico, Missouri, to Kansas City, thus confirming that the whole purpose of the earlier denial was to bar Santa Fe entry into St. Louis.[63]

Petitions to the Commission to *compel* main-line trackage agreements have generally been denied. First, the Commission has not been given any general power to compel trackage agreements other than those incidental to required terminal use.[64] Second, the Commission has refused to make the granting of trackage rights a condition to its approval of unifications under section 5(2) of the Interstate Commerce Act.[65] In *Detroit, T. & I.R.R. Control*,[66] for example, the Baltimore & Ohio intervened in an action of the Pennsylvania and the Wabash to control the Ironton. It asked that the Commission condition its approval of control of the Ironton granting the Baltimore & Ohio trackage over its line into Detroit. Noting that its right to impose such a condition in a control case was questionable, the Commission also found no public need for additional service into Detroit.

Trackage Agreements Incidental to Terminal Unifications.— Section 3(5) of the Interstate Commerce Act gives the Commission power to compel trackage agreements incidental to compulsory use of another's terminal facilities. It provides:

> If the Commission finds it to be in the public interest and to be practicable without substantially impairing the ability of a carrier owning or entitled to the enjoyment of terminal facilities to handle its own business, it shall have power to require the use of any such terminal facilities, *including main-line track or tracks for a reasonable*

---

was to allow the Burlington trackage rights over a Missouri section of the Santa Fe line from Chicago to Kansas City. As a result of this denial, the Burlington built a new line from Brookfield, Missouri, to Kansas City, paralleling those of the Santa Fe and the Wabash. This unneeded duplicate facility cost $16,000,000. See *Railway Age*, Feb. 12, 1951, p. 113.

[62] *Id.* at 166.

[63] *Chicago, B. & Q.R.R.*, 271 I.C.C. 675 (1949).

[64] *Wheeling & L. E. Ry.*, 267 I.C.C. 163, 187 (1946); *Baltimore & O.R.R.*, 261 I.C.C. 535, 544 (1945); *Alabama, Tenn. & N.R.R.*, 124 I.C.C. 114, 115 (1927) (dictum). See *Thompson* v. *Texas M. Ry.*, 328 U.S. 134, 146–47 (1946), holding that trackage rights begun under a voluntary agreement must continue until the ICC approves abandonment even though the agreement has expired or is terminated.

[65] 24 Stat. 380 (1887), as amended, 49 U.S.C. §5(2) (1958).

[66] 275 I.C.C. 455, 484–485 (1950); see *Toledo P. & W.R.R.*, 295 I.C.C. 523, 540–541 (1957).

distance outside of such terminal, of any carrier, by another carrier or other carriers, on such terms and for such compensation as the carriers affected may agree upon, or, in the event of a failure to agree, as the Commission may fix as just and reasonable for the use so required, to be ascertained on the principle controlling compensation in condemnation proceedings. . . .[67]

The scope of this section as a means to compel railroad trackage agreements is determined by the meaning of "public interest" in this context and the meaning of "reasonable distance outside of such terminal." In *Chicago & A. R. R.* v. *Toledo, P. & W. Ry.,*[68] the latter phrase was construed; the Commission held that 12 miles was a reasonable distance in relation to the Peoria, Illinois, terminal. In this case, compulsory trackage was ordered even though it was not into defendant's terminal, but to a connection with the Peoria and Pekin Union, a union terminal railroad in Peoria. Since this compulsory agreement replaced a voluntary agreement that had been terminated by defendant, public interest was found in the continuance of access to a major city by a large carrier. It is notable, however, that an action for compulsory trackage cannot be used to reduce charges by reforming an existing voluntary trackage agreement.[69] Also, if the local terminal railway has given adequate, proper, and equal service to the main-line carriers and to shippers, the public interest will not require that the carriers be given trackage over the terminal facility.[70]

A recent decision holds that section 3(5), together with section 1(21),[71] which gives the Commission power to require extensions of line, enables the Commission to order both the acquiring road and the owning road to enter a trackage agreement in a terminal area. In *City of Milwaukee* v. *Chicago & N. W. Ry.,*[72] the city asked that the Chicago, Milwaukee, St. Paul & Pacific be ordered to complete a cross-over track across the right-of-way of the North

---

[67] 41 Stat. 479 (1920), 49 U.S.C. §3(5) (1958); emphasis added. In the Transportation Act of 1920, this was §3(4). It was renumbered §3(5) in the Transportation Act of 1940. See 3A Sharfman, *The Interstate Commerce Commission* 411–421 (1935).

[68] 146 I.C.C. 171 (1928).

[69] *United States* ex rel. *Chicago Great W.R.R.* v. *I.C.C.,* 294 U.S. 50 (1935), affirming 71 F. 2d 336 (D.C. Cir. 1934), affirming *Missouri-Kan.-Tex. R.R.* v. *Kansas City Terminal Ry.,* 104 I.C.C. 203 (1925).

[70] *Stewart Inso Bd. Co.* v. *Atchison, T. & S.F. Ry.,* 188 I.C.C. 535 (1932).

[71] 41 Stat. 478 (1920), 49 U.S.C. §1(21) (1958).

[72] 283 I.C.C. 311 (1951), *modifying* 279 I.C.C. 521 (1950). One purpose of this agreement was to permit a third railroad, the Chesapeake & Ohio, to consolidate its Milwaukee terminal operations at a single car ferry slip. See Hilton, *The Great Lakes Car Ferries* 164 (1962).

Western to Milwaukee Harbor and that the North Western be ordered to grant such use of its right-of-way. Finding direct service to the harbor by the Milwaukee Road to be reasonably required by the public interest, the Commission issued the order. But it is unlikely that the Commission would order reluctant railroads to acquire terminal trackage over another line just to serve one shipper.[73]

The purpose of section 3(5) is to open terminals and terminal tracks to all main-line carriers serving a city.[74] If one or more main-line carriers acquire a local terminal railroad, the Commission will order that their terminal facilities and tracks ke kept open to the other main-line carrier serving the city.[75] Economic reasons underlie the issuance of mandatory trackage orders as opposed to service orders, which require the owning railroad to take over the cars of the other carrier and deliver them to industrial sidings. The carrier acquiring trackage is better able to coördinate terminal movements with arrivals and departures of its main-line trains, thus giving faster service to industrial shippers on the trackage line.[76] These shippers also favor such an arrangement because it gives them direct-line connections with all other businesses on the line of the carrier acquiring trackage, and it supplies them with an additional source of empty cars.

Under the statute, the carriers are given time to negotiate a compensation agreement when use of terminal tracks is ordered. Only when they are unable to negotiate such an agreement will the Commission undertake to set compensation. The statute states that the compensation shall be ascertained on the principle controlling compensation in condemnation cases—the difference between the value of the property before and after the taking. Since the trackage right is a license (a nonassignable personal privilege to perform acts of a temporary nature upon the lands of another) terminable by the Commission, compensation must be computed as an annual rental. The calculation of total operating and maintenance costs includes a return at market interest rates on the value, at the date of filing of the action, of property used.

[73] *Francis & Swaim* v. *Chicago, R.I. & Pac. Ry.*, 255 I.C.C. 633 (1943); see *Jamestown, N.Y., Chamber of Commerce* v. *Jamestown, W. & N.W.R.R.* 195 I.C.C. 289 (1933).

[74] *Railroad Comm'n* v. *Southern Pac. Co.*, 264 U.S. 331, 343–344 (1924) (dictum); *Hastings Commercial Club* v. *Chicago, M. & St. P. Ry.*, 69 I.C.C. 489, 493 (1922), *rev'd on other grounds*, 107 I.C.C. 208 (1926).

[75] *Erie R.R.*, 278 I.C.C. 425 (1950), *supplementing* 269 I.C.C. 493 (1947).

[76] *Erie R.R.*, 275 I.C.C. 679, 684–85 (1950).

The *Kansas City Terminal* case[77] is the leading decision on the determination of compensation for compulsory use of terminals. After the Commission determined the annual cost of operation of the property used under trackage rights, the question was how to divide this cost between the twelve carriers using the terminal line. The smaller carriers argued that the division should be on a user basis so that the larger carriers would pay a greater share of the total costs; the larger carriers argued that the total costs should be divided equally between the users. The Commission ruled in favor of equal division of costs; it felt that this method was supported by the procedure in condemnation cases.[78] Since the total line capacity was made available by the owner for the use of all tenants no matter how much one carrier's traffic might increase or decrease in any year, the Commission determined that each carrier was paying for an equal share of the owner's line capacity.[79]

CONCLUSION

Voluntary pooling-of-service and trackage agreements represent efforts by railroads to reallocate the utilization of fixed plant for more intensive use, thereby increasing operating efficiency. There is no situation where such an agreement, by itself, can be injurious to the public interest, for the interest of the general public is in adequate and efficient railroad service along those routes and to those towns where business is sufficient to pay for the carriers' services. The fact that almost all pooling and trackage agreements proposed by the railroads have been supported by the local shippers and approved by the ICC indicates the clear public benefit from such partial coördination. Unfortunately, the public-interest standard has no quantitative measure. Objections to pooling and trackage agreements by private interests in towns that lose some employment in railroad shops are clearly offset by gains to shippers and to the public of better through service. As noted in Chapter II, objections by such towns based on arguments favoring the preservation of interrailroad competition are based on a delusion.

The decisions on the two major voluntary trackage proposals to which the Commission denied approval seem wrong. In *Chicago, B. & Q. R.R.*,[80] the operation of the trackage agreement, by giving

[77] *Missouri-Kan.-Tex. R.R.* v. *Kansas City Terminal Ry.*, 198 I.C.C. 4 (1933).
[78] 198 I.C.C. at 8–13.
[79] *Id.* at 9–13.
[80] 271 I.C.C. 63 (1948); see text accompanying note 60 *supra*.

the Santa Fe an entry into St. Louis, would have shifted traffic from more circuitous routes and avoided interchange delays. Likewise, in *Lehigh Valley R.R. Trackage Rights*,[81] operation over the Erie lines would have enabled the Lehigh Valley to offer second-day service between the Midwest and New England, but would have sharply curtailed the carload freight delivered by applicant to smaller Eastern carriers. Neither case required significant new investment in an industry burdened with substantial overinvestment. Both applications were denied because of the prospect that smaller rivals would suffer financially and would have to curtail services. But this is the usual result of industrial reorganization in the direction of more efficient operation. In an industry like railroads, with substantial overinvestment in fixed plant, failure of some firms is the likely result of changes directed toward more efficient operations. Those sections of such failing carriers that can be rehabilitated and made viable operations will be acquired at bankruptcy sale by more efficient connecting roads and incorporated into them.

Pooling-of-service and trackage agreements as a technique for railroad coördination and cost reduction can lead to lower rates and thereby benefit all shippers. For this reason, such agreements should be promoted by statute rather than hindered by bureaucratic review. Regulation of such agreements should be terminated by the repeal of section 5(1) and the trackage portions of section 5(2) of the Interstate Commerce Act. This would leave the railroads free to enter such pooling-of-service and trackage agreements as they find desirable. It would not, however, end the regulation of abandonments of railroad lines or discontinuances of services even though such withdrawal of investment in plant may be a logical supplement to a pooling or trackage agreement. Arguments for relaxing the regulation of pooling and trackage agreements cannot be applied to abandonments and discontinuances because of their great long-run effect on the service that railroads are able to render.

Pooling and trackage agreements should be actively promoted by the ICC. The Commission should call conferences of carrier representatives in each metropolitan area to review the supply of and demand for railroad services in the area. Railroads that have neglected to review the efficiency of their fixed plant in any area would then have an opportunity to make such a review in coöpera-

---

[81] 312 I.C.C. 389 (1961); see note 59 *supra* and accompanying text.

tion with the other carriers serving the same area. At such conferences the relative efficiencies of pool, trackage, and joint-use agreements for any particular coördination project could be examined. The result should be the planning of agreements for coöperative, more efficient utilization of railroad lines and equipment.

The law relating to compulsory trackage agreements is also in need of revision. The present power of the ICC under section 3(5) to order only those trackage agreements that are incidental to required terminal unification should be expanded to cover all railroad lines.[82] Only such a general power in the Commission can guarantee the most efficient trackage systems. When, for example, the Baltimore & Ohio's trackage over the Pennsylvania Railroad from Philadelphia to New York was terminated in 1926, it had to lease rights over the less convenient routes and terminals of the Reading and Central Railroad of New Jersey.[83] In other cases, refusals to negotiate voluntary trackage agreements have resulted in wasteful building of unneeded parallel lines.[84] A voluntary trackage agreement of two parallel lines, although in the public interest, may fail to realize all possible economies if it is made to the exclusion of a third parallel line. Only a general power in the Commission to order main-line trackage agreements by compulsion and to set reasonable compensation for the use of such trackage will remedy this deficiency.

A strong argument can also be made in favor of giving a general power to the Commission to compel pooling-of-service agreements.[85] Two carriers with parallel losing services may both apply for a discontinuance when investigation might prove that one pooled service could be profitable. Both the Pennsylvania and the Baltimore & Ohio, for example, offer passenger service from Chicago to Washington, D.C. Both carriers report large passenger deficits, and the Baltimore & Ohio has threatened to apply to the Commission to discontinue all passenger service.[86] Since the

[82] See Note, "State Power to Order Railroad Trackage Agreements," 12 *Stan. L. Rev.* 674, 681 (1960).

[83] *Baltimore & O.R.R.*, 138 I.C.C. 171 (1928); see Hotelling, "The General Welfare in Relation to Problems of Taxation and of Railway and Utility Rates," 6 *Econometrica* 242, 264–265 (1938).

[84] *Atchison, T. & S.F. Ry.*, 261 I.C.C. 227, 233 (1945); *Alabama, T. & N.R.R.*, 124 I.C.C. 114, 115 (1927).

[85] See Note, "Regulation of Railroad Service Competition," 48 *Yale L. J.* 143, 148 (1938).

[86] *Wall Street Journal*, March 16, 1962, p. 22, col. 3.

Baltimore & Ohio segment of line from Pittsburgh to Washington, D.C., is much shorter, a pooled service operating over the Pennsylvania from Chicago to Pittsburgh and over the Baltimore & Ohio from Pittsburgh to Washington, D.C., may be a solution.[87] If the carriers, through inertia or deadlock, could not negotiate a pooling agreement, the Commission should have the power to compel one. The presence of such statutory power in the Commission should itself result in a greater readiness by the carriers to enter voluntarily into pooling-of-service agreements.

[87] See discussion in Chapter VII, pp. 132 ff.

VI

Regulation of Abandonments, 1946–1962

This chapter will review railroad abandonments and changes in their regulation since the publication of Professor Cherington's comprehensive study.[1] The economic benefits from consolidations and functional mergers for reducing excess capacity can be realized only by disinvestment in many present main lines through abandonments. A critical survey of current abandonment practices and recent decisions will be followed by suggestions for supplementary statutes to facilitate main-line abandonments.

NUMBER AND SIZE OF ABANDONMENTS

At the end of 1962, railroads in the United States owned 215,090 miles of road (first main track), compared with 252,588 miles of road owned at the beginning of federal regulation of abandonments in 1920.[2] The net decrease was 37,498 miles or 14.8 per cent. Since 8,424 miles of new lines were constructed in the period, the total line abandonments were 45,922 miles. The total abandonments of lines and of trackage rights permitted by the Interstate Commerce Commission from 1920 to June, 1963, were 49,374 miles.

As shown in Table 9, the Commission rendered 1,383 decisions on the merits in abandonment proceedings from 1946 to 1963. Data available for only the first eleven years of the period show

[1] Cherington, *Regulation of Railroad Abandonments* (1948).
[2] U.S. Interstate Commerce Commission, *Transport Statistics in the United States* 3 (1962) and Interstate Commerce Commission, *Statistics of Railways in the United States*, XI (1920).

TABLE 9

DECISIONS ON APPLICATIONS FOR CERTIFICATES OF PUBLIC CONVENIENCE
AND NECESSITY TO ABANDON LINES OR TRACKAGE RIGHTS
(1946–1963)

Year	Decisions on merits	Granted		Denied		Cases dismissed without decision	
		Number	Miles	Number	Miles	Number	Miles
1946	43	37	669.791	6	273.087	4	117.900
1947	64	63	1,241.114	1	2.000	1	2.000
1948	63	57	907.359	5	48.303	9	100.841
1949	59	56	1,185.263	3	28.715	3	38.726
1950	88	80	954.618	8	109.500	7	93.200
1951	60	55	564.001	5	181.089	5	98.470
1952	88	84	1,305.753	4	98.588	5	40.930
1953	78	77	1,101.684	1	6.220	5	64.587
1954	69	66	873.283	3	14.418	6	125.100
1955	62	62	513.917	0		5	73.140
1956	70	69	822.710	1	44.819	8	70.868
1957	67	65	588.514	2	88.819	8	61.138
1958	87	85	1,825.361	2	50.502	4	82.017
1959	98	94	1,179.733	4	136.720	5	127.190
1960	72	69	771.821	3	234.348	9	120.203
1961	105	101	1,167.159	4	139.900	6	376.320
1962	97	95	1,582.282	2	53.149	1	7.960
1963	113	110	1,688.404	3	72.652	6	76.820
TOTALS	1,383	1,325	18,942.767	57	1,582.829	97	1,677.410

SOURCE: Interstate Commerce Commission, Annual Reports 1946–1963. The Commission's reporting year ended on October 31 until 1956, and ended on June 30 in 1957 and succeeding years. The 1957 report has a 4-month overlap on the 1956 report.

that 34 per cent of these decisions were protested. Most unprotested cases concerned short segments of road for which adequate substitute lines existed or for which the need had disappeared. The important policy questions arose in the protested cases. The 57 denials in Table 9 or 4.1 per cent of the decided cases, were an estimated 13 per cent of the protested cases. In addition there were 97 cases in the period which were dismissed without decision. As to the denials, Cherington commented on the similar low ratio to total decisions in the period before 1946. He wrote:

Superficially these statistics would seem to indicate that the Commission has acceded to the wishes of the railroads and permitted abandonment in the great majority of cases. When an application is filed, the chances could appear to be nearly sixteen to one that a certificate would be granted. From such a record one might conclude that the

Commission has been liberal indeed in meeting the wishes of the applicants, and that relatively little controversy exists in the ascertainment of what the public convenience and necessity permits. Such a conclusion, however, would be entirely misleading. The formal denials of certificates of public convenience and necessity have been relatively few in number but they have been of great importance in curbing the natural trend toward railroad abandonments. Particularly in the early cases where certificates were denied, the Commission indicated in plain and unmistakable language the comparatively narrow limits and conditions within which it would permit abandonment to take place. The criteria laid down in these early cases and resorted to again in the later denials have served as warnings to prospective applicants. In consequence, many segments of railroad, particularly unprofitable branch lines of otherwise profitable systems, have been continued in operation.[3]

As shown in Table 9, the 1,325 abandonments permitted in the period covered a total of 18,943 miles or 14.3 miles per abandonment. The denials referred to longer segments. The 57 abandonments denied covered 1,583 miles or 27.7 miles per denial. The longer the segment, the more likelihood that entire villages or towns will be left without alternate rail service. Local shippers who depend on carload freight are almost sure to file protests. To the carriers, these longer segments are the ones causing the greatest losses, because loss is primarily a function of distance. For the cases where data were presented, the estimated annual loss or expected future savings per mile of line abandoned varied between $1,102 per mile in 1954 and $3,295 per mile in 1955. Since minimum maintenance of way per mile of line on branches carrying only slow freights would be about $1,000 per mile, higher losses would result from increased maintenance or from net operating losses on trains.

CAUSES OF ABANDONMENT

Before 1920 the largest cause of abandonment of rail lines was the exhaustion of natural resources on the particular branch line.[4] From 1920 to 1943, the competition of other modes of transport was the cause of most permitted abandonments. From 1946 to

[3] Cherington, *op. cit.*, at 102.
[4] For a detailed survey of the causes of abandonment, see Weissman, "Railroad Abandonments: The Impact of Competition," 44 *Iowa L. Rev.* 492, 500–510 (1959). See Cherington, *op. cit.*, chap. 5; I.C.C., Bureau of Transport Economics and Statistics, *Railroad Abandonments 1920–43*, Statement No. 453 (1945); Trumbower, "Railway Abandonments and Additions," 34 *J. Pol. Econ.* 37–60 (1926).

1955, the internal adjustment of routes by carriers was found to be the largest single cause. While earlier abandonments were mostly the result of declining demand for rail service, many recent ones are caused by rising costs resulting primarily from wage increases. Even with stable demand, rising costs may cause some branches to become net loss operations. Rising labor costs also promoted the substitution of capital for labor. Heavier diesel engines could pull longer trains with the same crews. But investment in track improvement to carry such engines would not be economic on branch lines presently operating just at the break-even point. Such lines would also become net loss operations. Railroad adjustment to these losses and prospective losses was to shift as much traffic to higher-density main lines and to abandon the losing secondary lines.[5]

Although most abandonments affect branch lines of less than 20 miles, the cases which best illustrate the problem of excess capacity in railroad lines are those which affect the abandonment of entire railroads. Table 10 summarizes the facts of five recent abandonments of entire lines. The longest of these was the *New York, Ontario and Western,* which included 473 miles of road and 72 miles of trackage rights over other railroads.[6] The carrier traversed an area which was served more efficiently by other carriers and had been in bankruptcy reorganization since 1937. In 1956 the court found that no feasible plan of reorganization could be approved and ordered operations discontinued.[7] Upon abandonment, only 38 miles of the line were purchased by other carriers for continued use.

The other two freight-only carriers in Table 10 also suffered from rivalry of other carriers that offered superior routes to main urban centers. In the *Lehigh and New England* case, 97 per cent of the traffic originating and terminating on its lines was on 40 miles of line sold to the Central Railroad Company of New Jersey.[8] The other 137 miles of lines were abandoned. At the time of the *Rutland Railroad* decision, its workers had been on strike for one year and freight had been carried to all major towns on

---

[5] See, e.g., *Missouri-K.-T. Co. Abandonment* (F.D. 19844), 295 I.C.C. 830 (1958), where the railroad abandoned a portion of its direct line between St. Louis and Kansas City in order to reduce costs and channel more traffic onto an alternate main line.

[6] *New York, O. & W. Ry. Co. Receivers Abandonment* (F.D. 19861), 295 I.C.C. 831 (1957).

[7] *New York, O. & W. Ry. Co. Reorganization,* 295 I.C.C. 346, 361 (1956).

[8] *Lehigh & New England R. Co. Abandonment,* 312 I.C.C. 645, 652 (1961).

TABLE 10

FIVE MAJOR ABANDONMENTS, 1957–1962

Carrier	Date of decision	Miles abandoned	Type carrier	Location
New York, Ontario & Western	October 10, 1957	545	Interurban Freight	New York, New Jersey and Pennsylvania
Chicago, Aurora & Elgin	May 2, 1961	53	Suburban Electric	Chicago
Lehigh & New England	September 26, 1961	177	Interurban Freight	Pennsylvania, New York and New Jersey
Chicago, North Shore & Milwaukee	May 28, 1962	106	Suburban and Interurban Electric	Chicago to Milwaukee
Rutland	September 21, 1962	331	Interurban Freight	Vermont and New York

SOURCE: New York, Ontario & Western Ry. Co., F.D. No. 19861, 295 I.C.C. 831 (1957); Chicago, A. & E. Corp., 312 I.C.C. 533 (1961); Lehigh & New England R. Co., 312 I.C.C. 645 (1961); Chicago, N.S. & M. Ry. 317 I.C.C. 191 (1962), aff'd 317 I.C.C. 363 (1962); Rutland Railway Corp., 317 I.C.C. 393 (1962).

the line by rival carriers.[9] In approving abandonment, the Commission ordered that the line might be sold to "any reasonable buyer" at a price not less than its salvage value of $5,765,912. In this case, unlike in most abandonments, no service was being offered on the line at the time of decision. The Commission's view was that upon abandonment, some other operator would be likely to acquire important segments of the line and thereby bring about a resumption of service. In December, 1963, the 132-mile segment of the Rutland between Burlington, Vermont, and White Creek, New York, was sold to the State of Vermont for $1,850,000. This line was leased to a new carrier, the Vermont Railway, which began operations in January, 1964.

The two electric railroads which were abandoned were both primarily passenger carriers. The *Chicago, Aurora & Elgin* had formerly used 2½ miles of elevated tracks of the Chicago Transit Authority to reach the center of the city. When these tracks were torn down in 1953, the railroad offered service from the western

[9] *Rutland Railway Corp.,* 317 I.C.C. 393 (1962), aff'd sub nom. *Brotherhood of Locomotive Engineers* v. *United States,* 217 F. Supp. 98 (N.D. Ohio 1963). See *State of Vermont and Vermont Railway Inc.,* I.C.C. Finance Docket 22830 (1963); "Vermont: New Life for an Old Road," *Railway Age,* March 23, 1964, p. 9.

suburbs only to the city limits. As a result passenger revenues declined by two-thirds, and in 1958 the Illinois Commission approved discontinuance of passenger service. In 1959, the Illinois Commission approved discontinuance of freight service. Since revival was proved hopeless, the Interstate Commerce Commission approved abandonment of the line.[10]

The *Chicago, North Shore & Milwaukee* was both a suburban and interurban electric railroad.[11] The carrier had shown net losses for every year since 1947. Its suburban service, like other similar lines, had lost much traffic to the private automobile upon the building of multiple-lane highways.[12] Its interurban passenger service between Chicago and Milwaukee was slower than its rivals, the Northwestern and the Milwaukee roads. Like other interurban electrics, it was unable to compete as a freight carrier against diesel-powered rivals.[13]

ECONOMIC AND LEGAL CRITERIA

Under free-market conditions, a firm will disinvest in those capital goods whose marginal cost to the firm exceeds the marginal revenue they earn for the firm.[14] If the net discounted value of a segment of railroad line is less than prospective replacement cost, making allowances for changes in technique, the owner will plan for abandonment. But the maximum recovery of capital values from a rail line will require the planning of gradual deterioration through decreased maintenance of way and structures. Abandonment planning to adjust to the decline in traffic on a line thus becomes an essential element of railroad management.

If carriers' costs and the social costs of abandoning a line were identical, there would be no regulation of railroad abandonments. Regulation by the states before 1920 and by the federal government since 1920 resulted from recognition that costs other than those of the railroads are affected by a line abandonment. Most abandoned lines carry only freight, and protestants are those busi-

---

[10] *Chicago, A. & E. Corp. Abandonment*, 312 I.C.C. 533 (1961).

[11] *Chicago, N. S. & M. Ry. Abandonment of Entire Operation*, 317 I.C.C. 191 (1962), *aff'd* 317 I.C.C. 363 (1962), *aff'd sub nom., State of Illinois* v. *United States*, 213 F. Supp. 83 (N.D. Ill. 1962), *aff'd* 373 U.S. 378 (1963).

[12] See *Chicago, N. S. & M. Ry. Abandonment*, 290 I.C.C. 765 (1955), permitting abandonment of its Shore Line Route of 37 miles.

[13] See *Texas Electric Ry. Co. Abandonment*, 271 I.C.C. 391 (1948); see generally Hilton and Due, *The Electric Interurban Railways in America* (1960).

[14] See detailed economic analysis in Troxel, *Economics of Transport*, chap. 22 (1955); Meyer, Peck, Stenason and Swick, *The Economics of Competition In The Transportation Industries* 252–258 (1959).

ness firms which have made investments in fixed plant in reasonable reliance on the continued existence of carload freight service. These usually include dealers in coal or building supplies, operators of grain elevators, or manufacturers. Such firms usually cannot operate economically with only higher-cost truck transport. The employees of such shippers and other citizens of a town losing all rail service may also suffer losses by becoming unemployed for a period of time or from a general decline in real estate values. But private parties paid no compensation to a railroad for the increase in their property values resulting from building of the railroad to their towns. Hence, there is no clear theoretical welfare principle for determining which of them, if any, should have a right to demand continued service at a loss to the carrier or to demand compensation upon abandonment of the line.

The Transportation Act of 1920 gave the Interstate Commerce Commission regulatory power over railroad abandonments, as follows:

No carrier by railroad subject to this chapter shall abandon all or any portion of a line of railroad, or operation thereof, unless and until there shall first have been obtained from the Commission a certificate that the present or future public convenience and necessity permit such an abandonment.[15]

In contrast to the regulation of rates where the public interest standard can be measured by comparing a railroad's rate of return on investment with other comparable industries, "public convenience and necessity" as applied to abandonments has no measurable meaning. It requires a balancing of interests between the carrier's losses from the line as a burden on its interstate rail system with the local public need for continued service.[16] The burden on interstate commerce of compelling operation on a losing branch line is that the losses from this division of the railroad must be paid for in higher rates for shippers in other divisions. On the other side are shippers dependent on carload freight for economic operations who stand to lose a greater part of their investment. The Commission decision requires the weighing of these incommensurables under the highly amorphous statutory standard. The Commission's discretion is limited only by decisions of the federal courts setting the statutory and constitutional boundaries of its

[15] Chap. 91, §402, 41 Stat. 477 (1920), 49 U.S.C. §1(18).
[16] *Colorado* v. *United States,* 271 U.S. 153, 168 (1926).

action.[17] The result has been a long series of cases, impossible of classification, developing no systematic detailed criteria on which later applicants can base their petitions.

The only small group of abandonment applications before the Interstate Commerce Commission which have estimable results are those to abandon the entire line of a net loss railroad. If the carrier establishes to the regulatory commission that it has present over-all losses from operation and that the prospect is for continued losses, the Commission must permit abandonment. Forcing an entire business to continue operations at a loss would be an unconstitutional taking of private property for a public purpose without compensation.[18] It can be argued that this same constitutional right would apply to a railroad showing over-all net losses which wished to abandon only those branches showing large losses hoping that the rest of the line could be revived to a net profit position.[19] To rule otherwise would grant the Commission power to force the railroad either to continue to consume its capital until forced to abandon all operations, or to abandon all operations immediately.

RECENT DECISIONS

The Commission decisions must be reviewed critically under the general question: When should a public regulatory agency overrule a managerial decision that a particular disinvestment in fixed plant is necessary to eliminate an operation loss as part of the continuing adjustment of the railroad to changing demand and cost conditions? When should the general public, the ultimate payers of increased shipping charges on the rest of the railroad, be asked to bear the cost of continued operation of a losing segment of railroad line? [20] A detailed survey of recent decisions will illustrate some of the important factors in the administrative discretion of the Interstate Commerce Commission.

In the usual abandonment case, the first burden of proof is on

[17] The courts will not reverse a finding of fact of the Commission unless it is shown to be unsupported by evidence. *Virginian Ry. Co.* v. *United States*, 272 U.S. 658, 665 (1926). See *Public Service Com'n of New York* v. *United States*, 56 F. Supp. 351, 356 (S.D.N.Y. 1944), *aff'd* 323 U.S. 675 (1944).

[18] *Brooks-Scanlon Co.* v. *R. R. Comm.*, 251 U.S. 396, 399 (1920). During the period that the abandonment petition is pending before the Commission, a carrier may be required to continue operations at over-all losses. *Meyers* v. *Jay Street Connecting Railroad*, 288 F. 2d 356 (2d Cir. 1961).

[19] *Crawford* v. *Duluth St. Ry.*, 60 F. 2d 212, 216 (7th Cir. 1932). See application of this rule to service discontinuances in Chapter VII.

[20] *New York Central R. Co. Ferry Abandonment*, 295 I.C.C. 385, 411 (1956).

the carrier to establish a recent history of losses on the segment concerned. Failure to prove these losses is in itself ground to deny the application.[21] Where the question of substantial losses from the line is contested by protestants, any reasonable doubt will be resolved in favor of denying the petition.[22] Estimated expenses which were not actually incurred will be disallowed in the Commission's calculations of the carrier's losses.[23] If the carrier's accounting methods showing losses is rejected in favor of protestants' methods which show the segment to be profitable, the abandonment petition will usually be denied. The present Commission rule for depreciation accounting is illustrative. In its abandonment petition, the carrier may not include the estimated wearing out of roadway and structures as an expense. Instead the expense accounts may show only out-of-pocket expenditures on replacement.[24] Thus, if in recognition of declining demand on a line and in contemplation of abandonment, a carrier makes no replacement expenditures, it may cause its accounts to show a profit although real costs of operation would show losses.[25] The historical cost data are not an accurate measure of future avoidable costs, which must be the tools of the business manager in decisions on disinvestment in plant.

Another accounting problem in calculating the losses on branch lines of profitable railroads relates to the apportionment of revenues and costs between the branch and the rest of the system's lines for shipments originating or terminating on the branch. The generally accepted method in recent cases is first to divide these revenues on a pro-rata mileage basis between the branch and the rest of the system. Then branch expenses are deducted from branch revenues. The pro-rata revenues apportioned to the other lines of the system are also credited to the branch with an estimated 50 per cent deducted as the out-of-pocket cost of carrying traffic beyond the line to be abandoned.[26] The 50 per cent formula

[21] *Great Northern Ry. Co. Abandonment,* 271 I.C.C. 207, 215 (1948).
[22] *Dawson Ry. Co. Abandonment,* 295 I.C.C. 273, 274 (1956).
[23] *Louisville & N. R. Co. Abandonment,* 307 I.C.C. 286, 290–291 (1959); *Chicago & N. W. Ry. Co. Abandonment,* 295 I.C.C. 31, 34 (1955).
[24] *Chicago & N. W. Ry. Co. Abandonment,* 275 I.C.C. 759, 772 (1951); *Chicago & N. W. Ry. Co. Abandonment,* 282 I.C.C. 525, 530 (1952).
[25] *Missouri Pac. R. Co. Abandonment,* 307 I.C.C. 189, 201 (1959).
[26] *Chicago & N. W. Ry. Co. Abandonment,* 275 I.C.C. 759, 774–776 (1951); *Norfolk S. Ry. Co. Abandonment,* 290 I.C.C. 268, 274 (1954), *aff'd sub. nom., State of North Carolina v. United States,* 124 F. Supp. 529 (M.D.N.C. 1954); *Chicago M. St. P. & P. R. Co. Abandonment,* 295 I.C.C. 157, 160 (1956); *Northwestern Pacific R. Co. Abandonment,* 312 I.C.C. 783, 785 (1962). See dissent of Chairman Splawn in *Texas & N. O. R. Co. Abandonment,* 282 I.C.C. 1, 12 (1951).

for the cost of handling shipments from or to the branch on other system lines is not absolute in that in any given case the railroad can prove a different formula more applicable.[27] But the carriers are not able to determine marginal costs of carrying one or more cars on a main-line freight train to or from a branch. Hence, they have not been able to rebut the 50 per cent formula. To the extent that carload revenues from shipments to or from the branch will not be lost upon abandonment because shippers will take delivery at the nearest main-line siding, the main-line revenues should not be credited to the branch. Historical revenue calculations, like historical cost calculations, though the basis of regulation, are not a good measure of the avoidable costs which must be the basis of business policy. But the Commission contends that all revenues generated by the branch must be credited to it in determining the burden on interstate commerce.[28]

A few recent decisions have permitted abandonments even though the affected branch had a history of net profits. These were branches connecting two towns on main lines and which carried overhead or bridge traffic between those towns. The Commission has permitted the carrier to exclude from calculations of expected savings the revenues and cost of carrying bridge traffic which upon abandonment will be transferred to another of the system's lines.[29] Traffic originating and terminating on the line will of course be insufficient to cover costs. Even if the alternate route which will carry all the bridge traffic is somewhat longer or steeper, the carrier may choose to retain it because it goes through major towns. These decisions are significant for main-line abandonments upon the merger of two parallel carriers. In such cases, only the subsequent transfer of all bridge traffic to one line will cause the other to show losses. Under these circumstances, a past history of losses should not be prerequisite to permitting abandonment.[30]

When a railroad has anticipated abandonment by curtailing maintenance and replacement on a line for a number of years, partial disinvestment has taken place before the abandonment pe-

[27] *Chicago & N. W. Ry. Co. Abandonment,* 282 I.C.C. 525, 530–532 (1952).
[28] *Northwestern Pac. R. Co. Abandonment,* 312 I.C.C. 783, 786 (1962).
[29] *Southern Pac. Co. Abandonment,* 312 I.C.C. 685, 692 (1961); *Chicago & N. W. Ry. Co. Abandonment,* 295 I.C.C. 31, 35 (1955); *St. Louis S. W. Ry. Co. of Texas Abandonment,* 290 I.C.C. 53, 73–74 (1953); *Chicago B. & Q. R. Co. Abandonment* 271 I.C.C. 261, 279 (1948). See *Gainesville Midland R. Co. Abandonment,* 267 I.C.C. 256, 262 (1947).
[30] *Duluth S. S. & A. R. Co. Merger,* 312 I.C.C. 341, 352 (1960). See *Louisiana & A. Ry. Co. Abandonment,* 290 I.C.C. 434 (1954).

tition is filed. If the petition is denied, the line must be rehabilitated—a reinvestment in fixed plant which the railroad's managers
believe can be operated only at a loss. The required reinvestment
may be twice the previous salvage value of the line.[31] And when
rehabilitation is completed, the total salvage value of the line may
be less than the reinvestment expenditure.[32] The Commission has
held that in abandonment cases the magnitude of the necessary
rehabilitation expenditures will be given weight,[33] especially if
sharply increased by a natural catastrophe such as a flood.[34] But
it has also held that abandonment cannot be permitted solely on
the prospect of heavy maintenance costs in the future arising from
previous deferred maintenance,[35] because allowing rehabilitation
costs to control abandonment decisions would enable the carriers
to predetermine petitions merely by neglecting maintenance of
lines.

In opposition to the losses of the petitioning carrier which are
alleged to burden interstate commerce, protestants argue a continuing local public need for the particular rail service. In estimating the inconvenience and loss to the protesting shippers from
abandonment of a line, the Commission will make a detailed examination of the economic factors. Some of these are:

The population of the area;

the number of stations on the line and distance by highway to
the nearest other railroad;

number of passengers handled;

commodities originating on or consigned to the line and costs
of alternate transport for them;

percentage of traffic on the line which is local as opposed to
through business;

local revenues in relation to system revenues;

number of trains daily and type of equipment;

substitute highway transport available; and

potential industrial development and growth of traffic.

In its opinions, the Commission sets forth the relevant facts
which support its findings. It generally does not, however, indicate

[31] *Leelanau Transit Co. Abandonment,* 307 I.C.C. 95, 96 (1959).

[32] *Missouri Pac. R. Co. Abandonment,* 307 I.C.C. 189, 190 (1959).

[33] *Sacramento N. Ry. Trustees Abandonment,* 295 I.C.C. 73, 85 (1955); *Chicago B. & Q. R. Co. Abandonment,* 271 I.C.C. 261, 268 (1948).

[34] *Chicago B. & Q. R. Co. Abandonment,* 271 I.C.C. 261, 268 (1948). For earlier denial see *Chicago B. & Q. R. Co. Abandonment,* 267 I.C.C. 38 (1946), *reversing* 261 I.C.C. 549 (1946).

[35] *Louisville & N. R. Co. Abandonment,* 307 I.C.C. 286, 291–292 (1959).

the relative weight of the different factors or which of them is controlling.[36]

Some recent denials of petitions to abandon branch lines center the decision on the investment loss to shippers of carload freight who will be unable to compete if they must shift to higher-cost truck transport. These include industrial firms shipping or receiving grain or steel,[37] lumber dealers,[38] grain elevators and warehouses,[39] and food processors.[40] Some of these same decisions and others emphasize the lack of adequate highways as substitute transport for the area,[41] or the expected economic growth of the region which should increase railroad traffic.[42] In another denial, applicant had conceded that it had made no attempt to reduce deficits on the branch by elimination of some station agents and operating fewer trains.[43] In many of these cases where abandonment is denied, the decision seems to be a mere delaying action.[44] Declining demand on a line or rising costs or both will result in eventual abandonment. The pleas of protestants that new industries may be founded on the line which will increase traffic, though given temporary recognition, will be overridden in a renewed petition a few years later.

The great majority of abandonment petitions are granted because the losses of the line in question are proved to be substantial and because there is no reasonable prospect of future profitable operations. They are found to be a burden on interstate commerce. In such cases, a clear public necessity must be shown by protestants before a carrier will be denied abandonment and ordered to

---

[36] 3A Sharfman, *The Interstate Commerce Commission* 338 (1935).

[37] *Northwestern Pac. R. Co. Abandonment,* 312 I.C.C. 783, 785 (1962).

[38] *Louisville & N. R. Co. Abandonment,* 307 I.C.C. 286, 290 (1959).

[39] *Missouri Pac. R. Co. Abandonment,* 307 I.C.C. 189, 197 (1959); *Chicago & N. W. Ry. Co. Abandonment,* 282 I.C.C. 525, 533 (1952), *subsequently permitted* (F.D. 19691) 295 I.C.C. 826 (1957); *Great Northern Ry. Co. Abandonment,* 271 I.C.C. 207, 213 (1948).

[40] *Leelanau Transit Co. Abandonment,* 307 I.C.C. 95, 103 (1959).

[41] *Missouri Pac. R. Co. Abandonment,* 307 I.C.C. 189, 203–204 (1959); *Leelanau Transit Co. Abandonment,* 307 I.C.C. 95, 103 (1959); *Chicago & N. W. Ry. Co. Abandonment,* 275 I.C.C. 759, 789 (1951).

[42] *Louisville & N. R. Co. Abandonment,* 307 I.C.C. 286, 289 (1959); *Chicago & N. W. Ry. Co. Abandonment,* 275 I.C.C. 759, 786 (1951).

[43] *Missouri Pac. R. Co. Abandonment,* 307 I.C.C. 189, 203 (1959).

[44] See, e.g., *New York Central R. Co. Abandonment,* 312 I.C.C. 271, 273 (1960); *Great Northern Ry. Co. Abandonment,* 271 I.C.C. 207, 215–216 (1948). Although the Interstate Commerce Commission may effect a redistribution of revenues between two carriers participating in the transport of through traffic in order to assist a weaker short line, this remedy is unlikely to be a permanent solution to declining traffic. See *United States* v. *Great Northern Ry. Co.,* 343 U.S. 562 (1952), *aff'g. Montana Western Ry. Co. Abandonment,* 275 I.C.C. 512 (1950).

suffer the losses into the indefinite future, when another petition to abandon will be filed. For this reason, loss of its investment in fixed plant by only one shipper usually will not be grounds to deny abandonment.[45] The Commission will give little weight to arguments that abandonment will decrease the taxable property of the territory, that costs of maintaining educational facilities will be increased, that a few shippers will curtail operations because of higher costs, that real estate will decline in value, or that future economic prospects of the area will be diminished.[46] Nor is it significant that the line to be abandoned is the shortest route between two towns so that abandonment will increase rates for shipment between them.[47] And a carrier cannot be compelled to continue a losing line merely for the purpose of furnishing employment.[48]

In one recent group of cases abandonments have resulted from the purchase of railroad rights-of-way by cities for use as local highways. Protestants carry little weight when a municipality intervenes in the case to argue that local public need requires the abandonment. Such abandonments have been granted for turnpike or thruway access in Oklahoma City, Buffalo, Boston, Syracuse, Savannah, and Santa Clara County, California.[49] Although these rights-of-way have been sold at high prices and their sale has reduced the local taxes of the railroads, the new highways have accentuated the movement of commuters away from railroad travel.

In recent abandonment cases, the Commission has attached to the permits many conditions found in earlier cases.[50] One of the

---

[45] *Moeller* v. *Interstate Commerce Commission,* 201 F. Supp. 583, 389 (S.D. Iowa 1962); *Illinois Term. R. Co. Abandonment,* 312 I.C.C. 607, 612 (1961); *Chicago A. & E. R. Corp. Abandonment,* 312 I.C.C. 533, 537 (1961). See *United States Feldspar Corp.* v. *United States,* 38 F. 2d 91, 95 (N.D.N.Y. 1930); *Town of Inlet* v. *New York Cent. R. Co.,* 7 F. Supp. 781, 785 (N.D.N.Y. 1934).

[46] *Village of Candor* v. *United States,* 151 F. Supp. 889, 893 (N.D.N.Y. 1957); *Boston & M. R. Co. Abandonment,* 290 I.C.C. 415, 422 (1954).

[47] *Texas & N. O. R. Co. Abandonment,* 282 I.C.C. 1, 11–12 (1951); *East Tennessee & W. N. C. R. Co. Abandonment,* 275 I.C.C. 547, 551 (1950).

[48] *Missouri & A. Ry. Co. Receivers Abandonment,* 271 I.C.C. 171, 187 (1948).

[49] *Chicago, R. I. & P. R. Co. Acquisition,* 282 I.C.C. 344 (1952); *Lehigh Valley R. Co. Abandonment,* 290 I.C.C. 427 (1954); *Boston & Albany R. Abandonment,* 312 I.C.C. 458 (1961); *New York Central R. Co. Abandonment,* 312 I.C.C. 587 (1961); *Seaboard Air Line R. Co. Trackage Rights,* 312 I.C.C. 797 (1962); *Southern Pacific Co. Abandonment,* 320 I.C.C. 278 (1963), reversing 317 I.C.C. 645 (1963).

[50] The Commission is empowered to attach conditions by Section 1(20) of the Interstate Commerce Act which provides in part: "The Commission . . . may attach to the issuance of the certificate such terms and conditions as in its judgment the public convenience and necessity may require." 49 U.S.C. §1(20). See Cherington, *op. cit.,* at 172–179.

most usual is that railroads offer to sell all or parts of the abandoned line to any responsible person, firm, or corporation at a price not less than the net salvage value of the properties.[51] This condition enables any shippers on the line to take over the rail service if they wish to continue the losing operations. It also assures parallel railroads the right to purchase those portions of track necessary to reach industries on the line.

In the *Lehigh Valley* case, the carrier voluntarily accepted a condition that it provide substitute connections for abutting industries to other nearby railroads.[52] Since the public agency which was purchasing the railroad right-of-way for thruway entry to Buffalo would pay the costs of these connections, the railroad had no objection to the condition. But the Supreme Court has held that even where a governmental agency would have to pay for substitute facilities, such a condition to the abandonment permit would not be ordered unless the traffic warranted the expenditure.[53] In the *Boston & Maine* case, the Commission refused to condition the abandonment on the applicant's being required to establish bus service as a substitute for the line and refused also to require applicant to pay to the affected towns a portion of the proceeds recovered from salvage and realized from tax savings.[54] It found insufficient evidence to warrant the bus service. It held that it had no statutory authority to order division of the carrier's proceeds with the affected towns.

The one condition found in most permits for abandonments is provision for payments to displaced labor. Specific statutory protection for labor is not provided in abandonment proceedings, as in mergers.[55] The courts have held, however, that such labor protection as is appropriate to the public convenience and necessity may be made a condition to abandonment.[56] The usual condition requires that the demoted or dismissed employee shall be com-

---

[51] See, e.g., *Lehigh & New England R. Co. Abandonment*, 312 I.C.C. 645, 652–653 (1961); *Jay Street Connecting R., Abandonment of Entire Line*, 307 I.C.C. 137, 162–163 (1959); *Texas & New Orleans R. Co. Abandonment*, 282 I.C.C. 1, 13 (1951). The salvage value must be determined by applicant railroad and will not be found by the Commission. *Missouri & A. Ry. Co. Receivers Abandonment*, 271 I.C.C. 171, 189 (1948).

[52] *Lehigh Valley R. Co. Abandonment*, 290 I.C.C. 427, 432 (1954).

[53] *Purcell v. United States*, 315 U.S. 381 (1942).

[54] *Boston & M. R. Abandonment*, 290 I.C.C. 415, 425 (1954).

[55] Interstate Commerce Act, §5(2)(f). 54 Stat. 906 (1940), 49 U.S.C. §5(2)(f). See *Railway Labor Executives' Ass'n. v. United States*, 339 U.S. 142 (1950); *New Orleans Union Passenger Terminal Case*, 282 I.C.C. 271 (1952).

[56] *Interstate Commerce Com'n v. Railway L. E. Ass'n*, 315 U.S. 373, 380 (1942).

pensated so that he does not suffer a drop in earnings for a period of up to four years or for the period of his previous employment, whichever is shorter.[57] This is essentially the same as the statutory protection for labor in mergers. In cases of partial abandonment such conditions will be imposed even though the payments use up most of the carrier's benefits from the abandonment during the first four years and even though the carrier is in a weak financial condition.[58] But no conditions for the protection of labor will be imposed if the entire line of the carrier is abandoned.[59] And the parent of a defunct and abandoned subsidiary carrier will not be required to pay allowances to the dismissed employees of the subsidiary.[60]

CONCLUSIONS AND PROPOSALS

The uncertainties of the present railroad-abandonment statute and procedures make them inadequate as a necessary part of planning a rational railroad system. Under present procedures, shippers of bulk products have valid objections that they have made fixed investment, perhaps recently, in reasonable reliance on the continued existence of railroad service. Carriers validly object that they cannot plan abandonments under present procedures because Interstate Commerce Commission decisions are in most cases completely unpredictable.[61] Public convenience and necessity is a vague and uncertain guide without any measurable standards.[62] The weight which the Commission will give the pleas of shippers and communities which are about to lose rail service, and whether

[57] *Chicago B. & Q. R. Co. Abandonment*, 257 I.C.C. 700, 704–707 (1944).

[58] *New York, N. H. & H. R. Co. Abandonment*, 312 I.C.C. 465, 469 (1961). Where partial abandonment of a railroad showing overall net losses is permitted, dismissal allowances to employees will not be ordered if the objective of financial recovery might thereby be defeated. *Maryland & P. R. Co. Abandonment*, 295 I.C.C. 719, 729 (1958).

[59] *Chicago, A. & E. R. Corp. Abandonment*, 312 I.C.C. 533, 537 (1961); *Texas Electric Ry. Co. Abandonment*, 271 I.C.C. 391, 397 (1948).

[60] *Cisco & N. E. Ry. Co. Abandonment*, 267 I.C.C. 139, 142 (1947). The Commission will not order payments to station employees of a connecting railroad who are dismissed because of the permitted abandonment. *United New Jersey R. & Canal Co. Abandonment*, 312 I.C.C. 530, 531 (1961).

[61] For a detailed history of the Chicago & North Western's sixteen years of proceedings before the Commission to discontinue its 37-mile branch line to What Cheer, Iowa, see Weissman, "Railroad Abandonments: The Competitive Ideal," 43 *Minn. L. Rev.* 251, 258–263 (1958).

[62] But see *New York Central S. Corp. v. United States*, 287 U.S. 12, 24–25 (1932), holding the "public interest" standard for regulating acquisitions of control under section 5(2) of the Transportation Act of 1920 not to be invalid because of uncertainty.

such losses will be found to overbalance the carrier's loss, cannot be estimated. Furthermore, the carrier's accounting methods showing losses may be rejected in favor of protestant's methods that show the line to be profitable.

Current prcoedures may actually impede any movement to large-scale consolidations and abandonments designed to decrease over-investment in railroad lines. In the consolidation of parallel main lines, carriers will usually be unable to show a history of losses on the line to be abandoned. Because each main line will have had a large amount of bridge or through traffic, each will have a record of profits. The carrier will have to rely on the few recent cases where the Commission has allowed profitable lines to be abandoned by not including in profit calculations the revenue and costs of carrying bridge traffic which will be moved to a parallel line.[63] But persuading the Commission to permit abandonment of such profitable lines over protests of large numbers of local shippers who will suffer losses may be extremely difficult.

The benefits of main-line consolidations can be realized only by a new, supplementary law of abandonments. The first requisite is that there be prior scheduling of abandonments. A period of notice, fixed in each case by the Interstate Commerce Commission, should precede a major abandonment. Only with adequate notice can shippers and carriers plan alternative routes and conserve and redirect investment accordingly. The second requisite is that carriers be given an absolute right of abandonment, subject to the notice requirement and certain other possible conditions. Long-run investment planning requires a degree of certainty that is presently precluded for railroads by the Commission veto over abandonments.[64] However, the right of abandonment in the new statute could be circumscribed by conditions for adequate protection of shippers without putting a power in the Commission to prevent the abandonment entirely. Types of conditions in abandonments are discussed below.

Under the new scheduled abandonments statute, the carrier would begin by filing an application for a hearing with the Interstate Commerce Commission. The application would indicate the line or segment to be abandoned and suggest a proposed period

---

[63] See notes 29 and 30 *supra,* and accompanying text.

[64] For a discussion of the decreased business risks when there is an absolute right to abandon a line, see *Wichita Falls & S. R. Co. Abandonment,* 290 I.C.C. 303, 314–319 (1954). In this case, the Rock Island agreed to purchase part of the abandoned line on the condition that it could abandon the line in three years if it considered the operation unprofitable.

of public notice before the abandonment would be effective. If no protest were filed within the protest period, the application would be automatically approved. Then the carrier would be obliged to post public notice in all terminals for the entire notice period. At the end of the notice period the line would be abandoned.

If protests were filed, the Interstate Commerce Commission would set the application down for hearing. Since the right to abandon would be absolute, the only question in contest would be the length of the appropriate notice period. At the hearing shippers could present evidence as to the nature of their products which must be shipped by rail, the amount and depreciation rates of their fixed plant, the sale value of their plant to other firms not requiring rail transport, and the cost of dismantling and moving fixed plant. The carrier could present its estimates as to these factors and offer plans to assist in relocating plants of protestants. After considering these factors, the Interstate Commerce Commission would set a period of public notice to elapse before abandonment. The statute might put an upper limit on the notice period of, say, seven years. In considering the new type of abandonment application, no questions of costs or revenues of the carrier would be material. The right to abandon, being absolute, would in no way depend upon past losses or profits.

The Interstate Commerce Commission should be given power to raise rates on any segment or branch during the period of public notice pending abandonment. It would probably use such power quite sparingly where one of two parallel main lines was to be abandoned, as it would create inequities between competing shippers on the two parallel lines. However, on branch lines higher rates are in many cases a workable alternative to abandonment. On many branch lines a few shippers have a vested interest in rail service only because of the unrealistically low rate structure imposed by government in the attempt to equalize geographical advantage. On such lines rate increases would correct inequities by making rates more consistent with costs. Such increases allowed during the period of public notice pending abandonment might cause the carrier in some instances to withdraw its abandonment application.

The new procedures, creating an abandonment of right, would not replace present permissive abandonments. The present procedures, while inadequate for large-scale abandonments, are nevertheless satisfactory for most cases of branch lines with an uncontestable history of losses. Hence, the new statute should not replace the present one, but merely supplement it. No conflict would arise between the two distinct procedures. A carrier would have a choice of filing initially under the old procedures or the new. If it filed first under the old procedures and immediate abandonment was denied, it could then file under the new scheduled abandonments statute. If it filed first under the new statute and if a long notice period was set, it could file an interim petition under the old statute before the notice ran out, requesting permission to abandon earlier because of sharp traffic declines causing losses.

Conditions precedent to abandonment are perhaps even more appropriate under the proposed new abandonment of right than under the old system. Under the new procedures, shippers and other protestants would be precluded from arguing in the Commission against the abandonment itself. They should, however, be given the possibility of easing their adjustment to this technological change by arguing for conditions precedent to the abandonment. Many types of conditions applied in past cases under the old statute might be used. The frequent conditions under the existing procedures that the carrier offer to sell the line at not less than scrap value to any responsible purchaser who will continue operations, or that carrier be required to build new connecting lines to a shipper's place of business, would also be appropriate under the new supplementary statute.

More difficult problems arise concerning conditions precedent to requiring compensation to private individuals. The Commission maintains that under the present statute it has no power to attach such a condition to an abandonment permit.[65] A strong argument can be made that firms which have invested in reasonable reliance on the continued existence of a rail line should not be forced to lose the greater part of their investment. The remedy would be to condition the abandonment of such line on the carrier's compensating bulk shippers for their investment loss. Such conditions would be available only to the types of businesses which cannot compete in their markets by shifting to truck transport. Grain elevators and shippers of coal, sand, stone, and clay products are in this class. The carrier could be required as a condition precedent to abandonment to pay these firms the difference between the net depreciated value of their plants and the amount realized by sale when the rail line is abandoned. In other cases,

[65] *Boston & M. R. Abandonment,* 290 I.C.C. 415, 425 (1954). See Cherington, *op. cit.,* 178.

the carrier might be required to move or pay the cost of moving dissembled plant and equipment from the abandoned line to another nearby line.

The final suggested statutory change is an alternative protection for shippers who would be unable to carry on without rail service. This is special tax relief. Accelerated depreciation allowances could be given on plant not convertible to other uses. The Internal Revenue Code would have to be amended to allow a shortened depreciation period. In each case the shipper would be allowed to adopt a depreciation period on plant equal to the period of notice required for abandonment by the railroad. These tax revisions would greatly facilitate the operation of the proposed abandonment procedures by allowing the disrupted shippers to spread the cost of readjustment over a number of income periods.

In considering the procedures suggested herein, one must keep in mind that the regulation of railroad abandonments is interdependent with the regulation of railroad rates. The more flexible rate structures recommended by President Kennedy and in the Doyle and Weeks reports,[66] if enacted, might raise railroad revenue substantially and thus lessen the carriers' pressure for consolidations and abandonments. However, consolidations and abandonments are problems of long-run resource allocation. The sooner the carriers correct the misallocation of resources, the sooner all shippers will gain by lower rates. For this reason, the supplementary procedures suggested above should be enacted regardless of legislative decision on the removal of minimum rate regulation.

[66] U.S. Cong., House, *The Transportation System of Our Nation*, House Doc. No. 384 (87th Cong. 2d Sess. 1962) pp. 4–5; U.S. Cong., Senate, Committee on Interstate and Foreign Commerce, *National Transportation Policy* (87th Cong. 1st Sess. 1961) pp. 440–444; U.S. Presidential Advisory Committee on Transport Policy and Organization, *Revision of Federal Transportation Policy* (1955).

VII

Railroad Service Discontinuances

Partial disinvestment in the railroad industry in response to declining demand and changing technology is necessary not only in the abandonment of lines, but also for some railroad services. Passenger service, less-than-carload freight service, and agency stations in small towns are among the outstanding losing services on some routes of railroads. One can infer from earlier studies on the railroad passenger deficit that direct operating losses from passenger services are the most important drain on railroad earnings.[1]

One suggested remedy for the deficits from losing services is to shift more of this burden on to freight shippers by increasing carload freight rates.[2] This remedy is limited by the fact that freight rates are now so high that small further rate increases for many commodities will make rail shipment more expensive than truck and cause shippers to shift to highway transport. The only other remedies are to discontinue operation of losing services, such as those passenger trains showing large losses, and perhaps to lower

---

[1] Nelson, *Railroad Transportation and Public Policy* 284–326 (1959); Berge, *Railroad Passenger Service Costs and Financial Results* (1956); U.S. Cong., Senate, Committee on Interstate and Foreign Commerce, *National Transportation Policy* (Doyle Report) 273-343 (87th Cong. 1st Sess. 1961); U.S. Cong., Senate, Committee on Interstate and Foreign Commerce, *Hearings on Problems of the Railroads* 63 (85th Cong. 2d Sess. 1958); *Railroad Passenger Train Deficit*, 306 I.C.C. 417–494 (1959).

[2] The Interstate Commerce Commission takes the passenger deficit into account in the adjustment of interstate freight rates and charges in a general rate case. *King* v. *United States*, 344 U.S. 254 (1952).

rates on more traveled segments where demand may be found to be elastic. On some railroads this might mean complete discontinuance of all passenger service. On most it means an appreciable number of discontinuances and a major revamping of passenger schedules.

This chapter will examine critically the law relating to railroad-service discontinuances. Before passage of the Transportation Act of 1958 there was no general federal jurisdiction over passenger-service discontinuances. Discontinuances were a matter of state statutes, and the regulatory standards developed by state commissions.[3] For this reason, passenger discontinuances under state law will be discussed first, followed by analysis of decisions under the 1958 statute. Freight discontinuances and station closings will be treated last.

The measurement of the escapable cost from the discontinuance of passenger services has been covered so thoroughly by other writers that, except for one comment, it will not be treated here.[4] The allocation of joint costs is a problem without adequate solution. The more recent statistical costing studies of the passenger deficit average the costs from many railroads whose traffic densities, operating conditions, and cost structures are so different that the conclusions are worthless.[5] The problem does not become determinative in many individual service discontinuances, because railroads usually do not petition to discontinue services until they show direct operating losses.

[3] The Interstate Commerce Commission had authority only to regulate abandonment of all or parts of a railroad line. 49 U.S.C. §§1(18–20). It had no jurisdiction over service discontinuances, which left such regulation to the states. *Alabama Public Service Com'n* v. *Southern Ry.*, 341 U.S. 341 (1951); *Palmer* v. *Massachusetts*, 308 U.S. 79 (1939); *Board of Public Utility Com'rs. of N.J.* v. *United States*, 158 F. Supp. 98 (N.J. 1957), *remanded* 359 U.S. 982 (1959); *New York Central R. Co. Abandonment*, 254 I.C.C. 745, 765 (1944); *Morris and E. R. Co. Abandonment*, 175 I.C.C. 49, 52 (1931); *Kansas City Southern Application*, 94 I.C.C. 691 (1925). See Roger B. Hendrix, "Railroads—Abandonments and Partial Discontinuances of Passenger Service—Jurisdiction," 31 *N.C.L. Rev.* 137 (1952). Federal courts may take jurisdiction in an action to enjoin enforcement of an order by a state commission to continue service where plaintiff alleges confiscation in violation of federal constitutional rights and state law does not afford similar equitable remedy. *Illinois Cent. R. Co.* v. *Mississippi Public Serv. Com'n.*, 135 F. Supp. 304 (S.D. Miss, 1955).

[4] Nelson, *op. cit.*, 286–301; Ladd, *Cost Data For the Management of Railroad Passenger Service* (1957).

[5] See Meyer, Peck, Stenason, Kraft and Brown, "Avoidable Costs of Passenger Train Service," Aeronautical Research Foundation report, in U.S. Cong., Senate, *Hearings on Problems of The Railroads* 237–284 (85th Cong. 2d Sess. 1958); Ulmer, *An Appraisal of the Aeronautical Research Foundation's Avoidable Costs of Passenger Train Service*, prepared for U.S. General Services Administration (1958).

ECONOMIC TRENDS IN PASSENGER SERVICE

The railroads' share of the passenger transport market has declined for more than thirty years. In 1939 railroads carried 8.4 per cent of total intercity passenger-miles and automobiles carried 87 per cent.[6] By 1962, the railroads' share was 2.5 per cent and that of automobiles 89.9 per cent. Of the commercial carriers of passengers, railroads had 67.7 per cent of total intercity passenger-miles in 1939 and only 24.7 per cent in 1962. Air carriers increased from 2 per cent of commercial passenger transport in 1939 to 45.9 per cent in 1962 in spite of the fact that average air fares per mile are twice rail coach fares.[7]

The adjustment of the railroads to declining demand is illustrated in Table 11. Revenue passenger-miles in 1962 of 15.9 billion, although only slightly below the 18.6 billion of 1939, were 46.9 per cent below the 29.7 billion passenger-miles in 1951. Miles of railroad on which passenger service was operated declined from 171,766 in 1939 to 139,269 in 1951 and to 85,908 in 1962.[8] The 1962 figure represented a decline of 50 per cent below 1939 and 38.3 per cent below 1951. Included in this decline were the seventeen railroads which discontinued passenger service entirely between 1945 and 1962. As a result of the discontinuances, the revenue passenger-miles per mile of road in passenger service declined only 13.6 per cent between 1951 and 1961.

Passenger revenues, excluding commutation, declined from $817 million in 1951 to $492.1 million in 1962, a drop of 39.8 per cent. The passenger revenue per mile of road in passenger service declined from $5866 in 1951 to $5728 in 1962, a drop of only 2.4 per cent. In spite of the fairly steady revenue per mile of road in passenger service from 1948 to 1961, railroad deficits from passenger service increased with continuously rising costs. Table 12 shows passenger service revenues and expenses per train-mile. The total expenses per train-mile, using the ICC formulas for distri-

[6] Computed from data assembled in U.S. Cong., Senate, Committee on Interstate and Foreign Commerce, *Hearings on Problems of the Railroads*, Part 1 at 61 (85th Cong. 2d Sess. 1958); U.S. Interstate Commerce Commission, *77th Annual Report* 74 (1963).

[7] U.S., I.C.C., Bureau of Transport Economics and Statistics, *Transport Economics* 13 (Dec. 1961).

[8] Of the total railroad mileage operated, 77.7 per cent had passenger service in 1939, 65.1 per cent had passenger service in 1951, and 43.2 per cent had passenger service in 1961.

TABLE 11

PASSENGER ROUTE MILES, REVENUE PASSENGER-MILES, AND PASSENGER REVENUE
(1939–1962)
CLASS I RAILROADS

Year	1 Miles of road operated in passenger service[a]	2 Revenue passenger-miles other than commutation (thousands)	3 = 2 ÷ 1 Revenue passenger-miles per mile of road operated in passenger service	4 Passenger revenue excluding commutation (millions of dollars)	5 = 4 ÷ 1 Passenger revenue per mile of road operated in passenger service
1939	171,766	18,644,825	108,548	$ 375.8	$2,188
1946	161,376	58,840,434	364,617	1,196.2	7,413
1947	160,857	39,921,110	248,178	895.6	5,568
1948	159,953	35,329,438	220,874	887.8	5,550
1949	157,000	29,622,262	188,677	782.0	4,981
1950	146,468	26,780,978	182,845	734.4	5,014
1951	139,269	29,749,578	213,612	817.0	5,866
1952	133,053	29,261,204	219,921	817.1	6,141
1953	129,048	26,904,794	208,487	749.1	5,805
1954	124,736	24,537,019	196,712	671.0	5,379
1955	119,745	23,747,177	198,315	641.1	5,354
1956	115,951	23,348,447	201,365	649.6	5,602
1957	112,724	20,988,507	186,194	619.2	5,493
1958	107,131	18,473,697	172,440	551.6	5,148
1959	100,243	17,501,737	174,593	525.8	5,245
1960	93,816	17,064,257	181,891	517.6	5,517
1961	88,854	16,154,160	181,806	497.5	5,599
1962	85,908	15,858,976	184,604	492.1	5,728

SOURCES: U.S., I.C.C., *Transport Statistics in the United States*, and *Statistics of Railways in the United States* (1939–1962).

[a] At end of year.

bution of joint costs, rose from $4.49 in 1948 to a high of $7.11 in 1960. The deficit or loss per train-mile rose from a low of $1.22 in 1950 to a high of $2.36 in 1955 and declined to $1.45 in 1962. The decline per train-mile since 1958 is the direct result of discontinuance of the most lightly patronized trains, those with the greatest train-mile deficits.

The financial results of passenger and allied service operations are shown for 1962 by region in Table 13. For the United States as a whole, $530 million or 46 per cent of these operating revenues were derived from the allied services. Of this, $342.7 million was from mail and $81 million was from express services. After

TABLE 12

PASSENGER SERVICE REVENUE AND EXPENSE PER TRAIN-MILE
(1948–1962)

Year	Revenue per train-mile	Expense per train-mile: transportation	total	Deficit per train-mile	Operating ratio passenger service
1948	$3.23	$2.15	$4.49	$1.23	127.4
1949	3.12	2.24	4.66	1.54	136.7
1950	3.61	2.35	4.83	1.22	124.0
1951	3.76	2.65	5.48	1.72	134.2
1952	4.00	2.73	5.72	1.72	131.6
1953	3.91	2.79	5.86	1.95	138.0
1954	3.80	2.82	5.72	1.92	138.2
1955	3.89	2.87	5.83	1.94	137.6
1956	4.06	3.08	6.22	2.16	140.7
1957	4.15	3.27	6.51	2.36	144.4
1958	4.52	3.43	6.66	2.14	136.5
1959	4.97	3.56	6.98	2.01	130.6
1960	5.22	3.64	7.11	1.89	126.6
1961	5.40	3.66	7.08	1.68	121.8
1962	5.53	3.69	6.98	1.45	121.4

SOURCE: Association of American Railroads, *Railroad Transportation—A Statistical Record 1921–1961* (1962), as computed from U.S., I.C.C., *Transport Statistics in the United States.*

apportionment of joint expenses, all regions showed losses from passenger and allied services. Four regions, however, had direct operating losses; revenues failed to cover even the solely related expenses and tax accruals.

PASSENGER DISCONTINUANCES UNDER STATE LAWS

Special constitutional issues arise in considering service discontinuances by railroads showing over-all net losses. For this reason the law relating to service discontinuances on railroads showing over-all net profits will be treated first, followed by a separate treatment of the special problems of service discontinuances on carriers showing over-all net losses.

Net Profit Railroads.—Discontinuance of passenger service is but one of the many operations of franchised carriers governed by statute in most states under the regulatory rule of public convenience and necessity. Whether explicit in the particular state's statutes or implicit in the general power of regulating railroad service, the carrier must apply to the state's commission for per-

TABLE 13

PASSENGER AND ALLIED SERVICES OPERATING REVENUES AND EXPENSES (EXCLUDING RENTS), 1962

(thousands of dollars)

	United States total	New England Region	Great Lakes Region	Central Eastern Region	Pocahontas Region	Southern Region	Northwestern Region	Central Western Region	Southwestern Region
Operating Revenue from:									
(1) Passenger Service	618,811	47,082	83,125	182,458	13,265	81,588	48,879	144,486	17,927
(2) Allied Services	530,072	17,947	85,753	102,458	16,503	77,877	43,058	152,663	33,814
Total	1,148,883	65,029	168,878	284,916	29,768	159,465	91,937	297,149	51,741
Operating expense and tax accruals related solely to passenger and allied services	1,117,523	50,149	164,387	264,534	35,148	163,687	101,883	280,597	57,136
Revenue less solely related expense = income before deducting joint expense	31,360	14,880	4,491	20,382	d 5,380	d 4,222	d 9,946	16,552	d 5,395
Joint expenses and tax accruals apportioned to passenger and allied services	406,353	24,565	42,519	73,707	15,268	64,621	43,706	121,749	20,218
Railway operating income	d 374,993	d 9,685	d 38,028	d 53,325	d 20,648	d 68,843	d 53,652	d 105,197	d 25,613

SOURCE: U.S. Interstate Commerce Commission, *Transport Statistics in the United States*, 138–146 (1962).

d = deficit.

mission to discontinue part or all of its passenger services.[9] As in the abandonment cases, the commission must weigh the carrier's losses against the public need for continued service. The public interest does not mean just those who use the service, but the entire public.[10] The general public's interest is in good freight service, and losing passenger services supported by high freight rates affect the entire public.[11]

In the usual case the carrier presents evidence of out-of-pocket losses on the particular service it wishes to discontinue. If the petition is for particular trains, accounts are presented to show that costs of labor and fuel on those trains exceed the fares collected. If the petition is to discontinue passenger service on an entire segment of line, other costs of terminals and special maintenance for passenger service are also included in calculating the particular passenger deficit.

The mere showing of out-of-pocket loss on a particular service of a railroad with over-all net profits has usually been ruled insufficient grounds for discontinuance.[12] Although inconvenience to users is insufficient ground to order continued service, proof of public need may require that a profitable railroad render some passenger services at a loss.[13] It is settled law that such a requirement is not confiscatory in the sense of an unconstitutional taking of property without just compensation.[14] But the requirement of continued service even though public need has not been proved is confiscation.[15]

[9] See *Great No. Ry.* v. *Board of R. R. Comm'rs,* 130 Mont. 627, 298 P. 2d 1093 (1956) and cases cited therein. See Annot., 70 A.L.R. 845 (1931).

[10] *St. Louis-San Francisco Ry. Co.* v. *City of Fall River,* 187 Kan. 23, 353 P. 2d 505, 507 (1960); *Application of Chicago & N. W. Ry. Co.,* 167 Neb. 61, 91 N. W. 2d 312, 315 (1958).

[11] *Maine Central R. Co.* v. *Public Utilities Com'n,* 156 Me. 284, 163 A. 2d 633, 637 (1960); *St. Louis-San Francisco Ry. Co.* v. *State,* 319 P. 2d 592, 594 (Okl. 1957).

[12] *Southern Pac. Co.* v. *Public Util. Comm'n,* 41 Cal. 2d 354, 367, 260 P. 2d 70, 77 (1953), *appeal dismissed,* 346 U.S. 919 (1954); *Illinois Cent. R. R.* v. *Public Serv. Comm'n,* 225 Ind. 643, 75 N.E. 2d 900 (1947); *Chicago, M., St. P. & P. R. R.* v. *Board of R. R. Comm'rs,* 126 Mont. 568, 255 P. 2d 346 (1953), *cert. denied,* 346 U.S. 823 (1953).

[13] *Application of Chicago, B. & Q. R. Co.,* 166 Neb. 567, 89 N. W. 2d 837, 839 (1958).

[14] *Chicago, M., St. P. & Pac. R. R.* v. *Illinois,* 356 U.S. 906 (1958); *Cheasapeake & O. Ry.* v. *Public Serv. Comm'n,* 242 U.S. 603 (1917); *Missouri Pac. Ry.* v. *Kansas ex. rel. R. R. Comm'rs,* 216 U.S. 262, 278 (1910); *Atlantic Coast Line* v. *North Carolina Comm'n,* 206 U.S. 1 (1907). See Mr. Justice Frankfurter concurring in *Alabama Publ. Serv. Comm'n* v. *Southern Ry.,* 341, U.S. 341, 352–353 (1951).

[15] *Atlantic Coast Line R. Co.* v. *Public Service Com'n,* 77 F. Supp. 675, 686 (1948); *Ann Arbor R. Co.* v. *Michigan Public Serv. Com'n,* 91 F. Supp. 668, 671–672 (E.D. Mich. 1950).

Public convenience and necessity is an amorphous concept. As a regulatory standard for railroad-service discontinuances, it is, for practical purposes, vague and unworkable. Even though a railroad is not required to prove its losses or the absence of public need with mathematical precision,[16] there is no definable method for weighing losses against public need. The relevant factors considered in applying the test of public convenience and necessity to passenger service discontinuances were summarized in *Illinois Cent. R. R. v. Illinois Commerce Com'n* as: the cost (direct operating loss) of providing the service; the use made by the public of the service; and the availability and adequacy of other transportation facilities.[17] In a Virginia case, reversing a commission denial of discontinuance, five criteria were listed as follows: the character and population of the territory served; the public patronage or lack of it; the facilities remaining; the expense of operation as compared with the revenue from it; and the operations of the carrier as a whole.[18] The last two standards in the *Illinois* case and the first three in the Virginia case, "the elements of public need," cannot be measured in dollars. Hence, in different cases, even before the same commission, they may be given different weights. In some cases, local political pressures are alleged to play a part in a commission's determination that public need outweighs the carrier's losses.[19] And one federal court enjoined a commission order to restore trains where no public necessity was shown, labeling the proceeding an illegal dissipation of the railroad's assets through the device of sham hearings.[20]

Since the criteria of public convenience and necessity are unmeasurable, there is no way to predict how courts hearing an appeal will react to the frequent commission holding that passenger services operated at a large deficit are still a public necessity. In those courts where the commission's finding of fact is unreviewable on appeal except if clearly against the manifest weight

[16] *Application of Chicago & N. W. Ry. Co.*, 167 Neb. 61, 91 N. W. 2d 312, 317 (1958).

[17] *Thompson v. Illinois Commerce Comm'n*, 1 Ill. 2d 350, 115 N. E. 2d 622 (1953); *Illinois Cent. R. R. v. Illinois Commerce Comm'n*, 410 Ill. 77, 101 N. E. 2d 588 (1951). See *Commuters' Comm. v. Pennsylvania Pub. Util. Comm'n*, 170 Pa. Super. 596, 88 A. 2d 420 (1952); *Susquehanna Transit Commuters Ass'n. v. Board of Public Utilities Com'rs.*, 55 N. J. Super. 377, 151 A. 2d 9 (1958).

[18] *Southern Ry. v. Commonwealth*, 196 Va. 1086, 1093, 86 S. E. 2d 839, 841 (1955).

[19] Martin, "Legal Problems of the Railroad Passenger Deficit," 22 *ICC Prac. J.* 275, 277 (1955).

[20] *Chicago, B. & Q. R. Co. v. Illinois Commerce Com'n*, 82 F. Supp. 368, 374 (N. D. Ill. 1949).

of the evidence, the court is likely to affirm the commission.[21] Where the court hears the facts *de novo* and makes its own findings, there is a greater chance of reversal in favor of discontinuance.[22]

Recently a number of state supreme courts have taken a new view of public necessity in appeals from commission denials of passenger service discontinuances. Numerous commission denials of discontinuances have been reversed by the courts as arbitrary and without reason.[23] The change has been in the evidence required. The burden of proof of lack of public necessity is of course on the carrier petitioning to discontinue services presently rendered pursuant to its franchise.[24] The new approach to sustaining this burden, which has been approved by the courts of many states, requires the carrier to prove its direct operating loss plus only one of the two elements of public necessity outlined in the *Illinois Central* case. Proof of direct operating losses on the trains to be discontinued plus adequate substitute bus service is sufficient to reverse a commission denial of discontinuance.[25] In such cases the carrier does not have to prove lack of use, although usually the patronage is slight. Likewise, proof of direct operating losses on the trains together with evidence that the public has virtually abandoned use of the trains is sufficient ground to reverse a commission denial of discontinuance.[26] In such case, ade-

---

[21] *Chicago, R. I. & Pac. R. R. v. State Corp. Comm'n*, 177 Kan. 697, 282 P. 2d 405 (1955); *New York Cent. R. R. v. Public Serv. Comm'n*, 278 App. Div. 725, 103 N. Y. S. 2d 217 (1951); *Sherwood v. Pennsylvania Pub. Util. Comm'n*, 177 Pa. Super. 6, 109 A. 2d 220 (1954).

[22] *Corporation Comm'n v. Southern Pac. Co.*, 55 Ariz. 173, 99 P. 2d 702 (1940).

[23] Orders of regulatory commissions within the area of their expertise are accorded great weight on appeal to the courts. They will not be overturned unless abuse of power is clearly shown. See *Texas & N. O. R. Co. v. Louisiana Public Service Com'n*, 233 La. 787, 98 So. 2d 189, 190 (1957).

[24] *In Matter of Union Pac. R. R.* 64 Idaho 597, 605, 134 P. 2d 1073, 1076 (1943); *Gardner v. Commerce Comm'n*, 400 Ill. 123, 129, 79 N. E. 2d, 71, 75 (1948).

[25] *Corporation Comm'n v. Southern Pac. Co.*, 55 Ariz. 173, 99 P. 2d 702 (1940); *Illinois Cent. R. R. v. Illinois Commerce Comm'n*, 410 Ill. 77, 101 N.E. 2d 588 (1951); *Chicago, R. I. & Pac. R. R. v. Louisiana Pub. Serv. Comm'n*, 234 La. 462, 100 So. 2d 471 (1958); *Chicago & N.W. Ry. v. Michigan Pub. Serv. Comm'n*, 329 Mich. 432, 45 N. W. 2d 520 (1951); *Application of Chicago, R. I. & Pac. R. R.* 166 Neb. 32, 87 N. W. 2d 616 (1958); *St. Louis-San Francisco Ry. v. State*, 262 P. 2d 168 (Okla. 1953); *Chicago, M. St. P. & P. R. Co. v. Public Service Com'n*, 98 N. W. 2d 101, 106 (N. D. 1959); *Maine Cent. R. Co. v. Public Utilities Com'n.*, 156 Me. 284, 163 A. 2d 633, 638 (1960); *Portland Traction Co. v. Hill*, 231 Ore. 354, 372 P. 2d 501, 509 (1962).

[26] *Thompson v. Illinois Commerce Comm'n*, 1 Ill. 2d 350, 115 N. E. 2d 622 (1953); *Atchison, T. & S. F. Ry. v. State Corp. Com'n*, 182 Kan. 603, 322 P. 2d 715 (1958); *Texas & N. O. R. R. v. Louisiana Publ Serv. Com'n*, 233 La. 787, 98 So. 2d 189

quate substitute public transportation did not have to be proved. In effect this is a recognition that in many areas the private automobile has replaced public transportation. An entire passenger train will not be required to operate to carry the very few people who prefer trains to bus or private automobile. The transportation convenience of a few persons who wish to continue riding trains is distinguished from the general public necessity that would require continued train service.[27] Individuals or municipalities protesting a discontinuance petition must present some clear evidence of the public's need for the service.[28] On the other hand, the effect of the direct operating loss of the trains concerned on the financial health of the carrier is a factor of public need favoring discontinuance.

Three states have been found that have statutes more favorable to passenger-service discontinuances. In Texas, a finding that particular passenger services do not and will not pay their costs plus a reasonable return on property employed, makes a discontinuance order *mandatory*.[29] In Kentucky, if operating loss is proved, discontinuance must be allowed if either there is no reasonable probability that such conditions will change for the better or the service has become unnecessary in the public interest. Where the first of these alternatives was proved, denial of discontinuance is in error.[30] In Tennessee, authorization for discontinuance of any passenger train is mandatory where for twelve

---

(1957); *Chicago, M., St. P. & Pac. R. R.* v. *Michigan Pub. Serv. Comm'n*, 338 Mich. 9, 12, 61 N. W. 2d 24, 26 (1953); *Application of Chicago, B. & Q. R. R.*, 166 Neb. 29, 87 N. W. 2d 630 (1958); *Baltimore & O. R. R.* v. *Public Util. Comm'n*, 160 Ohio St. 67, 113 N. E. 2d 240 (1953); *Missouri-Kansas-Texas R. R.* v. *State*, 319 P. 2d 590 (Okla. 1957), citing many earlier Oklahoma cases; *City of Princeton* v. *Public Serv. Comm'n*, 268 Wis. 542, 68 N. W. 2d 420 (1955); *State* ex rel. *Chicago R. I. & P. R. Co.* v. *Public Service Com'n.*, Mo., 312 S. W. 2d 791 (1958); *Western Maryland Ry. Co.* v. *Public Service Com'n*, 144 W. Va. 110, 106 S. E. 2d 923, 61 *W. Va. L. Rev.* 331 (1959); *Alabama Public Service Com'n* v. *Southern Ry. Co.*, 269 Ala., 63, 111 So. 2d 214 (1959).

[27] *Illinois Cent. R. R.* v. *Illinois Commerce Comm'n*, 397 Ill. 323, 327, 74 N. E. 2d 545, 547 (1947); *Application of Chicago, R. I. & Pac. R. R.*, 166 Neb. 32, 87 N. W. 2d 616, 618 (1958).

[28] In *Baltimore & O. R. R.* v. *Public Util. Comm'n*, 160 Ohio St. 67, 113 N. E. 2d 240 (1953), the court reversed a commission denial of discontinuance where the facts showed large operating losses and very little patronage on the trains, and there was no evidence offered in opposition to the discontinuance.

[29] *Texas & N. O. R. R.* v. *Railroad Comm'n*, 145 Tex. 541, 545, 200 S. W. 2d 626, 629 (1947).

[30] *Commonwealth* v. *Illinois Cent. R. R.* 299 S. W. 2d 803 (Ky. App. 1957); *Railroad Comm'n* v. *Illinois Cent. R. R.* 265 S. W. 2d 797 (Ky. App. 1954).

months or more the direct operating costs of the train exceeded its aggregate gross revenue by more than 30 per cent.[31]

One should not infer from this discussion that public convenience and necessity in discontinuance cases is developing into a predictable body of rules. In a number of recent cases courts have affirmed denials of discontinuance by commissions even though the carriers showed large out-of-pocket losses on the trains and slight use of the services.[32] In *State* v. *Duluth M. & I. R. Ry. Co.*,[33] for example, the court upheld a commission order requiring restoration of passenger service on a line where the 1952 average number of passengers carried per train-mile was 4.62, or slightly less than the five-man crew. The 1952 net out-of-pocket loss on this service was $223,127. In *Chicago M. St. P. & P. R. Co.* v. *Board of R. R. Comr's*,[34] the Montana Supreme Court upheld a denial of discontinuance of two trains on a 199-mile line which showed a net out-of-pocket loss in 1950 of $83,690. In other states, courts have reversed some of the more blatant antirailroad policies of legislatures and commissions. The New Jersey legislature passed a resolution against further discontinuances pending a public study of the problem, but the court refused to give it the status of a legislative act.[35] In North Dakota, the commission refused to combine a railroad's petition for passenger service discontinuance with the railroad's subsidiary's petition to offer substitute highway service until a mandamus was issued ordering combination of these petitions in the interest of a fair hearing.[36] In Missouri, a commission whose order to continue service was reversed by the courts attempted to order substitute service for the carriage of chickens without granting a new hearing on the need for this service.[37] The prejudice of some commissions in favor of local protestants and the lack of detailed regulatory criteria

---

[31] *Louisville & N. R. R.* v. *Fowler*, 197 Tenn. 266, 271 S. W. 2d 188 (1954).

[32] *State* v. *Duluth M. & I. R. Ry.*, 246 Minn. 383, 75 N. W. 2d 398 (1956); *Chicago, M., St. P. & P. R. R.* v. *Board of R. R. Comm'rs*, 126 Mont. 568, 255 P. 2d 346 (1953); *Pennsylvania R. R.* v. *Board of Pub. Util. Comm'rs*, 48 N. J. Super. 216, 137 A. 2d 76 (1957); *Delaware & H. R. R.* v. *Public Serv. Comm'n*, 285 App. Div. 326, 136 N. Y. S. 2d 510 (1954); *State* ex rel. *Utilities Com'n* v. *Southern Ry. Co.*, 254 N. C. 73, 118 S. E. 2d 21 (1961).

[33] 246 Minn. 383, 75 N. W. 2d 398, 402 (1956).

[34] 126 Mont. 568, 255 P. 2d 346, 349 (1953).

[35] In re *New York S. & W. R. R.*, 25 N. J. 343, 136 A. 2d 408 (1957).

[36] *State* ex rel. *Northern Pacific Transport Co.* v. *Public Service Com'n*, 82 N. W. 2d 597 (N. D. 1957).

[37] *State* ex rel. *Chicago, R. I. & P. R. Co.* v. *Public Service Com'n*, Mo., 355 S. W. 2d 45 (1962).

mean that there still remains no way to predict future commission reaction to a petition for discontinuance of passenger services.

While the rule of public convenience and necessity gives no measurable standards for railroad-service discontinuances, designing a better rule is not easy. Much of the trouble in commission denials of discontinuances, in spite of heavy losses and little use, appears to stem from the presumption that the public needs all trains now running. The trouble can largely be eliminated by discarding the public-convenience-and-necessity test and adopting a "fixed amount" or "percentage of loss on the specific service" test for discontinuance. A rule of this type was adopted in the Tennessee statute. If public convenience and necessity is kept as the standard, a legislative revision of the burden of proof could be adopted in order to eliminate the presumption that the public does indeed need all trains currently operated. Such a statute would put the burden of coming forward with evidence on the carrier requesting a service discontinuance to prove its out-of-pocket losses on the trains concerned, namely, that the direct operating expenses that would be escaped by discontinuing the train or trains exceeds the gross revenue from the train or trains. Once such a case is made, the statute would shift the burden of persuasion to the protestants to show public necessity for continued service and convince the commission that public necessity outweighs the operating losses of the carrier, thereby eliminating the presumption. In a period of sharply declining passenger traffic, it is only sensible to shift to the few remaining users the burden of showing why the service should be continued in spite of proved out-of-pocket losses. Such a statute would not cure the basic weaknesses of the public-convenience-and-necessity test—the incomparability of dollar losses and the elements of public need. It would, however, give the commissions a test more consistent with the economic facts of life. To the extent that the test would facilitate the discontinuance of loss services, both freight shippers and railroad stockholders could gain some relief from the burden of the passenger deficit.

Net Loss Railroads.—Railroads operating with *over-all* net losses over the foreseeable economic horizon are particularly anxious to get off the road to bankruptcy by discontinuing the specific services causing out-of-pocket losses. There is little law on the subject. The few decisions ruling directly on the rights of a net-loss railroad to discontinue particular losing services tend to confuse two related but separate constitutional issues. The first is the usual standard of review for all commission rulings based on public convenience and necessity, the due-process question of whether the commission's action was reasonable; that is, not arbitrary or capricious. The second, the one to be analyzed here, is an eminent-domain question. The gist of the holdings on this latter issue is that refusal of a state commission to permit a net-loss railroad to discontinue specific services showing losses of such magnitude that they jeopardize possible recovery to profitable operations is an unconstitutional taking of private property for a public use without just compensation.[38] The practical effect of this rule is that railroads operating at over-all net losses have an *absolute* right to mitigate the loss by discontinuing specific services showing very large direct operating losses. Commission attempts to block the discontinuances are confiscatory and therefore unconstitutional.

Before the discontinuance cases on net-loss roads are discussed it will be helpful to survey the legal and logical background to these cases found in the law relating to complete and partial abandonments by net-loss railroads. As noted in Chapter VI, a net-loss railroad has a constitutional right to abandon its entire operations, forfeit its charter, and retire from business.[39] In *Brooks Scanlon* v. *Railroad Comm'n,* Mr. Justice Holmes stated that "A carrier cannot be compelled to carry on even a branch of business at a loss, much less the whole business of carriage."[40] This dictum on the constitutional right to abandon particular net-loss branches of an over-all net-loss railroad is supported by court decision.[41] The rule follows logically from the right of the directors, when they decide that there is no reasonable prospect of recovery, to abandon an entire net-loss road. Where the remedy of partial abandonment will save the profitable parts of the line for the

[38] Although the eminent domain protection of the Fifth Amendment to the Constitution was originally held by the Supreme Court not to be operative against the states, the Fourteenth Amendment has been held to incorporate this section as a protection against state action. *United Ry. & Elec. Co.* v. *West,* 280 U.S. 234 (1930); *Chicago, B. & Q. R. R.* v. *Chicago,* 166 U.S. 226, 241 (1897); *Scott* v. *Toledo,* 36 Fed. 385, 395 (N. D. Ohio 1888).

[39] See Chapter VI, page 120.

[40] *Brooks-Scanlon Co.* v. *Railroad Comm'n,* 251 U.S. 396, 399 (1920). See *Railroad Comm'n* v. *Eastern Texas R. R.,* 264 U.S. 79 (1924); *Bullock* v. *Railroad Comm'n,* 254 U.S. 513 (1921); see Annot., 11 A.L.R. 252 (1921).

[41] *Iowa* v. *Old Colony Trust Co.,* 215 Fed. 307 (8th Cir. 1914); *Board of Comm'rs* v. *Public Util. Comm'n,* 107 Ohio St. 442, 140 N. E. 87 (1923); *Sherwood* v. *Atlantic & D. Ry.,* 94 Va. 291, 26 S. E. 943 (1897). See Annot., 10 A.L.R. 2d 1121, 1130–1134 (1950).

public use, denial of such remedy is confiscation.[42] The total value of the profitable parts of the carrier, if continued as an operating railroad, will surely be greater than the salvage value of the assets used on those parts if immediate, entire abandonment must be adopted as the only alternative to slow dissipation of its capital. Denial of the partial abandonment would confiscate this difference in value. Therefore, the net-loss railroad has a constitutional right to discontinue branches causing that loss so that the remainder of the road may recover and survive.

A constitutional right to *discontinue* specific net-loss services on a railroad showing over-all net losses follows the same logic as the right to partial abandonments on a net-loss road. Whether the railroad's possibility of recovery to profitable operation is jeopardized by heavy-loss branches that it wishes to abandon or by heavy-loss services that it wishes to discontinue, the consequences of denial are the same. In either case its revenue will be insufficient to replace its equipment, and eventually total abandonment must result. The passenger-service deficits imperiling the future of many major railroads operating at over-all net losses in 1958 make discontinuance of part or all of those services on most lines imperative. The constitutional right to discontinue such services on roads showing over-all net losses in spite of commission denials should enable many roads to survive the present railroad crisis.

The leading case on the constitutional right to discontinue particular loss services on a railroad showing over-all net losses is *Mississippi R. R. Comm'n v. Mobile & O. R. R.*[43] While operating at a deficit and without obtaining permission from the Mississippi Railroad Commission, the Mobile & Ohio discontinued the operation of six passenger trains. The commission ordered the service restored. The carrier obtained an order from a three-judge district court enjoining enforcement of the commission's order. It submitted evidence of its over-all net losses and of the operating losses on each of the six discontinued trains. The Supreme Court affirmed the injunction:

[42] "The loss was traced to the three branch lines. By discontinuing that service it is possible to operate the remainder. If the branches are not abandoned the whole system is lost. . . . The action of the city council [denying abandonment] . . . must be held to be unreasonable, and the enforcement of the regulatory statute in the circumstances found to amount to a deprivation of rights protected by the Constitution." *Crawford v. Duluth St. Ry.*, 60 F. 2d 212, 216 (7th Cir. 1932).

[43] 244 U.S. 388 (1917); see Annot., 123 A.L.R. 922, 930–33 (1939).

[We] fully agree with the district court in concluding that the order of the Commission at the time and under the circumstances when it was issued was arbitrary and unreasonable and in excess of the lawful powers of the Commission, and that if enforced it would result in such depriving of the railroad company of its property without due process of law as is forbidden by the 14th Amendment to the Constitution of the United States.[44]

The rule of the *Mobile* case was followed in *Delaware & H. R.R* v. *Public Serv. Comm'n*.[45] The carrier, which had lost money for three years, was ordered by the New York Public Service Commission to restore operation of one train it had discontinued. In the light of its over-all losses the court held the order arbitrary and unreasonable. Holding its enforcement would be repugnant to the Constitution, the commission's order was annulled:

The state has the right to regulate the conduct of railroads within its borders and may require that reasonable and adequate facilities be provided to serve, not only the necessities, but the convenience of the communities which are tributary, but the property used is entitled to the full protection of the law and cannot be taken from its owners without just compensation.[46]

Only one other case has put the confiscation issue in discontinuance cases by net-loss roads before the courts, and there the carrier failed to prove its over-all losses. While in receivership, the New Jersey & New York Railroad petitioned to discontinue one passenger train, which the carrier's accountants showed would reduce its *net* operating loss of $165,303 by $34,000 or 20 per cent. The New Jersey Public Utility Commission denied the petition and found public necessity for continuance of the train.

---

[44] 244 U.S. at 396 (1917). A similar ruling was made when the State of Maryland passed a statute requiring a net loss railroad to operate two additional trains. "In the long run all attempts to secure for the public so costly a facility must prove futile no matter what the courts do or leave undone. If that facility cannot be furnished otherwise than by the expenditure of the capital invested, sooner or later the exhaustion of the corporation's capital will make it impossible for the corporation to render any service whatsoever. . . . If legislation of the character of that under consideration can be upheld, a public service corporation may be forced first to consume all its property and then have its charter taken away in the end." *Washington, P. & C. Ry.* v. *Magruder,* 198 Fed. 218, 231 (C.C.D. Md. 1912).

[45] 245 App. Div. 66, 281 N. Y. Supp. 155 (1935).

[46] *Id.* at 68, 281 N. Y. Supp. at 157.

The Superior Court affirmed the commission.[47] It held that there was no constitutional right, regardless of public convenience and necessity, to discontinue one train on a net-loss railroad. In effect it held that the railroad had no remedy. Its only alternatives were either to abandon business entirely or expire slowly.

On appeal the Supreme Court of New Jersey subscribed to this same theory but held that it was not necessary to determine the question.[48] It held that although the business was in receivership and conducted by a trustee, its joint operations with the Erie Railroad and the ownership of 80 per cent of its stock by the Erie made it part of the Erie. Since Erie was showing over-all net profits, it held that petitioner had failed to prove a loss in its entire business. Mr. Justice Brennan (now of the United States Supreme Court) dissented from this decision, pointing out that the railroad could not go on indefinitely as a losing venture. He did not, however, take the next logical step and say that forcing continued operation of the train was a taking of property from the creditor-owners without just compensation.

No other cases have been found that put in issue the constitutional right to discontinue losing services on an over-all net-loss railroad. Commissions are much more likely to grant discontinuances when the *entire* road is operating at a loss. For this reason the carriers have not often been forced to appeal to the courts in those cases. Frequently where the carrier has secured review of the denial of discontinuance, the courts have reversed the commission on the grounds that its findings of public necessity were against the weight of the evidence and hence arbitrary and unreasonable. In doing so they found it unnecessary to reach the constitutional issue of confiscation.[49]

It can be argued that there has never been a case decided in the courts where public necessity for specific services of a net-loss

---

[47] In re *New Jersey & N. Y. R. R.*, 23 N. J. Super. 1, 92 A. 2d 515 (App. Div. 1952).

[48] In re *New Jersey & N. Y. R. R.*, 12 N. J. 281, 96 A. 2d 526 (1953), *appeal dismissed*, 346 U.S. 868 (1953).

[49] E.g., *Atlantic Coast Line* v. *Public Serv. Comm'n*, 77 F. Supp. 675 (E.D.S.C. 1948); *New York Cent. R. R.* v. *Public Serv. Comm'n*, 257 App. Div. 558, 13 N.Y.S. 2d 614 (1939); *Southern Ry.* v. *Public Serv. Comm'n*, 195 S.C. 247, 10 S.E. 2d 769 (1940); see *Pennsylvania-Reading Seashore Lines* v. *Board of Pub. Util. Comm'rs*, 5 N. J. 114, 74 A. 2d 265 (1950), *cert. denied sub nom. Brotherhood of R. R. Trainmen* v. *Pennsylvania-Reading Seashore Lines*, 340 U.S. 876 (1950), holding that denial of discontinuance after a finding by the commission of no public necessity was arbitrary and hence without due process.

road was clearly found and a constitutional right to discontinue was upheld. In both the *Mobile & Ohio* and *Delaware & H. R.R. v. Public Serv. Comm'n* cases there were holdings that the commissions' conclusions of public necessity for the trains were unreasonable. The courts did not have to reach the eminent-domain issues in those cases. In the *New Jersey* case, the constitutional discussion became dictum by virtue of the finding that the road was part of the Erie, which was showing over-all net profit. Hence, the court which next meets the issue of a constitutional right to discontinue services on a net-loss road can correctly hold that there is no clear law on the subject.

How should a court treat the subject? Assume there is a clear finding by the commission and courts that the public necessity for the train or trains outweighs the specific loss from those services to be discontinued by the net-loss carrier. Assume that the losses from those particular trains jeopardize the entire carrier's future by precluding possible recovery to net-profit operations. The situation is analogous to the partial abandonment case, discussed earlier. The carrier, if denied these discontinuances, must either abandon operations entirely or slowly consume its capital, and, when unable to replace its equipment, be forced to abandon operations. When there is possible recovery to net profit operations by specific service discontinuances, forcing the road either to leave business or to piecemeal exhaustion of its assets results in taking property for a public purpose without just compensation.

The managers of the net-loss railroad would probably first petition the state commission for permission to discontinue unprofitable trains on the conventional ground of lack of public necessity. If the commission denied the petition, the railroad would discontinue the services anyway. The commission would then file an action in the appropriate local court demanding that the trains be restored. The railroad would defend the action on the ground that it was showing over-all net losses, and that the specific unprofitable trains which it had discontinued jeopardized its possible recovery to net profit operations. If the railroad successfully carried the burden of proof of these two elements of its defense, the court would enter judgment for it in recognition of its constitutional immunity from confiscation.

One further analogy supporting the above rule must be mentioned. When railroad rates are *set* so low that a well-managed carrier loses money in its over-all business, the rate statute or order has the effect of taking private property for public use without just compensation.[50] In such a case specific confiscatory rate statutes or orders which do not enable the carrier to earn out-of-pocket costs will be set aside.[51] Any other holding would allow regulatory commissions to set rates so low that the carrier would be forced to consume its capital in rendering its public service and eventually have to abandon operations entirely. The similarities to the service discontinuance cases are apparent. If the source of over-all net losses can be traced to specific rates or to specific services not earning out-of-pocket costs, the rates must be raised or the services discontinued. Forcing a net-loss road to operate at rates that do not return direct operating costs or to continue services which show very large direct operating losses, is confiscatory in both cases.

Passenger Discontinuances Under Federal Law

The Transportation Act of 1958 gave the Interstate Commerce Commission its first jurisdiction over passenger-service discontinuances by the addition of section 13a to the Interstate Commerce Act.[52] The act was designed to remedy the defects of state regulation of discontinuances, extensive delay, and alleged political bias of state commissioners.[53] Section 13a(1) gives the Interstate Commerce Commission initial jurisdiction of discontinuances of trains operating between two states. Section 13a(2) gives the Commission jurisdiction of discontinuances of trains operating wholly within one state only after denial of permission to discontinue by a state commission or failure of the state commission to act. The differing procedures under these two sections of the

[50] *Baltimore & O. R. R.* v. *United States*, 345 U.S. 146 (1953) (dictum); *Bellamy* v. *Missouri & N.A.R.R.*, 215 Fed. 18 (8th Cir. 1914); *Capital Transit Co.* v. *Bosley*, 191 Md. 502, 62 A. 2d 267 (1948); 13 C.J.S., *Carriers* §296 (1939). See *Norfolk & W. Ry.* v. *Conley*, 236 U.S. 605 (1915) and analysis of rule in *Central R. R. of N.J.* v. *Department of Pub. Util.*, 10 N.J. 255, 263, 90 A. 2d 1, 6 (1952), *appeal dismissed*, 345 U.S. 931 (1953); compare this rule as to particular services with *Baltimore & O. R. R.* v. *United States, supra.* See Harbeson, "A New Judicial Test of Reasonable Rates," 22 *ICC Prac. J.* 789 (1955).

[51] The only exception to this rule on a net-loss railroad is where no possible rate increase will save the carrier from failing. It has no value as a going concern and entire abandonment is its only out. *Market St. Ry.* v. *Railroad Comm'n*, 324 U.S. 548 (1945). See *Baltimore Transit Co.* v. *Hessey*, 196 Md. 141, 75 A. 2d 76 (1950) *cert. denied*, 340 U.S. 896 (1950), where application of this rule is explained.

[52] 72 Stat. 571, 49 U.S.C. 13a (1958). See note, 57 *Mich. L. Rev.* 1258 (1959).

[53] U.S. Cong., Senate, Committee on Interstate and Foreign Commerce, *Report on Problems of the Railroads* 15–16 (85th Cong. 2d Sess. 1958); see Priest, "Discontinuance of Railroad Service," 61 *Pub. Util. Fort.* 656 (1958); Thomas, "Public Utilities: Discontinuance of Railroad Service," 14 *Rutgers L. Rev.* 345 (1960).

act is discussed in detail below. The statutory test for permitting discontinuance under the two sections, however, is the same. The Commission must find that the train operation is no longer required by public convenience and necessity and that continued operation will constitute an unjust and undue burden on interstate commerce.[54]

The Supreme Court has ruled on the jurisdictional boundary between sections 13a(1) and 13a(2). The New York, Susquehanna & Western applied to the Commission under section 13a(1) to discontinue two trains operating between Butler and North Bergen, New Jersey, 90 per cent of whose passengers transferred to connecting buses for travel to New York. The buses were owned by an unaffiliated carrier and operated under contract with the railroad. The Commission dismissed the notice of discontinuance under section 13a(1) on the ground that the trains were wholly intrastate and the carrier must apply first to the New Jersey state commission. The Supreme Court affirmed the Commission,[55] holding that the plain words of the statute and the legislative history both supported the Commission's interpretation. The purpose of the statute was remedial, but it was conditioned by a desire to protect state jurisdiction over local operations. But if a train starting in one state terminates in a town on the border of the next state so that at least part of the train crosses a state line, section 13a(1) applies to the railroad's petition for discontinuance.[56]

Table 14 records the discontinuance proposals and decisions under the Transportation Act of 1958. More than half the proposals under section 13a(1) to discontinue interstate passenger trains received affirmative decisions. The expedited procedures of this act make it much superior to petitioning for discontinuance under state regulatory statutes. Only one-third of the petitions filed under section 13a(2) resulted in permits to discontinue service. Some of the petitions were dismissed on jurisdictional grounds. Of the fifty-one intrastate trains required to continue operation in 1961–62, twenty-one were commuter trains of the Pennsylvania

---

[54] The latter phrase, "Undue burden on interstate commerce," although often used by the courts, became a statutory standard for railroad regulation for the first time in the 1958 act. See Wells, "A Review of Interstate Commerce Commission Section 13a Decisions," 27 *ICC. Prac. J.* 821, 825 (1960).

[55] *New Jersey v. New York, Susquehanna & W. R. Co.*, 372 U.S. 1 (1963). See *Pennsylvania R. Co.*, 317 I.C.C. 737 (1963).

[56] *Texas & P. Ry. Co.*, 307 I.C.C. 259, 264 (1959).

TABLE 14

<small>PASSENGER SERVICE DISCONTINUANCES UNDER THE TRANSPORTATION ACT OF 1958</small>
(1958–1963)

Section 13a(1): Interstate Trains

	Discontinuance proposals		Discontinuances permitted		Discontinuances denied	
	Number of notices	Number of trains	Number of railroads	Number of trains	Number of railroads	Number of trains
1958–59	31	75	8	20	2	6
1959–60	21	61	14	85	5	12
1960–61	14	61	4	18	3	6
1961–62	16	58	8	50	5	26
1962–63	13	31	6	16	2	7
TOTALS	95	286	40	189	17	57

Section 13a(2): Intrastate Trains

	Discontinuance proposals		Discontinuances permitted		Discontinuances denied	
	Petitions filed	Number of trains	Number of railroads	Number of trains	Number of railroads	Number of trains
1958–59	12	40	0	0	0	0
1959–60	8	32	2	4	1	8
1960–61	4	65	7	27	0	0
1961–62	3	12	3	15	2	51
1962–63	1	1	1	1	1	2
TOTALS	28	150	13	47	4	61

SOURCE: U.S. Interstate Commerce Commission, *Annual Reports* 1959–1963.

Railroad at Pittsburgh and thirty were Pennsylvania-Reading Seashore trains between Camden, N.J., and southern New Jersey points.

Interstate Train Discontinuances.—Section 13a(1) authorizes railroads to discontinue trains operating between two states by giving 30 days notice to the Interstate Commerce Commission. If the Commission decides not to enter upon an investigation of the proposed discontinuance, it becomes effective at the end of the 30-day notice period. If the Commission decides to enter an investigation, it must notify the railroad 10 days before the expiration of the 30-day-notice period and may suspend the discontinuance for four months pending its decision. If the Commission finds that the particular train service is required by public convenience and necessity and that it will not unduly burden interstate commerce, it may order continuance or restoration of service for a period not to exceed one year.

The summary procedures of section 13a(1), in permitting discontinuance merely by notice when the Commission concludes not to enter upon an investigation of the proposal, have been held constitutional. In *State of New Jersey* v. *United States*,[57] the New York Central filed notice under section 13a(1) and discontinued its Weehawken passenger ferries when the Commission concluded not to enter upon an investigation. The Commission was fully aware of the facts in the case, because, before passage of section 13a, it had permitted discontinuance of these ferries under the abandonments section of the act[58] only to be reversed by the district court.[59] In upholding the later discontinuance under section 13a(1), the court held that it had no jurisdiction to enjoin the Commission decision not to enter upon an investigation, since this was not an *order* of the Commission requiring the carrier to do or to refrain from an act. It held that under its constitutional power to regulate commerce, Congress could make this mere filing with the Commission sufficient procedure for service discontinuances.[60]

In more than 90 per cent of the notices filed under section 13a(1), the Commission has undertaken an investigation. A first issue in many of these cases has been which party must carry the burden of proving existence or nonexistence of public convenience and necessity for continued operation and whether the burden on interstate commerce is undue. The Commission has consistently followed an early decision under the act where it refused to decide whether applicant or protestants must carry the

[57] 168 F. Supp. 324 (N.J. 1958), *aff'd per curiam*, 359 U.S. 27 (1959).

[58] 41 Stat. 477 (1920), 49 U.S.C. 1(18) (1958). See *New York Central R. Co. Ferry Abandonment*, 295 I.C.C. 385 (1956), *aff'd* 295 I.C.C. 519 (1957).

[59] *Board of Public Utility Commissioners of N.J.* v. *United States*, 158 F. Supp. 98 (N.J. 1957). In this decision, the Court held the Commission was without jurisdiction to authorize the New York Central to discontinue passenger ferry service from Weehawken to New York City while continuing to operate its waterborne freight transportation between the same cities. It held that discontinuance of passenger ferry service only was not an abandonment of a portion of a line of railroad under section 1(18).

[60] See *Sludden v. United States* 211 F. Supp. 150 (M.D. Pa. 1962), for a similar dismissal of an action by a labor union to enjoin discontinuance.

burden of proof.[61] It has held the question to be of only theoretical importance, stating that the burden of proof would be controlling only if no substantial evidence were adduced or if the evidence were equally balanced. In the hearings, the carrier is always given the first duty of going forward, so that the procedure is like that under the abandonments section of the Interstate Commerce Act where the burden of proof is on the carrier. In one denial of a petition to change service by merging two trains, the Commission decision was based on the carrier's failure to prove that the consolidated trains would provide the same service as the separate trains.[62]

The Commission decision under this act is in two interrelated steps. First it must decide if there is a definite and substantial public need for the service. If such need is found, the service is ordered to continue unless outweighed by the resulting loss to the carrier, this constituting an undue burden on interstate commerce.[63] In many of these decisions, the factors to be considered are summarized from *Colorado* v. *United States*,[64] a leading abandonments decision by the Supreme Court.[65] Among other factors, the Court emphasized the populations of the communities served; the use made by the public of the service sought to be discontinued; other means of transportation in the area; and the financial losses sustained by the carrier in providing the service.

In deciding the issue of public convenience and necessity, the Interstate Commerce Commission has taken an approach similar to that of the state commissions. Where insubstantial use and little public support for the passenger train is shown, no public necessity will be found even though some of the towns have no other common-carrier passenger service.[66] Since the people of the

---

[61] *Great Northern Ry. Co.*, 307 I.C.C. 59, 60–61 (1959). See *Chicago & N. W. Ry. Co.*, 307 I.C.C. 271 (1959); *Chicago & N. W. Ry. Co.*, 307 I.C.C. 463 (1959); *Chicago Great W. Ry. Co.*, 317 I.C.C. 99 (1962).

[62] *Southern Pacific Co.*, 312 I.C.C. 437 (1961). See *Southern Pacific Co.*, F.D. No. 21946 (1962) approving this train consolidation.

[63] *Louisville & Nashville R. Co.*, 307 I.C.C. 173, 186 (1959); *Southern Pacific Co.*, 312 I.C.C. 437, 454 (1961).

[64] 271 U.S. 153 (1926).

[65] See *New Jersey & N.Y. R. Co.*, 307 I.C.C. 533, 537 (1959); *Chicago, M., St. P. & P. R. Co.*, 307 I.C.C. 565, 576 (1959); *Delaware L. & W. R. Co.*, 307 I.C.C. 627, 634 (1959); *Missouri Pacific R. Co.*, 307 I.C.C. 787, 796 (1960); *Chicago & N. W. Ry. Co.*, 312 I.C.C. 313, 320 (1960); *Chicago & N. W. Ry. Co.*, 312 I.C.C. 517, 527 (1961); *St. Louis-S.F. Ry. Co.*, 312 I.C.C. 713, 727 (1960).

[66] *Great Northern Ry. Co.*, 307 I.C.C. 59, 64, 70 (1959); *Minneapolis, St. P. & S.S.M.R. Co.*, 307 I.C.C. 125, 130 (1959); *Chicago, M. St. P. & P.R. Co.*, 307 I.C.C.

area have overwhelmingly adopted automobile transport, neither train nor bus service is needed. In most cases, however, there is both insubstantial use and adequate substitute-common-carrier service.[67] If the discontinued trains are the last ones on that line, both air and bus service are usually available.[68] In the case of the St. Louis Southwestern discontinuance of its last passenger trains, the Missouri Pacific paralleled applicant's entire line from 21 to 64 miles away with adequate train service.[69] Many of these cases involve discontinuance of the last train on the line which hauls only one coach, and the average number of passengers per train-mile is often less than the train crew. In such a situation, the general prosperity of the carrier is no grounds to continue the burden on interstate commerce of the losing trains. The Commission has described such particular losses on a prosperous railroad as "an infection which might spread as a cancerous growth and sap the strength of the entire system." [70] Furthermore, railroads may not be forced to continue little-used passenger trains just for the convenience of mail and express carriage, because railroads are not common carriers of mail and express;[71] they are contract carriers for these items.

In the cases where discontinuance is denied, the Commission

565, 571 (1959); *Missouri Pacific R. Co.*, 307 I.C.C. 787, 792 (1960); *Louisiana & A. Ry. Co.*, 317 I.C.C. 155, 160 (1962).

[67] *Chicago & N. W. Ry. Co.*, 307 I.C.C. 271, 278 (1959); *Chicago & N. W. Ry. Co.*, 307 I.C.C. 463, 468–469 (1959); *Minneapolis & St. L. Ry. Co.*, 307 I.C.C. 79, 83 (1959); *Texas & Pacific Ry. Co.*, 307 I.C.C. 259, 261 (1959); *New Jersey & N.Y. R. Co.*, 307 I.C.C. 533 (1959); *Chicago M. St. P. & P. R. Co.*, 307 I.C.C. 669, 671 (1960); *Chicago & N. W. Ry. Co.*, 312 I.C.C. 517, 520 (1961); *Chicago & N. W. Ry. Co.*, 312 I.C.C. 621, 626 (1961); *Boston & M. R.*, 317 I.C.C. 165, 168 (1962); *Southern Pacific Co.*, 317 I.C.C. 519 (1962). Even when there has been substantial use of the trains but there are large losses and adequate substitute service on other trains of the same or nearby railroads, the Commission will find the trains are not required by public convenience and necessity. *Baltimore & O. R. Co.*, 317 I.C.C. 673 (1963); *Chicago & N. W. Ry. Co.*, Finance No. 22425 (1963).

[68] *Wabash R. Co.*, 307 I.C.C. 353, 358 (1959); *St. Louis-S. F. Ry. Co.*, 307 I.C.C. 477, 479 (1959); *Delaware L. & W. R. Co.*, 307 I.C.C. 627 (1959); *Chicago & N. W. Ry. Co.*, 312 I.C.C. 313, 317 (1960); *Lehigh Valley R. Co.*, 312 I.C.C. 339, 406–407 (1961); *Chicago Gt. W. Ry. Co.*, 317 I.C.C. 99, 105 (1962).

[69] *St. Louis S. W. Ry. Co.*, 307 I.C.C. 639 (1959).

[70] *Great Northern Ry. Co.*, 307 I.C.C. 59, 70 (1959). See *St. Louis S. W. Ry. Co.*, 307 I.C.C. 639, 650 (1959); *Missouri Pacific R. Co.*, 307 I.C.C. 787, 796 (1960); *Chicago & N. W. Ry. Co.*, 312 I.C.C. 517, 527 (1961). Over-all system losses are a factor of public necessity supporting a petition to discontinue trains. *Chicago & N. W. Ry. Co.*, 312 I.C.C. 313, 316 (1960); *Lehigh Valley R. Co.*, 312 I.C.C. 399, 408 (1961).

[71] *Pennsylvania R. Co.*, 317 I.C.C. 737, 741 (1963); *Chicago & N. W. Ry. Co.*, 307 I.C.C. 775, 781 (1960). See *Minneapolis, St. P. & S.S.M. R. Co.*, 307 I.C.C. 125, 131 (1959).

must first find that the public convenience and necessity requires continued service. In those cases where the last trains on a line have been denied authority to discontinue in spite of heavy losses, the Commission has found need for some common-carrier service to the small towns along the route. Thus, the Soo Line was required to continue two trains over 561.8 miles of lines in spite of a 1960 out-of-pocket loss of $406,609 because 232 miles of the line would lose all public transport by discontinuance.[72] And the St. Louis-San Francisco was required to continue two trains over a 305.4-mile route in spite of a $99,772 out-of-pocket loss in 1959 where twelve intermediate towns would lose all public transport.[73] In both cases the average passenger load per train was less than fifty and could easily have been carried in one bus. In two cases, portions of losing service were ordered continued to accommodate long-distance commuters.[74] In those denials of train discontinuances where other trains operate on the same line, the basis of public need for the losing service is not so clear. In some cases the Commission seems to have found public need because the carrier's proof of losses was incomplete.[75] In still other cases, the Commission, having found public need for the train services from their substantial use and required service for one year, has permitted discontinuance at the end of the year upon showing of declining use.[76]

Direct operating losses of the trains to the carrier are not only one element in determining public convenience and necessity of the service but are also a burden on interstate commerce. Since any direct or out-of-pocket loss is a burden on interstate commerce, the crucial question is when is there an *undue* burden on interstate commerce. In a few cases where discontinuance was denied, the Commission held that the carrier failed to establish the existence of a burden on interstate commerce. Expenses for maintenance of way, traffic, general administration and station

[72] *Soo Line R. Co.*, 312 I.C.C. 729 (1961).

[73] *St. Louis-S.F. Ry. Co.*, 312 I.C.C. 713 (1960).

[74] *New York Central R. Co.*, 307 I.C.C. 167 (1959) (29 miles of 50-mile route ordered to continue); *Louisville & N.R. Co.*, 307 I.C.C. 173 (1959) (63 miles of 89-mile route ordered to continue). See *Pennsylvania R. Co.*, 317 I.C.C. 111 (1962).

[75] *Louisville & N.R. Co.*, 307 I.C.C. 392, 398 (1959); *Texas & N.O. R. Co.*, 307 I.C.C. 725, 731 (1960); *Chicago R.I. & P. R. Co.*, 307 I.C.C. 655, 661–664 (1959) and 312 I.C.C. 324, 325 (1960).

[76] *Lehigh Valley R. Co.*, 307 I.C.C. 239 (1959), *discontinuance permitted* 312 I.C.C. 399 (1961); *Chicago & N. W. Ry. Co.*, 307 I.C.C. 585 (1959), *discontinuance permitted* 312 I.C.C. 517 (1961); *Southern Pacific Co.*, 312 I.C.C. 437 (1961), *train consolidation permitted* Finance No. 21946 (1962).

services used also by other trains were wrongly included as out-of-pocket costs in some instances.[77] Only those direct costs which are avoidable and thus savable by discontinuance may be used to calculate the burden on commerce.[78] In addition, joint terminal facilities expense, which the railroad will save by discontinuance, may not be included in calculating avoidable costs because the other carriers using the terminal will have to pay this expense.[79] That terminal expense would remain a burden on commerce even if the discontinuance by the one carrier was allowed.

In cases where the Commission held that public need and direct losses constituting a burden on interstate commerce both were proved, the balancing of these two interests in reaching a decision was similar to that in the cases in state commissions. Since there are no measurable standards for making this decision, there is no way to predict the outcome of such cases. The smaller the direct loss in relation to the distance the train must run, the less likely the Commission will find an undue burden on interstate commerce from continuing the trains. On a 50-mile line with substantial use, for example, two trains were ordered continued over 29 miles of the line in spite of a previous $21,815 out-of-pocket annual loss.[80] Likewise, an $84,898 annual direct loss on a 265-mile line, where $52,000 of this loss was joint terminal expense that would remain a burden on other railroads, would not be sufficient loss to allow discontinuance of two trains.[81]

There were some denials of discontinuance of trains, however, where the losses from operations were very large and the prospects were for them to get larger. In the first *Lehigh Valley* case,[82] the carrier was operating at an over-all loss and petitioned to discontinue all passenger service over its 400-mile route. Its out-of-pocket losses were estimated at $2,388,000 per year. Nevertheless, the carrier was required to continue four trains for one year at an estimated loss of $756,000. At the end of the year, the Com-

---

[77] *Texas & N.O. R. Co.*, 307 I.C.C. 725, 731 (1960); *Southern P. Co.* 312 I.C.C. 437, 452 (1961).

[78] *St. Louis-S.F. Ry. Co.*, 312 I.C.C. 713, 718 (1960); *Missouri Pacific R. Co.*, 312 I.C.C. 765, 770 (1961); *Missouri Pacific R. Co.*, Finance No. 22341 (1963).

[79] *Louisville & N.R. Co.*, 307 I.C.C. 173, 181–182 (1959); *Chicago & N. W. Ry. Co.*, 307 I.C.C. 585, 607 (1959); *Texas & N.O. R. Co.*, 307 I.C.C. 725, 731 (1960); *Chicago R.I. & P. R. Co.*, 312 I.C.C. 324, 325 (1960); *St. Louis-S.F. Ry. Co.*, 312 I.C.C. 713, 721 (1960).

[80] *New York Central R. Co.*, 307 I.C.C. 167 (1959).

[81] *Louisville & N.R. Co.*, 307 I.C.C. 392, 398 (1959).

[82] *Lehigh Valley R. Co.*, 307 I.C.C. 239 (1959).

mission found this loss to be a burden on interstate commerce and allowed the Lehigh Valley to discontinue all passenger service.[83] A similar reversal of position by the Commission after initial denial of discontinuance occurred for four Chicago and North Western trains where minimum estimated savings from discontinuance were $372,634.[84] The one denial of discontinuance which resulted in a dissent involved eighteen Pennsylvania Railroad trains between Philadelphia and southern New Jersey.[85] The four dissenting commissioners stated that a railroad with such large passenger losses should at least be allowed to dicontinue those trains where revenues were less than crew expense.

From an economic viewpoint, the most significant partial denial was on the Milwaukee road 1,806-mile line from Minneapolis to Tacoma.[86] The last two trains on this line had out-of-pocket losses of more than $2 million per year. The western 1,200 miles of the line roughly paralleled the Northern Pacific, which offered alternate passenger service from Minneapolis to Tacoma. Nevertheless, and in spite of the heavy losses and small patronage, the Commission's decision in 1961 permitted discontinuance only on the western 700 miles. This ended transcontinental service, but left the carrier with the cost of running the trains on 60 per cent of the line. In 1964, after the carrier proved $905,360 annual losses on this eastern portion, it was permitted to discontinue the 855 miles of service west of Aberdeen.

Intrastate Train Discontinuances.—For trains operating wholly within one state, the Interstate Commerce Commission may hear a petition for discontinuance only after the state commission has denied discontinuance or has failed to act on a discontinuance petition within 120 days. Under section 13a(2), unlike the interstate trains section, there is no option in the ICC to conclude not to make an investigation of the proposed discontinuance.

The Commission may grant such authority only after full hearing and upon findings by it that (a) the present or future public convenience and necessity permit of such discontinuance or change, in whole or in part, of the operation or service of such train or ferry, and (b) the continued operation or service of such train or ferry without

[83] *Lehigh Valley R. Co.*, 312 I.C.C. 399 (1961).
[84] *Chicago & N.W. Ry. Co.*, 307 I.C.C. 585 (1959), *discontinuance permitted*, 312 I.C.C. 517 (1961).
[85] *Pennsylvania R. Co.*, 317 I.C.C. 111, 136 (1962).
[86] *Chicago M. St. P. & P. R. Co.*, 317 I.C.C. 691 (1961). See Chicago, Milwaukee, St. Paul and Pacific Railroad Company, *Annual Report 1963*, 11.

discontinuance or change, in whole or in part, will constitute an unjust and undue burden upon the interstate operations of such carrier or carriers or upon interstate commerce.[87]

Section 13a(2) has been held constitutional by a district court.[88] Since the statute concerns effects upon interstate commerce, it clearly comes under the commerce power given Congress. The court further held that this section removes the common-law prohibitions of *res judicata* from such actions and allows them to be reheard even though they were given a full hearing before a state regulatory authority. Other jurisdictional matters have also been settled. Section 13a(2), like 13a(1), applies not only to single trains but can be applied to a group or all the trains on a line in one action.[89] If partial relief is granted by a state commission, the railroad may petition the ICC under 13a(2) to discontinue those trains for which the state denied relief, and the railroad does not have to continue all trains operating before the state action while its petition before the ICC is pending. Furthermore, the denial of discontinuance by the state must have occurred after the passage of the Transportation Act of 1958, and the petition under section 13a(2) must be substantially the same as the previous one before the state commission.[90]

Most of the petitions filed under section 13a(2) have been granted. Typically they involve a single pair of trains with one or two coaches on which the state commission has denied discontinuance in spite of little use and large out-of-pocket losses.[91] In such cases, it is usually clear that the state commission in denying discontinuance has put the needs of a few travelers above the needs of the public generally for efficient freight service at the lowest possible rates consistent with a financially sound railroad system.[92] In all appeals from ICC decisions under section 13a(2) permitting discontinuance except one, the courts have held the

[87] 72 Stat. 571, 49 U.S.C. §13a(2) (1958).

[88] *State of North Carolina* v. *United States,* 210 F. Supp. 675, 678 (M.D.N.C., 1962).

[89] *Southern Pacific Co.,* 312 I.C.C. 631, 633 (1961); *Pennsylvania R. Co.,* 317 I.C.C. 111, 117–120 (1962).

[90] *Northern Pacific Ry. Co.,* 312 I.C.C. 150 (1960), 312 I.C.C. 309 (1960), 312 I.C.C. 311 (1960).

[91] See, e.g., *Missouri Pacific R. Co.,* 312 I.C.C. 105 (1960); *Great Northern Ry. Co.,* 312 I.C.C. 580 (1961), *aff'd. sub. nom, State of Montana* v. *United States,* 202 F. Supp. 660 (Mont. 1962); *Pennsylvania R. Co.,* 317 I.C.C. 5 (1961).

[92] See *Pennsylvania R. Co.,* 317 I.C.C. 5, 11 (1961).

Commission's findings to be supported by substantial evidence and affirmed the Commission.[93]

The one Commission permit to discontinue service under 13a(2) which was reversed in a trial court was the *Southern Railway* between Greensboro and Goldsboro, North Carolina.[94] On these last two trains on the route, passenger revenues for the first five months of 1961 were $10,653 or approximately $26,000 less than train- and engine-crew wages. The district court set aside the discontinuance permit, holding that there was clear evidence of public need and that the test of whether there is an undue burden on interstate commerce is whether the segment of line (freight and passenger service combined) is contributing a fair share to over-all company operations.[95] Since the avoidable passenger loss was $90,000 per annum and the annual freight profit on the line was $630,000, the court held that there was not an undue burden on interstate commerce. The Supreme Court reversed the District Court and upheld the ICC permit of discontinuance, holding that it was within the ICC exercise of its expertise to decide (regardless of profitable freight operations on a line) what effect discontinuance of particular trains will have upon public convenience and necessity and upon interstate operations or commerce.[96]

There are three reported denials of discontinuance by the ICC under section 13a(2).[97] In the *New York Central* case permission was denied to discontinue eight trains on its St. Lawrence division. The Commission found a public need for the service in that substitute bus and air service were held to be inadequate. Since there was no evidence on the feeder value of the line, the estimated $250,000 annual saving was not considered a burden on interstate commerce. Six of the eight trains were later permitted to be discontinued. The second reported Commission denial under section 13a(2) was for thirty trains in southern New Jersey of the *Pennsylvania-Reading Seashore* Lines. In spite of

[93] *State of Montana* v. *United States*, 202 F. Supp. 660 (Mont. 1962); *City of Philadelphia* v. *United States*, 197 F. Supp. 832 (E.D.Pa. 1961); *People of State of California* v. *United States*, 207 F. Supp. 635 (N.D. Calif. 1962).

[94] *Southern Ry. Co.*, 317 I.C.C. 255 (1962). For court affirmance of earlier denial of discontinuance by the state commission, see *State ex rel. Utilities Comm.* v. *Southern Ry. Co.*, 254 N.C. 73, 118 S.E. 2d 21 (1961).

[95] *State of North Carolina* v. *United States*, 210 F. Supp. 675 (M.D.N.C. 1962).

[96] *Southern Railway Company* v. *North Carolina*, 373 U.S. 907.

[97] *New York Central R. Co.*, 312 I.C.C. 4 (1960); *Pennsylvania R. Co.*, 317 I.C.C. 111 (1962); *Denver & R.G.W.R. Co.*, 317 I.C.C. 722 (1963).

estimated savings of more than $2 million, the Commission found a paramount public need for these trains in commuter service. The *Rio Grande* service between Denver and Craig, Colorado, was the third denial under section 13a(2). The commission found that the isolation of the territory, the lack of adequate alternative service, and the strong financial condition of the carrier were grounds to order continuance of the admittedly unprofitable service.

FREIGHT-SERVICE DISCONTINUANCES

Freight-service discontinuances take the form of closing agency freight stations and the refusal by carriers to accept less-than-carload (LCL) freight in small towns. Before the time of paved highways and motor trucks, railroads in the East and Midwest usually built stations along their lines 7 to 10 miles apart for the LCL freight needs of a farm economy. Recent studies show that trucks are the lowest-cost transport for most LCL shipments of less than 150 miles and that most LCL freight is now carried by trucks.[98] Total LCL freight originated on the railroads declined from 36 million tons in 1929 to 2.6 million tons in 1961.[99] Part of this drop was the result of another technological change. Much LCL traffic still moves by rail, but only after being combined into carloads by freight forwarders.[100]

The decline of rail LCL shipments has caused a large percentage of agency freight stations to become net-loss operations. Since freight-car pickup and delivery for carload freight can be negotiated by telephone from central agency stations as much as 30 miles away from a shipper's plant, avoidable costs of other agency stations must be calculated on the basis of revenues and costs of LCL freight. A Chicago and North Western study showed that local agents in one-man stations worked as little as 12 minutes per day, and the average daily work time in its one-man stations

[98] Poole, *Costs—A Tool for Railroad Management* 78–88 (1962); Meyer, Peck, Stenason, and Zwick, *The Economics of Competition in the Transportation Industries* 150–155 (1959). See U.S. Board of Investigation and Research, *Comparison of Rail, Motor and Water Carrier Costs*, S. Doc. 84 (79th Cong. 1st Sess. 1944); *Pickup and Delivery—Official Territory—L.C.L. & A.Q.*, 314 I.C.C. 313 (1961).

[99] Association of American Railroads, *Railroad Transportation—A Statistical Record 1921–1961*, 23 (1962). See "Commodity Transportation: Competition Among Carriers," 41 *Survey of Current Business* 6 (1961); Phillips, "Diversion of Freight Traffic from the Railroads," 16 *J. of Land and Pub. Util. Econ.* 403 (1940).

[100] See Nelson, *Railroad Transportation And Public Policy* 32 (1959).

was only 59 minutes.[101] Pay computed for time actually worked ran in some cases as high as $300 per hour.

The net loss on agency freight stations has resulted in the closing of many of them and the dualization of others. Dualization cuts agency hours in half by assignment of one agent to two stations, requiring the agent to spend mornings in one station and afternoons in the next station on the line.[102] Table 15 shows the

TABLE 15

NUMBER OF FREIGHT STATIONS AND COSTS OF OPERATIONS, 1951 AND 1959

District or Region	Number of agency freight stations		Percentage change	Variable costs of operating freight stations— agency and nonagency[a]		Percentage change
	1951	1959	1951–1959	1951	1959	1941–1959
Eastern District	6,674	4,870	−27.0	$190,008,256	$169,115,342	−11.0
Pocahontas Region	832	625	−24.9	16,252,867	16,447,212	1.2
Southern Region	3,298	2,802	−15.0	66,804,969	60,685,071	−9.2
Western District	10,078	8,532	−15.3	191,582,991	199,223,542	4.0
U.S. TOTAL	20,882	16,829	−19.4	$464,649,083	$445,471,167	−4.1

SOURCES: U.S. Interstate Commerce Commission, Bureau of Accounts, *Summary of Returns to Cost Inquiry On Railroad Freight Station Costs And Other Performance Factors* (Statement No. 1-53, 1953), and *ibid.*, (Statement No. 1-60, 1960); U.S., Interstate Commerce Commission, Bureau of Transport Economics and Statistics, *Preliminary Abstract of Railway Statistics* (1951) and *Transport Statistics in the United States* (1959)ı
[a] Includes station maintenance, station employees, and station supplies and expenses in Interstate Commerce Commission uniform accounts 227, 373, and 376.

decline in the number of agency freight stations by districts. From 1951 to 1959, the total decline was 19.4 per cent. Cost data are available only for all freight stations, agency and nonagency. From 1951 to 1959, the decline in total costs was only 4.1 per cent. This includes a 17.6 per cent decline in total station maintenance costs, a 4.9 per cent decline in total wages, and an increase of 24.1 per cent in station supplies and other expenses.[103]

[101] *Telegraphers* v. *Chicago & N.W. R. Co.*, 362 U.S. 330, 343 (1960). See *Village of Cobb* v. *Public Ser. Com'n.*, 12 Wis. 2d 441, 107 N.W. 2d 595 (1961).
[102] See, e.g., *Atlantic Coast Line R. Co.* v. *King*, Fla., 135 So. 2d 201 (1961); *Application of Chicago B. & Q. R. Co.*, 172 Neb. 321, 109 N.W. 2d 369 (1961).
[103] Freight-station maintenance declined from $32,684,449 to $26,926,923; total freight station wages declined from $405,023,194 to $385,111,878; freight station supplies and expenses increased from $26,941,440 to $33,432,366.

Since the termination of an agency at a freight station is a local matter over which the Interstate Commerce Commission has not been delegated jurisdiction, regulation is left to state statutes and state commissions.[104] Public convenience and necessity as the standard of state commissions in station agency terminations is not the same as in train discontinuances. A railroad's duty to transport freight and passengers is absolute, but its duty to furnish agency stations is only incidental to this main purpose.[105] Station service in one town is not an issue of public need but merely one of local convenience.[106] In such a case, the expense or loss to the carrier is of much greater weight than in a case requiring public necessity. The factors to be considered by the state commission have been summarized as follows:

(1) The volume and nature of the business transacted at the station; (2) proximity and accessibility of other stations; (3) ratio of cost of maintaining the station agency (including both out-of-pocket and overall expense) to revenues received from the station; (4) the inconvenience to the public resulting from removal of the agent; and (5) the nature of the service remaining or to be substituted.[107]

The important test in these cases is whether the cost of maintaining the agency is out of proportion to the benefit to and the convenience of the public as a whole, because economic waste cannot be justified or excused by the showing that the service has been in the convenience and necessity of some individuals.[108] The overwhelming majority of appellate-court decisions concerning the closing of agency stations sustain a commission permit to terminate an agency or set aside a commission denial of a permit. *Village of Cobb* v. *Public Ser. Com'n.*[109] is the case of greatest economic significance, sustaining a commission permit for the Chicago and North Western to withdraw agency service from 104

---

[104] See *North Carolina Corporation Com'n* v. *Southern Ry. Co.*, 185 N.C. 435, 117 S.E. 563, 573 (1923), treating analogous case of commission order to railroad to erect a new station; *Pennsylvania R. Co.* v. *Department of Public Utilities*, 14 N.J. 411, 102 A. 2d 618, 625 (1954).

[105] *Commonwealth* v. *Illinois Central R. Co.*, Ky., 358 S.W. 2d 533, 536 (1962); *Arizona Corporation Com'n* v. *Southern Pacific Co.*, 87 Ariz. 310, 350 P. 2d 765, 768 (1960).

[106] *Application of Chicago, R.I. & P. R. Co.*, 169 Neb. 867, 101 N.W. 2d 448, 452 (1960).

[107] *Rydal-Meadowbrook C. Ass'n.* v. *Pennsylvania P.U.C.*, 173 Pa. Super. 380, 98 A. 2d 481, 485 (1953).

[108] *Illinois Cent. R. Co.* v. *Illinois Commerce Commission*, 397 Ill. 323, 74 N.E. 2d 545, 547 (1947).

[109] 12 Wis. 2d 441, 107 N.W. 2d 595 (1961).

of its 196 one-man stations in Wisconsin. Applicants' evidence showed that only 26 per cent of the prior working hours of agents were needed to do all the work of its one-man stations. The expected annual saving of $523,000 in wages alone was of crucial importance to a railroad operating at a net loss and without sufficient working capital for necessary maintenance of way and repair of equipment.

Given the great presumption accorded administrative findings of fact, the reversal of a commission denial of a permit to close an agency must hold that the commission's order was clearly erroneous and unsupported by evidence.[110] Yet large numbers of appeals have resulted in state commission denials being set aside. In some of these cases, the commissions have ignored the fact that carload freight can be continued to a town without an agent. In New Hampshire, for example, a commission denial of an agency closing was reversed where the railroad's annual savings would be $7,177 and carload freight of $11,000 could be billed as easily from the next station, leaving shippers of $460 LCL freight the only ones inconvenienced by the closing.[111] In other cases, commissions have failed to give weight to the ready availability of nearby stations.[112] In a number of others, commissions have been held to give insufficient weight to the out-of-pocket losses incurred in relation to the incidental nature of an agency station to transport service.[113]

The few recent cases where courts have sustained commission denials of permits to close agencies are subject to question. In a Virginia case, the commission and court included carload as well as LCL revenues in holding the five stations to be profitable, even though carload shipments could be handled as conveniently from the next retained agency station.[114] In a Minnesota case, the court affirmed commission denial of permission to close an agency in a

---

[110] See, e.g., *Texas & Pacific Ry. Co. v. Louisiana Public Serv. Com'n.*, 243 La. 322, 143 So. 2d 86, 88 (1962).

[111] *Boston & M. R. R. v. State*, 102 N.H. 9, 148 A. 2d 652, 653 (1959). See *Illinois Cent. R. Co. v. Illinois Commerce Com'n.*, 399 Ill. 67, 77 N.E. 2d 180 (1948).

[112] *Pennsylvania R. Co. v. Pennsylvania Publ. Serv. Com'n.*, 197 Pa. Super. 382, 178 A. 2d 856, 858 (1962).

[113] *Commonwealth v. Illinois Cent. R. Co.*, Ky., 358 S.W. 2d 533, 534 (1962); *Pennsylvania R. Co. v. Pennsylvania Pub. Ser. Com'n.*, 197 Pa. Super. 382, 178 A 2d 856, 858 (1962); *Illinois Central R. Co. v. Illinois Commerce Com'n.*, 397 Ill. 323, 74 N.E. 2d 545, 546 (1947); *Chicago R.I. & P. R. Co. v. Louisiana Pub. Ser. Com'n.*, 243 La. 680, 146 So. 2d 161 (1962); *Missouri Pacific R. Co. v. Louisiana Pub. Ser. Com'n.*, 244 La. 175, 151 So. 2d 362 (1963); *Atlantic Coast Line v. King*, Fla., 135 So. 2d 201 (1961).

[114] *Pennsylvania R. Co. v. Commonwealth*, 195 Va. 538, 79 S.E. 607 (1954).

town served by only two trains per week even though the next agency station was only one and one-half miles away.[115] In Arkansas, the carrier was required to continue a station agent in a town of 700 people at large out-of-pocket loss although the next agency station was only seven miles away.[116] Since the modified application of public convenience and necessity to agency closings puts much greater emphasis on carrier losses, it is hard to see how the courts could find evidence to support the commission rulings that the losses in these cases were outweighed by the benefits and convenience to the public as a whole.

The *New York Central* case[117] was the one federal court decision dealing with the attempt of carriers to terminate losing LCL freight service. The railroad issued an embargo, announcing it would no longer accept interstate LCL shipments of less than trap- or ferry-car quantity except from twelve listed cities. The Interstate Commerce Commission issued an order annulling the embargo, and the carrier petitioned the court to set aside the ICC order. The court upheld the Commission's power to annul the embargo under its authority to issue orders enforcing carriers' statutory duty to furnish reasonable transportation upon request therefor. The embargo was lifted and the judgment vacated when the ICC granted the New York Central permission to transport LCL freight to and from smaller towns and cities on the highways via its motor subsidiary.

CONCLUSIONS

The public-convenience-and-necessity criterion for railroad-service discontinuances under state law and the additional standard of undue burden on interstate commerce under federal law are vague and unmeasurable. They enable regulatory commissions which are under heavy political pressure of local interests to confuse the private interests of a few passengers or station patrons with the public interest in adequate and efficient transportation.[118] It is the thesis of this chapter that it would be to the long-run advantage of all parties that the test of public convenience

[115] *State* v. *Chicago & North Western Ry. Co.*, 246 Minn. 403, 75 N.W. 2d 411 (1956).

[116] *Louisiana & A. Ry. Co.* v. *Arkansas Commerce Com'n.*, 235 Ark. 506, 360 S.W. 2d 763 (1962).

[117] *New York Central R. Co.* v. *United States*, 201 F. Supp. 958 (S.D.N.Y. 1962), *vacated with direction to dismiss* 83 S. Ct. 19 (1962).

[118] See U.S. Cong., Senate, Committee on Interstate and Foreign Commerce, *National Transportation Policy* (Doyle Report) 324 (87th Cong. 1st Sess. 1961).

and necessity be discarded. For losing services that consume the revenues of carriers is likely to mean higher rates for all shippers and ultimately higher prices for all goods shipped. If the Commission should deny rate increases, losing services will be borne by the railroad stockholders through lower profits or overall losses. An alternative criterion should give carriers an absolute right either to raise rates or to discontinue services which they prove to the commission are showing direct operating losses. A less extreme statute would at least shift to those who protest discontinuance of a service which has direct operating losses the burden of proving a clear public necessity for continuance. The present statutes, both state and federal, cause carriers seeking discontinuance of passenger, LCL freight, or station services to bear a burden which is poorly apportioned relative to the affected economic interests. Roads showing over-all net losses may, of course, urge in addition to the arguments made above, their constitutional right to compensation for the assets used to sustain the services. In such a case, a showing that the losses sustained by the services are of such magnitude that the financial stability of the road is seriously threatened, or that the road, if losses continue, may or will not be able to recover to a status of net profit operation, should require a mandatory order of discontinuance. If discontinuance is denied, the order should be subject to appeal and be reversed on the ground that the denial under such circumstances is unconstitutional in that just compensation is being denied the road for property taken for "public" use.

VIII

Administrative Regulation of Resource Allocation

The standard of public interest in railroad mergers and the standard of public convenience and necessity in abandonments and service discontinuances have been shown to be ambiguous and amorphous. In spite of the ruling of the Supreme Court upholding the public interest concept in *New York Central Securities Corp.* v. *United States*,[1] the vagueness of the public-interest standard[2] in merger and trackage cases is clear. The worst example was the protection of other lines from traffic diversion to the detriment of better through service for shippers, the intended and effective result of the merger denial in the *Chicago, B. & Q. R. Co.* decision.[3] The weight given alleged interrailroad competition in merger cases when such competition is at most minimal further indicates the confusion of the Commission. In the abandonment and service-discontinuance cases, one finds the same lack of measurable or even estimable standards. Denials of permits effectively order losing services continued for small minorities while increased rates for other lines and services pay for this subsidy.

The members of the Interstate Commerce Commission and of the state commissions generally fail to remember or to recognize that the public as consumers ultimately pay shipping costs. The Commissions' duty to police the minimization of costs as part of maximum-rate regulation is slighted or even overlooked. Mergers and abandonments with clear expectations of cost savings should

---

[1] 287 U.S. 12, 24–25 (1932). For arguments on vagueness of the public-interest concept, see U.S., I.C.C., *Railroad Consolidations and the Public Interest—A Preliminary Examination* 51–54 (1962).

[2] See generally, Miller, "Public Interest Undefined," 10 *J. Pub. L.* 184 (1961).

[3] *Chicago, B. & Q. R. Co., Control,* 271 I.C.C. 63 (1948).

be viewed first as a basis for the lowering of rates or as an offset to rising labor costs which may at least defer rate increases. This interest of the general public in lowest rates consistent with adequate service surely takes precedence over the private interest of a few shippers in a marger case who would find themselves in one-railroad towns instead of two-railroad towns. Yet no administrative decision is more unpredictable than a railroad merger or abandonment petition.

The inconsistencies in merger regulation between the general public interest and the specific supplementary criteria of the Transportation Act of 1940 create further difficulties. Allowing intervention of the railroads and of labor unions to assert their private interests against the public interest cannot help but confuse the issues. No clear priorities of interests are stated in the statute. As a result, the Commission has no guidelines for weighing the opposing contentions in a merger case. Failure to include an intervening railroad as a coöwner in a control proposal, for example, may make for continued, costly excess capacity in a region of light traffic.[4] But allowing the protests of intervening carriers to block an entire merger may prevent the public from realizing new savings in transport service.[5]

The clear need is for new definitive standards in merger and abandonment cases to replace the vague public-interest criterion.[6] The statute that is required would have rules which would limit some of the almost unlimited discretion now exercised by the ICC in merger and abandonment cases under the public-interest concept. A number of possible changes in regulation have been noted in the previous chapters. A more general approach to regulatory solutions will be explored here. New controls will be surveyed under the following categories: partial deregulation; voluntary mergers under general and detailed economic rules; voluntary mergers pursuant to an overall national plan; and compulsory mergers and nationalization.

PARTIAL DEREGULATION

Partial deregulation is a solution to ineffective or inefficient government control whenever economic conditions change so that

---

[4] *Spokane Int'l R. Co., Control,* 295 I.C.C. 425 (1956), *aff'd sub. nom. Canadian Pac. Ry.* v. *United States* 158 F. Supp. 248 (D. Minn. 1958).

[5] See *Chicago, B. & Q. R. Co., Control,* note 3 *supra.*

[6] See Tucker and O'Brien, "The Public Interest in Railroad Mergers," 42 *Boston U. L. Rev.* 160, 183–186 (1962).

new competitive economic forces appear that will automatically control business practices. Thus President Kennedy's transportation message suggested an end to much of minimum-rate regulation on this basis.[7] As to mergers, the argument for partial deregulation has little force. New competitive forces in the transportation industry as a whole, although increasing the financial pressures on the railroads, will not have the effect of directing mergers toward the most efficient combinations of railroads. Likewise, as was shown in Chapter II, the lack of effective competition between railroads has been a factor promoting excess capacity and misallocation of resources in the railroad industry. Rational railroad executives are likely to plan mergers with carriers that will maximize their combined profits. But this will not necessarily coincide with the efficiency criterion of maximizing the combined resultant savings. Railroads with the largest number of parallel lines and common terminals may be unable to reach agreement on the financial terms for merger, or executives of the roads may block negotiations in order to protect their own positions of authority. The parallel Chicago and North Western and Milwaukee roads, for example, have had numerous unsuccessful merger negotiations in spite of the very large savings that the merger studies indicate would result from their combination.[8]

Strong railroads may be especially reluctant to merge with parallel lines that are financially weak because the owners of the weak railroads will usually refuse to lower the price of their shares or assets sufficiently to reflect the fact that major portions of the line are losing investments. Strong railroads are more likely to find it financially advantageous to merge with other strong railroads, regardless of whether real economies of operation exist. Thus a carrier may find it most profitable to merge with a connecting line in order to establish longer through routes and divert traffic from other through carriers. Although an end-to-end merger may be the most profitable for the carriers, it may actually impede the merger of those railroads with parallel lines and thereby block combinations which would foster the social function of reducing excess capacity. The Norfolk & Western-Nickel Plate merger would seem to be of this character.[9]

[7] U.S. Cong., House, *The Transportation System of Our Nation*, House Doc. No. 384 (87th Cong. 2d Sess. 1962).

[8] See *Wall Street Journal*, Feb. 24, 1961, at 2; and *Chicago & North Western Railway Co. Reorganization*, 230 I.C.C. 548 (1939).

[9] See Conant, "Two, Not Three, Eastern Rail Systems Make Economic Sense," 3 *Transportation Journal* 35 (1963).

In contrast to mergers, a strong argument can be made for partial deregulation of abandonments and service discontinuances. Rational railroad executives would not abandon a profitable service or a losing one which is likely to become profitable within the foreseeable future. They will be motivated to abandon clearly losing lines and services in an effort to minimize over-all costs. Such cost reductions, under effective regulation, should be reflected in lower rates for remaining lines and services, a direct benefit to the general public. A free-abandonments statute would have to be limited by allowing the Commission to protect vested interests. It would be empowered to condition any abandonment on the carrier building new connections to its line or to another near-by line for those shippers who can show they cannot survive without rail service. An alternative condition would require payments to shippers for the cost of moving plants or compensation for those deciding to quit business entirely.

It should be emphasized that under partial deregulation with conditions to protect affected parties, the burden of proof on whether particular conditions should attach is crucial. Deregulation is based on the premise that private decisions to abandon lines or discontinue services will foster the economic allocations of resources and thus minimize long-run shipping costs. Conditions to protect private interests affected by abandonment or service discontinuance limit the full reallocation of resources and increase long-run carriage costs. The conditions are rightly justified by the fact that business firms made investments in fixed plant in reliance on the existence of the railroad and its continuance of some specific level of service. Since the conditions are designed to protect private interests from the impact of resource reallocation designed to benefit the general public, a strong argument can be made that the intervenors who request such conditions should have the burden of proving to the Commission that they are necessary.

Voluntary Mergers with New Economic Standards

If railroad mergers and abandonments are to continue under general regulation, new definitive economic criteria are needed for satisfactory regulation. The long-run criteria of classical economics are not sufficient for commissioners who must face the day-to-day regulatory decisions. As was noted in Chapter IV, the basic economic criterion for mergers is that the proposed combination will result in greater over-all savings than any other possible combination made by either of the two railroads. More detailed standards would relate to the elements of potential savings from any proposed merger.[10] These elements can be summarized as follows:[11]

Savings primarily from parallel mergers: Consolidation of terminals; Consolidation of parallel lines; Elimination of duplicate lines; Elimination of duplicate trains; Use of shorter or more economical routes; Economical handling of less-carload freight; Lower property taxes.

Savings from parallel or end-to-end mergers: Consolidation of office-managerial and accounting; Reduced interchange of cars; Carriage of freight over longer hauls; Pooling of equipment; Consolidation of heavy repairs; Reduce materials and supplies inventories.

Rules for merger control based on these two categories of savings could be both internal and comparative. The internal rule would be based on the absolute amount and percentage of savings for each item of operating expenses. If a savings estimate is found reasonable, a rule could make operating-cost savings of over 10 per cent presumptive ground to approve a merger. In this case, protesting intervenors would have the burden of overcoming this presumption by proving why approval should be denied. In the alternative, even more detailed cost-saving rules might be adopted based on particular key items such as terminals, duplicate lines, interchanges, and car accounting.

Comparative cost-saving criteria for mergers would also have to be based on the individual items of saving. Under such a system, the Commission would have to collect cost data from all existing railroads and from these data create a set of standards for optimum lines and terminals for different traffic densities. If the estimated cost savings of a proposed merger were to cause individual functions of the combined line to approximate more closely the optimum than were the separate lines, the merger would be approved. Rules of this type would encourage merger of parallel lines to a size that it would pay to invest in electronic controlled yards and lines with the most advanced systems of centralized traffic control. Savings estimates would be increased by showing the net effects of such investments after deducting the interest costs.

[10] See U.S. Cong., Senate, Committee on Interstate and Foreign Commerce, *National Transportation Policy* (Doyle Report) 244–246 (87 Cong. 1st Sess. 1961).

[11] Compare U.S. Congress, Senate, Committee on the Judiciary, Report on *The Railroad Merger Problem* 24 (88th Cong. 1st Sess. 1963).

Simple merger rules relating to cost savings presume that merged railroads will offer the same service as the previous individual roads offered. In this case all advantages gained from merger can be measured in dollars. In fact, a merged road may be able to offer better service than either of its component roads did. Combining the lowest grades and shortest routes of two parallel lines will likely make for faster service. Although this does not appear in the merger estimates as a cost saving, it may increase revenues by making the combined railroad better able to meet highway competition. Estimating possible revenue effects of faster service is more difficult than making estimates of cost savings. Nevertheless, some method of accounting for this benefit must enter the decision calculations on a railroad merger.

VOLUNTARY MERGERS PURSUANT TO NATIONAL PLAN

Although national planning of mergers under the Transportation Act of 1920 was clearly a failure, there are still some proponents of national planning.[12] The existing system of regulation creates the possibility that the Commission will approve merger of railroads where cost savings are minimal or even questionable, to the detriment of more economic mergers. The pending merger of the unconnected Norfolk & Western and the Nickel Plate are a possible example of this. The danger of national or regional consolidation plans, as were drawn up under the 1920 statute, is that protection of weak carriers or preservation of interrailroad competition will become criteria of the plan. Weak carriers, with substantial segments operating at net losses, will usually be unwilling to join a merger at prices for their lines that reflect their true low market values. If major lines' mergers are dependent on reaching agreement with such weak carriers, mergers are effectively blocked. Likewise, the preservation of minimal or nonexistent interrailroad competition as a basis of national merger plans will bar those mergers which would result in the greatest cost savings.

If protection of weak carriers and preservation of interrailroad competition are clearly rejected as standards, national planning of railroad mergers can have general economic benefit. The economic staff of the Commission can draw on the statistical data of the carriers to assemble consolidation plans which would result in the greatest possible economies. The ultimate least-cost combinations which are indicated in the plan would act as a directive

---

[12] See Barriger, "Why Consolidation?" in Ruppenthal, ed., *Challenge to Transportation* 66, 75–83 (1961).

to the carriers. Mergers negotiated according to the plan have the presumption in favor of Commission approval. If the requirements of sound financing are met, such mergers should be approved with much shorter administrative proceedings and much less expense to the carriers. Protesting carriers would have a much greater burden in upsetting mergers following the plan. They would thus be more likely to lower their asking prices to amounts which realistically reflect their value to a regional railroad system when they bargain to join a major merger.

National or regional planning of mergers is advantageous also in that it is not bound by the existing railroad structures. A plan can be based on best estimates of cost savings regardless of ownership of component lines. If one main segment of a railroad does not fit economically into the merger that the other segments should join, the plan can propose sale of the first segment as a condition to merger. The Pere Marquette branch of the Chesapeake and Ohio, for example, may be most economically operated as a division of the parallel New York Central; the main Pocahontas divisions of the Chesapeake and Ohio may be most economically merged with the Norfolk & Western. A plan requiring such divorcement of railroad segments as a condition of merger may seem to create barriers to merger. Since it is based on greatest cost savings, however, the gains to each carrier in the mergers should clearly offset possible losses.

National planning of abandonments could easily accompany merger planning. Any plan proposing the merger of parallel lines or lines with net-loss branches could, on the basis of data submitted by the carriers to the planning officials, indicate lines probably to be abandoned. If a merger application is then filed by the railroads, it could contain a supplementary petition to abandon those lines which the national plan had indicated as probably dispensable in that region. The abandonment petition would still have to demonstrate existing losses on the affected sections or estimated losses when traffic is to be diverted to another line of the same railroad. The abandonment planning, like merger planning, would serve the function of creating a presumption in favor of those specific abandonments which protestants would have to overcome in order to defeat the petition.

COMPULSORY MERGERS OR NATIONALIZATION

There is little sentiment in the United States either for compulsory railroad mergers or nationalization of railroads. Both approaches to government control would necessitate extended con-demnation proceedings. Railroads refusing to merge would raise, in defense of an action under a compulsory merger statute, that the exchange price of shares deprived them of property without just compensation. As for nationalization, few owners would volun-tarily sell shares to the government if they thought more could be realized by forcing the government to condemn the shares. But, this procedural barrier is not as important as other objections. Compulsory mergers would put a governmental agency in the position of forcing creation of new business firms. Executives in an organizational structure not of their own creation and which they oppose are not likely to function effectively. Thus the likeli-hood of operational breakdown is great. In nationalization, the cost to the nation of buying the railroads is a first objection. Even more important is the general public sentiment against "distress socialism," the belief that nationalization of failing or near-failing businesses will result in management that is even less efficient than present management. Some of the nationalized railroads in West-ern European countries, operated at losses because political pres-sures prevent the abandonment of net-loss lines and services or the discharge of redundant labor, indicate the kind of continuous cost to the taxpayers that a general railroad deficit could mean.[13]

A strong argument can be made that any social control of re-source allocation which is to be effected by compulsion can more easily be accomplished by reward. Instead of compulsory mergers following a national plan, rewards in terms of special tax relief are likely to accomplish the same result at even lower costs. Ad-ministration of awards of tax relief by a regulatory commission is clearly less costly than legal action to force combinations which are resisted as a violation of the eminent-domain protection. Sim-ilar arguments can be made about nationalization. Attempts to better railroad administration in the United States by nationaliza-tion are likely to be frustrated by political interference. In the alternative, special rewards to private firms for most efficient operations and subsidies for carrying on public functions which are not profit-making are likely to accomplish public objectives most economically. Special tax relief to railroads which innovate the most modern techniques to shorten freight delivery time is one example.

[13] See Gt. Britain. British Railways Board, *The Reshaping of British Railways* 4–18 (1963). Note the critical comment of Munby, "The Reshaping of British Rail-ways," 11 *Journal of Industrial Economics* 161 (1963).

ICC PROCEDURES

Procedures in United States regulatory agencies, including the Interstate Commerce Commission, have been under severe criticism for excessive delay and high costs.[14] The Landis Report criticises the Interstate Commerce Commission for its lack of positive direction, decentralization of responsibility, unwieldy size, poor opinion-writing, and its generally poor organizational structure.[15] The attack on the hearing examiners and their position in the regulatory process has been especially strong. The discussion here, though confined to mergers, abandonments, and service discontinuances, will suggest changes in procedure that may be applicable to many other regulatory functions of the Commission.

As a background to suggested changes in the procedural sections of the Interstate Commerce Act, it is essential to note that power to approve mergers and abandonments is an executive or purely administrative function of the Commission. This is significant because none of the constitutional constraints on procedure applicable to legislative functions or to judicial functions apply. Approval power over individual mergers and abandonments is executive because it requires carrying laws into effect, applying statutory rules to specific fact situations, and securing their observance.[16] It is not legislative because it does not create or abolish general classes of rights and duties for prospective application.[17] It is not judicial because it does not enforceably determine a controversy over alleged existing legal rights nor does it award a remedy for wrongful deprivation of legal rights.[18] Any common-law rights of railroads to merge or to abandon lines or services were extinguished by the Transportation Act of 1920.[19] Therefore,

---

[14] For a survey of the critical literature, see Woll, "Administrative Law Reform: Proposals and Prospects," 41 *Neb. L. Rev.* 687 (1962).

[15] U.S. Cong., Senate, Committee on the Judiciary, *Report on Regulatory Agencies to the President Elect* 37–41 (87th Cong. 2d Sess. 1960), cited hereinafter as *Landis Report*. See McFarland, "Landis' Report, The Voice of One Crying in the Wilderness," 47 *Va. L. Rev.* 373 (1961).

[16] Executive functions include all actions necessary to carry laws into effect other than clearly judicial functions. See *Mitchell Coal Co.* v. *Pennsylvania R.R.* 230 U.S. 247, 273 (1913).

[17] For definitions of the legislative function, see *Dash* v. *Van Kleeck,* 7 Johns. (N. Y. Ch.) 477, 502 (1811); *San Diego Land & Town Co.* v. *Jasper,* 189 U.S. 439, 440 (1903); *Prentis* v. *Atlantic Coast Line,* 211 U.S. 210, 226 (1908).

[18] For definitions of the judicial function, see *Rhode Island* v. *Massachusetts,* 12 Pet. 657, 718 (1838); *Prentis* v. *Atlantic Coast Line,* 211 U.S. 210, 221 (1908); *Muskrat* v. *United States,* 219 U.S. 346, 356 (1911).

[19] Chap. 91, 41 Stat. 456.

a carrier's application to the Commission for permission to merge or to abandon lines is a request for a public benefit. Dispensing public benefits is an executive function, administered in the individual case pursuant to statute by executive officers. Within the limits set by the statute the executive officer may use his administrative discretion, constrained only by the constitutional duty not to act arbitrarily or discriminatorily.

Since regulation of mergers and abandonments is an executive function, the constitutional requirements of judicial proceedings do not apply. Yet, by statute the procedures under the Interstate Commerce Act have been highly judicialized.[20] This has probably been the principal cause of excessive delay. The requirement of oral hearing and cross-examination with a relaxed hearsay-evidence rule interposes a long and unnecessary step in order to present economic data to the Commission. The recent management study of the Interstate Commerce Commission recommends the termination of judicial-type procedure in nonjudicial cases by amendment of section 17 of the Interstate Commerce Act.[21] The study concludes:

The ICC act itself should be amended to indicate that it is not the intent of Congress *to require* a court-like hearing or decision on the record for any rule making or adjudication required of the ICC. Such amendment should make clear that, in fact, it is the intent of Congress to encourage less formal methods whenever, in the opinion of the Commission, a full and fair judgment can be attained by such methods. This modification is needed to avoid the forced applications of the Administrative Procedure Act "exception" procedures to the full range of ICC cases as a result of such Supreme Court decisions as the *Wong Yang Sung* immigration case, the *Riss ICC* case, and the *Reliance Steel ICC* case. Such modification, of course, should not prevent use of more formal processes where the Commission believes them desirable.[22]

Facts, evidence, or argument in support of or in opposition to a specific action in carrying out an executive function of an administrative agency can most easily be filed with and reviewed by the Commission in written form. Replacement of oral presentation by written filings would have many advantages to petitioners, to intervenors, and to the Commission. Legal expenses of petitioners

[20] Interstate Commerce Act, Section 17, 49 U.S.C. 17.
[21] Booz, Allen & Hamilton, *Organization and Procedures Survey of the Interstate Commerce Commission,* Chap. IX (1960). See Hutchinson, "I.C.C. Organization and Procedure," 31 *Geo. Wash. L. Rev.* 29 (1962).
[22] Booz, *op. cit.,* IX, 63.

and intervenors would be reduced greatly. Time within which to file opposing written evidence and argument could be granted to intervenors after petitioner's evidence is thoroughly studied by them without delaying a formal proceeding. The Commission could eliminate all problems relating to delegation of function to hearing examiners by dispensing with them altogether. Instead, the law clerks and economic analysts assigned to assist each member of the Commission would perform the function of sifting through the written materials filed in each case and preparing summaries for the commissioners' review. In this way, the initial decision function would remain in the commissioners, not in examiners.

Cases could be expedited by requiring written filings in support of or in opposition to a merger or abandonment petition to follow a form designated in the Commission's rules. A primary rule could require all filings to be divided in three main parts: verified statements of fact; unverified opinions on the significance of the facts and predictions of future economic events; and legal argument. More detailed rules for each type of petition could designate the form to present the basic facts, with open permission to add at the end any other classes of facts not designated by the Commission rules. These procedural rules would follow in form the revised regulatory statutes which designated the economic criteria for mergers and abandonments. For petitions to abandon a railroad line, for example, the Commission rules could designate the form in which the net loss condition of the line must be presented. Such form could require historical tables showing the number of carloads of each type of goods and revenues to and from each town on a line. Other rules could require statements of alternative transport available to each carload shipper on the line.

The great advantage to the Commission of requiring economic evidence in written form pursuant to detailed Commission rules is that the minor part of the total filings which is material to decision can be easily isolated for decision purposes. Large parts of the opinion evidence and legal argument filed in administrative proceedings are trivial and immaterial to the basic economic regulation. Opinion evidence, especially by intervenors to merger and abandonment petitions, is typically characterized by unsupported generalities. Legal argument based on past administrative decisions usually fails to recognize that even slight differences in fact make each case of economic regulation unique.

Not only will such segmented, detailed methods of filing written evidence expedite Commission procedures, but they will assist courts on appeal. If a petitioner or intervenor should charge violation of due process in Commission procedures, a reviewing court can easily review the economic facts upon which Commission findings were based. A charge of arbitrary or discriminatory action by the Commission would have to be substantiated by plaintiff by reference to the verified economic facts in the record before the Commission. The rigor of proof in terms of organized economic data would thus facilitate review decisions and discourage frivolous appeals.

The elimination of oral hearings and hearing examiners and the substitution of written filings in support of merger and abandonment petitions would allow the Commission to terminate the two-stage decision process. No longer would there be need for a hearing examiner's report and recommendations. This alone would be a great time saver. More important, it would eliminate the complex question of what weight the Commission should give to the decisions of hearing examiners. The present unnecessary judicialization of the administrative process can make the witnesses appear more significant than the data they present, and raises the issue of what presumption should be given to the findings of the presiding officer who observed the witnesses. This issue exists even though the responsibility for determining the question of public convenience and necessity is that of the Commission, and it is not bound by the recommended finding of a hearing examiner.[23]

The ideal system would be a one-stage review and decision process for cases of major significance. Copies of the evidence filed by the parties and intervenors in each case would be transmitted directly to the commissioners in each case. Each commissioner would review the evidence with the assistance of his law clerk and economic assistant and arrive at his decision. Then, after a conference on the case and vote by the commissioners, the chairman would assign one commissioner to write the opinion for the majority. This recommendation is consonant with the revised Commission rule of procedure of March 1, 1961, which placed the opinion-writing responsibility in the hands of individual commissioners in the more important cases.[24] It would eliminate the need for the

---

[23] *Burlington Truck Lines, Inc.* v. *I.C.C.*, 194 F. Supp. 31, 50 (S.D. Ill. 1961), *reversed on other grounds* 371 U.S. 156 (1962); *W. J. Dillner Transfer Co.* v. *I.C.C.*, 193 F. Supp. 823, 828 (W.D. Pa. 1961), *aff'd* 368 U.S. 6 (1961).

[24] U.S. Interstate Commerce Commission, *75th Annual Report* 5 (1961).

present, much criticized opinion-writing staffs and would surely raise the quality of ICC opinions.[25] Even though his law clerk did a large part of the drafting of any opinion, the commissioner would still bear complete responsibility for its content.

It may seem paradoxical to dispense entirely with the judicial-type hearing in administrative regulation of resource allocation and still require a written opinion by a commissioner similar to a judge's opinion. Yet the reasons for both are clear. The oral hearing and cross-examination are a distinct waste of time when existing legal rights are not in contest. The application for permission to engage in a specific economic action is based on economic facts which can most easily be filed in written form. In contrast, procedural protections for the parties require the form of decision of the Commission to have some close analogies to the form of a court decision. Both a court decision and an executive order must conform to due process of law; that is, they must not be arbitrary or discriminatory. An opinion must be written to demonstrate to a court on review that the decision was based on reason and not on caprice. In the administrative case, the reasoning from the economic facts in the record to a regulatory decision can be known only if a written opinion demonstrates that reasoning.

In order to expedite the great volume of cases in the Commission, one copy of the petition and written data filed in each case could be forwarded to an economic-analysis section. This group would make digests and summaries of the economic data and do further economic analyses of the data. Copies of these summaries and analyses would then be forwarded to each commissioner to assist him in his decision of the case. These economic analyses would not be accompanied by a recommendation for decision and thus would not take on the status of the present hearing examiners' reports. Consequently, they would not have to be released to the parties or the public. The procedure would be designed only to assist the commissioners in analysis of materials and not to create an intermediate decision group. Hence it would conform to the policy of having a one-stage decision process in the commissioners themselves.

Another method of expediting Commission procedures would be initial assignment of all cases either to the entire Commission for cases of major significance or to panels of three members for

[25] See *Landis Report* 39; Westwood, "The Davis Treatise: Meaning to the Practitioner," 43 *Minn. L. Rev.* 607, 614–617 (1959).

cases of minor significance, together with a policy eliminating all appeals or review within the Commission. The Commission would have to adopt rules of case classification. For merger and abandonment cases, these rules could be according to value of railroad assets or miles of line affected. A supplementary rule would allow any panel of three members, upon its preliminary review of a case in the minor class, to recommend its transfer to the whole Commission because of the importance of the issues. The transfer would be made forthwith, without preliminary decision on the merits by the panel of three. These initial decisions on the major or minor importance of cases would eliminate any need for review procedures within the Commission. The importance of each case would be determined when it was filed, and hence a single decision on the issues would be sufficient to final determination.

This suggested procedure is different from the present petition for a finding in that a proceeding concerns an issue of general transportation importance. These petitions may be filed only after a decision by a division of the Commission has become final. Under the present statutes a division may make a final decision on a petition for rehearing.[26] It is probable that a statutory revision would be necessary to make the decision of a panel of three members final on the issue of whether an application contained a matter of general transportation importance requiring summary transfer to the entire Commission.

Concluding Comments

As to railroad mergers and abandonments, administrative regulation of resource allocation has been a failure. Restrictive and vague regulatory statutes have been the primary cause. Secondly, commissioners untrained in economics have until recently shown little understanding of the transportation industry's development. The result has been static regulation in a dynamic economy. Technological change in terms of heavier rails, larger cars, more efficient locomotives, centralized traffic control, and electronic yards have made the optimum sizes of railroads in many market areas much larger than they were forty years ago. Technological change in motor transport has made less-than-carload railroad freight a relatively more expensive form of carriage and caused many branch lines to operate at net losses. In spite of these technological

[26] *Malone Freight Lines, Inc.* v. *United States*, 204 F. Supp. 745 (N.D. Ala. 1962). See Hutchinson, *op. cit.*, note 21, at 34–36.

innovations, the Commission approach to mergers and abandonments has retained its 1940 character. The questions of excess
capacity in railroad lines and yards and of who pays to maintain
this excess capacity, crucial issues of resource allocation, are consistently ignored by the Commission. Instead of fostering mergers
of parallel lines and disinvestment in redundant and unprofitable
plant, the Commission approach until recently has been centered
on how to maintain the status quo in railroad investment. Diversion of traffic to the most efficient routes has been disdained because some inefficient railroad lines in the same markets may become bankrupt. The fact that some of these unprofitable lines
should never have been built and that the rest are technologically
redundant has been overlooked. And, as a corollary to this policy,
the Commission has permitted one general rate increase after
another so that the consuming public would pay the rising costs of
inefficient railroad organization.

Dynamic technology and aggressive intermodal rivalry in transportation can be expected to continue.[27] If railroads are to survive
and continue to perform their valuable economic function as the
low-cost, long-distance carriers, regional mergers on a much larger
scale must take place. As noted in Chapter I, the fast freight train
of the next decade, moving at 100-120 miles per hour, will necessitate large investment in the shortest, most level, and straight
lines with no road-level crossings. In order to pay for such super-
lines and the equipment on them, the highest possible density of
traffic will be required. As a result of this traffic diversion, excess
capacity and losses on investment in secondary main lines will
increase. Abandonment of many of these lines will be a necessary
condition to concentrate investment and maintenance on the
fewer superlines. Mergers and abandonments are thus interrelated
policies in the adjustment of railroads to dynamic technology in
a competitive transport market.

Regulation of investment and disinvestment in railroad plant
must be as dynamic as railroad technology and intermodal transport rivalry. Dynamic regulation must be based on definitive economic standards. When underlying economic conditions change,
regulatory rules should automatically work to encourage any
needed compensatory changes in railroad fixed plant. These rules

[27] See Barriger, *Super-Railroads for a Dynamic American Economy* (1956); Magee,
"U.S. Railroaders Inspect Japanese 'Super-Railroad,'" 59 *Railway Track and Structures* 23 (June, 1963).

would require disinvestment in any plant showing net losses and expected to continue unprofitable in the future. If most people want such plant to continue in operation in spite of losses, they must be prepared to pay such losses from the public treasury. Efficient allocation of resources will not permit higher rates for service on profitable lines in order to subsidize the continued operation of net-loss lines.

APPENDIX to Chapter VIII

Comment on Report of the Interagency Committee on Transport Mergers

On March 6, 1963, the White House released the Report of the Interagency Committee on Transport Mergers, containing a statement of the general criteria applicable to mergers in the railroad and airline industries.[28] These criteria are purported to have general applicability to mergers in other modes of transport, although the committee recognized that the particular character of one or more of these modes may call for some modification. The criteria purportedly are based on those objectives already included in existing law and therefore are not proposals to amend the present regulatory statutes. The merger criteria are stated in the form of questions, and are as follows:

1. Will the proposed merger restrict effective competition in the provision of transportation services in the areas affected?

2. Will the proposed merger permit an economically more efficient use of resources, through fuller utilization over a period of time of plant and equipment and/or reduction in direct costs per unit of output, which will reduce costs while maintaining or improving the general quality of service offered to users?

3. Can the economies sought by the proposed merger be achieved by alternatives more easily revocable which promise to be of comparable effect in accomplishing the improvement in over-all efficiency?

4. Will the cost and quality benefits resulting from the merger be reflected in the benefits to the public? To what extent will potential passengers or shippers retain a choice of services from this or other modes of transportation?

5. Will the proposed merger, with the increased market power

---

[28] U.S. Office of the President, *Criteria to Implement the Merger Provisions of the President's Transportation Message* (March 6, 1963).

of the merged carrier, have substantial undesirable repercussions on other carriers in the industry?

6. Will the proposed merger serve the long-run interests of the public and of the carriers concerned or is it merely an attempt to meet a short-run crisis arising because of unfavorable economic conditions in general, or a particular transitory problem?

7. Is the merger proposed, in part, because of the imminent failure of one or more of the merging carriers and is it the most appropriate solution to this difficulty?

8. Are the legitimate interests of existing creditors and equity holders of the merging carriers adequately protected?

9. Does the merger provide adequate protection and assistance to affected employees, and take into account community employment effects?

10. Will the proposed merger serve other objectives of public policy?

The first critical issue raised by the published criteria is whether they should have been written to lump regulatory policy for railroads and airlines. The structures of the railroad and airline industries are radically different. The fixed roadbeds and yards of railroads result in proportionately high fixed costs, put severe limitations on the entry of new firms, and make effective interrailroad competition impossible. Airline-industry structure has lower fixed costs, rented terminal space, and much greater likelihood of effective competition.[29] Thus criterion 1—the amount of restriction on competition—is sure to have completely different application to the two industries. And the regulatory statutes reflect this; there is no mention of interrailroad competition in section 5 (2) of the Interstate Commerce Act, but both sections 102 and 408 (b) of the Federal Aviation Act maintain competition as a standard.

The objectives of efficiency in criteria 2 and 3 are of course the key to the long-run public interest in railroad mergers. The Interstate Commerce Act unfortunately does not mention the efficiency standard. The emphasis on cost and quality benefits to the public in criterion 4, is a needed change in regulatory outlook from the present particularist approach to the public-interest concept. The retention of choice of services, however, may be inconsistent with efficiency in the railroad industry. Likewise, concern with in-

[29] On the possibility of enforcing greater competition in the airline industry, see Caves, *Air Transport and its Regulators* 428–449 (1962).

creased market power in detriment to rival carriers in criterion 5 seems misdirected in regulated industries. Structural conditions precluding competition are the rationale for regulation; increased market power should be curtailed and channeled to the public benefit by the regulation. Criteria 3, 4, and 5 all seem cast under the assumption that the present amount of investment in transport industries is optimum. In railroad lines and yards, this is not true. The committee ignored the integral interdependence of merger and abandonment policies as they apply to railroads.

Criteria 6 and 7 are important as guides to regulatory pitfalls. Criterion 7 is stated in too limited terms. Financial distress can never be a sound economic standard for approving mergers, even though it is presently established by the Interstate Commerce Commission as one element of the public interest in approving railroad mergers.

Parts of criteria 8 and 9 are presently standards of section 5 (2) of the Interstate Commerce Act. Protection of creditors as primary claimants on the assets of firms is based on sound financial principles. Protection of equity holders is possible only at the expense of creditors or the public and is not a standard in the statutes presently regulating rail and airline mergers. Assistance to employees is presently part of our merger statutes; it should not give them power to intervene and oppose the mergers entirely.

Criterion 10 is noted in the report to include, *inter alia,* the maintenance of a common-carrier system; protection of the national-security interest; and protection of the public health and safety. This raises the prime deficiency in the entire process of listing of merger criteria: no method is suggested to assign weights to the individual criteria. To the extent that the criteria are contradictory, they will have to be weighted in the individual case. Perhaps the key example is the conflict between the efficiency criterion 2 as opposed to the retention of choice of services in criterion 4 and protection of investors in criterion 8. If mergers of railroads are approved by the Interstate Commerce Commission in an effort to create most efficient service, nearby carriers with less efficient routes may be forced into bankruptcy. Can the Commission recognize the primary importance of efficiency to shippers and consumers and the fact that bankruptcy of some uneconomic lines may be the only route to needed disinvestment? Neither the statutes nor the Interagency Committee offer a solution to this problem.

Bibliography

Bibliography

BOOKS

GENERAL

Adams, Walter, and Horace M. Gray. *Monopoly in America.* New York: Macmillan Co., 1955.

Bain, Joe S. *Barriers to New Competition.* Cambridge: Harvard University Press, 1956.

———. *Industrial Organization.* New York: John Wiley & Sons, Inc., 1959.

Bernstein, Marver H. *Regulating Business by Independent Commission.* Princeton: Princeton University Press, 1955.

Chamberlin, Edward H., ed. *Monopoly and Competition and Their Regulation.* London: Macmillan & Co. Ltd., 1954.

———. *The Theory of Monopolistic Competition.* Cambridge: Harvard University Press, 1933.

Clark, James Maurice. *Studies in the Economics of Overhead Costs.* Chicago: University of Chicago Press, 1923.

Committee on Price Determination. *Cost Behavior and Price Policy.* New York: National Bureau of Economic Research, 1943.

Dean, Joel. *Managerial Economics.* New York: Prentice-Hall, Inc., 1951.

Edgeworth, F. Y. *Papers Relating to Political Economy.* Vol. I. London: Macmillan Co., 1925.

Fellner, William. *Competition Among the Few.* New York: Alfred A. Knopf, 1949.

Friendly, Henry J. *The Federal Administrative Agencies: the Need for Better Definition of Standards.* Cambridge: Harvard University Press, 1962.

Hutt, W. H. *The Theory of Idle Resources.* London: Jonathan Cape, 1939.

Jones, Eliot. *The Anthracite Coal Combinations in the United States.* Cambridge: Harvard University Press, 1914.

Kelf-Cohen, Reuben. *Nationalization in Britain; the End of a Dogma,* 2d ed. London: Macmillan Co., 1961.

Lerner, Abba P. *The Economics of Control.* New York: Macmillan Co., 1946.

Lewis, W. Arthur. *Overhead Costs: Some Essays in Economic Analysis.* London: George Allen & Unwin Ltd., 1949.

Machlup, Fritz. *The Economics of Sellers Competition.* Baltimore: Johns Hopkins Press, 1952.

Marshall, Alfred. *Industry and Trade.* London: Macmillan and Co., 1919.

National Bureau of Economic Research, Conference on Research in Income and Wealth. *Problems of Capital Formation: Concepts Measurement and Controlling Factors.* Princeton: Princeton University Press, 1957.

Pigou, A. C. *Economics of Welfare.* London: Macmillan Co., 1932.

Robinson, E. A. G. *Monopoly.* London: Pitman Publishing Corp., 1941.

———. *The Structure of Competitive Industry.* London: Pitman Publishing Corp., 1935.

Robson, William A. *Nationalized Industry and Public Ownership.* London: George Allen & Unwin, Ltd., 1960.
———, ed. *Problems of Nationalized Industry.* London: Allen & Unwin Ltd., 1952.
Stigler, George J. *The Theory of Price.* New York: Macmillan Co., 1946.
Universities-National Bureau Committee for Economic Research. *Business Concentration and Price Policy.* Princeton: Princeton University Press, 1955.

TRANSPORTATION INDUSTRIES

Association of American Railroads. *American Railway Signaling and Practices.* New York: Signal Section, Association of American Railroads, 1946.
———. *Report on Coordination.* Washington, D.C.: Association of American Railroads, 1942.
———, Railroad Committee for the Study of Transportation. *Consolidation of Railroads.* Washington, D.C.: Association of American Railroads, 1945.
Barger, Harold. *The Transportation Industries 1889–1946: A Study of Output, Employment, and Productivity.* New York: National Bureau of Economic Research, 1951.
Barriger, John W. *Super-Railroads for a Dynamic American Economy.* New York: Simmons-Boardman Publishing Corp., 1956.
Beckmann, Martin, C. Bart. McGuire and Christopher Winsten. *Studies in the Economics of Transportation.* New Haven: Yale University Press, 1956.
Berge, Stanley. *Railroad Passenger Service Costs and Financial Results.* Evanston: Northwestern University School of Commerce, 1956.
Booz, Allen & Hamilton. "Organization and Procedures Survey of the Interstate Commerce Commission." Washington, D.C.: mimeographed, 1960.
Burnie, Nadreen A., ed. *Transportation Mergers and Acquisitions.* Evanston: Northwestern University Transportation Center, 1962.
Caves, Richard E. *Air Transport and Its Regulators.* Cambridge: Harvard University Press, 1962.
Chapman, John Will. *Railroad Mergers.* New York: Simmons-Boardman Pub. Corp., 1934.
Cherington, Charles R. *Regulation of Railroad Abandonments.* Cambridge: Harvard University Press, 1948.
Daggett, Stuart. *Railroad Consolidation West of the Mississippi River.* Berkeley: University of California Press, 1933.
Dearing, Charles L., and Wilfred Owen. *National Transportation Policy.* Washington, D.C.: The Brookings Institution, 1949.
Drayton, Charles D. *Transportation Under Two Masters.* Washington, D.C.: National Law Book Co., 1946.
Frederick, John H., F. T. Hypps, and J. M. Herring. *Regulation of Railroad Finance.* New York: Simmons-Boardman Publishing Corp., 1930.
Fulda, Carl H. *Competition in the Regulated Industries: Transportation.* Boston: Little, Brown and Co., 1961.
General Railway Signal Company. *G.R.S. Siding Length and Non-Stop Meet Formulas.* New York: General Railway Signal Co., Pamphlet 635, January, 1947.
Grodinsky, Julius. *Railroad Consolidation: Its Economics and Controlling Principles.* New York: D. Appleton and Co., 1930.
———. *The Iowa Pool: A Study in Railroad Competition.* Chicago: University of Chicago Press, 1950.
Hay, William W. *Introduction to Transportation Engineering.* New York: John Wiley & Sons, Inc., 1961.
Healy, Kent T. *The Effects of Scale in the Railroad Industry.* New Haven: Yale University Committee on Transportation, 1961.
Herring, James Morton. *The Problem of Weak Railroads.* Philadelphia: University of Pennsylvania Press, 1929.
Hilton, George W. *The Great Lakes Car Ferries.* Berkeley: Howell-North Press, 1962.

Hilton, George W., and John F. Due. *The Electric Interurban Railways in America.* Stanford: Stanford University Press, 1960.

Hudson, C. J. *A Computer Simulation of Railroad CTC Operations.* Toronto: Joint ASME-AIEE-EIC Railway Conference, April 10, 1962.

Hypps, Frank T. *Federal Regulation of Railroad Construction and Abandonment Under the Transportation Act of 1920.* Philadelphia: University of Pennsylvania Press, 1929.

Ladd, Dwight R. *Cost Data for the Management of Railroad Passenger Service.* Boston: Harvard University Graduate School of Business Administration, 1957.

Latham, Earl. *The Politics of Railroad Coordination, 1933–1936.* Cambridge: Harvard University Press, 1959.

Lemly, James Hutton. *The Gulf, Mobile and Ohio: A Railroad That Had to Expand or Expire.* Homewood: Richard D. Irwin, Inc., 1953.

Leonard, William Norris. *Railroad Consolidations Under the Transportation Act of 1920.* New York: Columbia University Press, 1946.

Locklin, D. Philip. *Economics of Transportation,* 5th ed. Homewood: Richard D. Irwin, Inc., 1960.

———. *Railroad Regulation Since 1920.* New York: McGraw-Hill, 1928.

Mayer, Harold Melvin. "The Railway Pattern of Metropolitan Chicago." Chicago: Lithoprinted doctoral dissertation, University of Chicago, 1943.

Meyer, B. H. *A History of the Northern Securities Case.* Madison: University of Wisconsin Bulletin No. 142, 1906.

Meyer, John R., Merton J. Peck, John Stenason, Gerald Kraft, and Robert Brown. *Avoidable Costs of Passenger Train Service.* Cambridge: Aeronautical Research Foundation, 1957.

Meyer, John R., Merton J. Peck, John Stenason, and Charles Zwick. *The Economics of Competition in the Transportation Industries.* Cambridge: Harvard University Press, 1959.

Milne, A. M. *The Economics of Inland Transport,* revised ed. London: Pitman & Sons, Ltd., 1960.

Moulton, H. G. and associates. *The American Transportation Problem.* Washington, D.C.: The Brookings Institution, 1933.

Nelson, James C. *Railroad Transportation and Public Policy.* Washington, D.C.: The Brookings Institution, 1959.

Nelson, Robert S., and Edward M. Johnson. *Technological Change and the Future of the Railways.* Evanston: Northwestern University Transportation Center, 1961.

Newcomb, H. T. *Railway Economics.* Philadelphia: Railway World Publishing Co., 1898.

Oppenheim, Saul Chesterfield. *The National Transportation Policy and Rail-Motor Rate Competition.* Harrisburg: Evangelical Press, 1945.

Poole, Ernest C. *Costs—a Tool for Railroad Management.* New York: Simmons-Boardman Publishing Corp., 1962.

Prince, Frederick H. "A Plan for Coordinating the Operations of Railroads in the United States." Mimeographed, March 15, 1933, revised September, 1933.

Ripley, William Z. *Railroads: Finance and Organization.* New York: Longmans, 1915.

Ruppenthal, Karl M., ed. *Challenge to Transportation.* Stanford: Stanford University Graduate School of Business, 1961.

———. *Revolution in Transportation.* Stanford: Stanford University Graduate School of Business, 1960.

———. *Transportation Frontiers.* Stanford: Stanford University Graduate School of Business, 1962.

Sampson, Roy J. *Obstacles to Railroad Unification.* Eugene: University of Oregon Bureau of Business Research, 1960.

Sharfman, I. L. *The Interstate Commerce Commission.* New York: The Commonwealth Fund, 1935.

Shott, John G. *The Railroad Monopoly.* Washington, D.C.: Public Affairs Institute, 1950.

Splawn, Walter M. W. *Consolidation of Railroads.* New York: Macmillan Co., 1925.

Troxel, Charles Emery. *Economics of Transport.* New York: Rinehart & Co., Inc., 1955.

Ulmer, Melville J. "An Appraisal of the Aeronautical Research Foundation's Avoidable Costs of Passenger Train Service." Mimeograph, prepared for U.S. General Services Administration, 1958.

Union Switch and Signal Company. "Signals and Track Capacity." Swissvale, Pa.: Typewritten memorandum, June 26, 1936.

Williams, Ernest W. *Freight Transportation in the Soviet Union.* Princeton: Princeton University Press, 1962.

————. *The Regulation of Rail-Motor Rate Competition.* New York: Harper, 1958.

Wiprud, Arne C. *Justice in Transportation.* New York: Ziff-Davis Pub. Co., 1945.

ARTICLES

GENERAL

Adams, Walter. "Dissolution, Divorcement, Divestiture: The Pyrrhic Victories of Antitrust," *Indiana Law Journal,* Vol. 27 (Fall, 1951), 1–37.

Adelman, M. A. "Effective Competition and the Antitrust Laws," *Harvard Law Review,* Vol. 61 (September, 1948), 1289–1350.

Apel, H. "Marginal Cost Constancy and Its Implications," *American Economic Review,* Vol. 38 (December, 1948), 870–885.

Averch, Harvey, and Leland L. Johnson. "Behavior of the Firm Under Regulatory Constraint," *American Economic Review,* Vol. 52 (December, 1962), 1052–1069.

Bishop, Robert L. "Cost Discontinuities, Declining Costs and Marginal Analysis," *American Economic Review,* Vol. 38 (September, 1948), 607–617.

Brems, Hans. "Cartels or Competition," *Weltwirtschaftliches Achiv,* Vol. 66 (Part 1, 1951), 51–67.

Cassels, John M. "Excess Capacity and Monopolistic Competition," *Quarterly Journal of Economics,* Vol. 51 (May, 1937), 426–443.

Chenery, Hollis B. "Overcapacity and the Acceleration Principle," *Econometrica,* Vol. 20 (January, 1952), 1–28.

Clark, James M. "Toward a Concept of Workable Competition," *American Economic Review,* Vol. 30 (June, 1940), 241–256.

Coase, Ronald H. "Monopoly Pricing with Interrelated Costs and Demands," *Economica N.S.,* Vol. 13 (November, 1946), 139–156.

Conant, Michael. "In Defense of Administrative Regulation," *Indiana Law Journal,* Vol. 39 (Fall, 1963), 29–68.

Cox, Hugh B. "Trends in the Application of the Antitrust Laws to Regulated Industries," *Public Utilities Fortnightly,* Vol. 66 (November 10, 1960), 773–782.

de Leeuw, Frank. "The Concept of Capacity," *Journal of the American Statistical Association,* Vol. 57 (December, 1962), 826–840.

Dewey, Donald J. "Imperfect Competition No Bar to Efficient Production," *Journal of Political Economy,* Vol. 66 (February, 1958), 24–33.

Eiteman, W. J. "Factors Determining the Location of the Least Cost Point," *American Economic Review,* Vol. 37 (December, 1947), 910–918.

Ezekiel, Mordecai. "Is Government Intervention or Planning Consistent with Antitrust Policy?" *American Economic Review, Supplement,* Vol. 36 (May, 1946), 190–204.

Fuchs, Ralph F. "Fairness and Effectiveness in Administrative Agency Organization and Procedures," *Indiana Law Journal,* Vol. 36 (Fall, 1960), 1–50.

Haines, Walter W. "Capacity Production and the Least Cost Point," *American Economic Review,* Vol. 48 (September, 1948), 617–624.

Hall, Hugh M. "Responsibility of President and Congress for Regulatory Policy Development," *Law and Contemporary Problems,* Vol. 26 (Spring, 1961), 261–282.

Handler, Milton. "Industrial Mergers and the Anti-Trust Laws," *Columbia Law Review,* Vol. 32 (February, 1932), 179–271.

Heady, Ferrel, and Eleanor Tabor Linenthal. "Congress and Administrative Regulation," *Law and Contemporary Problems,* Vol. 26 (Spring, 1961), 238–260.

Heflebower, Richard B. "Stability in Oligopoly," *The Manchester School of Economics and Social Studies,* Vol. 29 (January, 1961), 79–93.

Hines, Howard H. "The Effectiveness of 'Entry' by Already Established Firms," *Quarterly Journal of Economics,* Vol. 71 (February, 1957), 132–150.

"Judicial Application of Antitrust Law to Regulated Industry," *Harvard Law Review,* Vol. 64 (May, 1951), 1154–1181.

Klein, Lawrence R. "Some Theoretical Issues in the Measurement of Capacity," *Econometrica,* Vol. 28 (April, 1960), 272–286.

Levi, Edward H. "The Antitrust Laws and Monopoly," *University of Chicago Law Review,* Vol. 14 (February, 1947), 153–183.

Lewis, Ben W. "Ambivalence in Public Policy Toward Regulated Industries," *American Economic Review, Supplement,* Vol. 53 (May, 1963), 38–52.

McFarland, Carl. "Landis' Report, the Voice of One Crying in the Wilderness," *Virginia Law Review,* Vol. 47 (April, 1961), 373–438.

Miller, Arthur S. "Public Interest Undefined," *Journal of Public Law,* Vol. 10 (Fall, 1961), 184–202.

Patinkin, Don. "Multi-plant Firms, Cartels, and Imperfect Competition," *Quarterly Journal of Economics,* Vol. 61 (February, 1947), 173–205.

Phillips, Almarin. "An Appraisal of Measures of Capacity," *American Economic Review, Supplement,* Vol. 53 (May, 1963), 278–292.

Schultze, Charles L. "Uses of Capacity Measures for Short-Run Economic Analysis," *American Economic Review, Supplement,* Vol. 53 (May, 1963), 293–308.

Schwartz, Louis B. "Legal Restriction of Competition in the Regulated Industries," *Harvard Law Review,* Vol. 67 (January, 1954), 436–475.

Stigler, George J. "The Case Against Big Business," *Fortune,* Vol. 45 (May, 1952), 123, 158, 162, 164.

Von Mehren, Robert B. "The Antitrust Laws and Regulated Industries: The Doctrine of Primary Jurisdiction," *Harvard Law Review,* Vol. 67 (April, 1954), 929–966.

Whitlow, J. A. "The Failure of Competition in Public Utility Regulation," *Public Utilities Fortnightly,* Vol. 39 (May 8, 1947), 597–606.

Woll, Peter. "Administrative Law Reform: Proposals and Prospects," *Nebraska Law Review,* Vol. 41 (June, 1962), 687–722.

Transportation Industries

Adkins, L. D. "Roadblocks to Railroad Mergers," *Business Lawyer,* Vol. 17 (April, 1962), 519–531.

"Administrative Law—Powers of Agencies—the Interstate Commerce Commission and Discontinuance of Railroads Under the Transportation Act of 1958," *Michigan Law Review,* Vol. 57 (June, 1959), 1258–1260.

Aitchison, Clyde B. "Bulwinkle Bill—Commissioner Aitchison's Prepared Statement," *I.C.C. Practitioners' Journal,* Vol. 13 (May, 1946), 685–731.

Allen, Margaret P. "The Administrative Conference of the United States: Its Final Report and the Interstate Commerce Commission," *I.C.C. Practitioners' Journal,* Vol. 30 (June, 1963), 1113–1122.

Ames, H. C. "The Reed-Bulwinkle Bill," *I.C.C. Practitioners' Journal,* Vol. 15 (October, 1948), 3–4.

Ansnes, Bliss. "Federal Regulation of Railroad Holding Companies," *Columbia Law Review,* Vol. 32 (June, 1932), 999–1016.

"Application of the Sherman and Clayton Acts to Holding Companies Organized by Parent Railroad Corporations," *University of Pennsylvania Law Review*, Vol. 78 (March, 1930), 652–656.

Arpaia, A. F. "Future of Public Transportation," *I.C.C. Practitioners' Journal*, Vol. 21 (April, 1954), 265–276.

———. "Brass Tacks of the I.C.C. Administrative Problem," *Public Utilities Fortnightly*, Vol. 65 (March 31, 1960), 433–442.

Arragon, A. V. "Railroad Co-ordination: A Plan to Strengthen Railroad Credit Through Systematic Correlation of the Railways Under Government Supervision," *Journal of Political Economy*, Vol. 25 (June, 1917), 542–560.

Ashton, Herbert. "Some Aspects of Rail Transport Service," *Transport and Communications Review*, Vol. 14 (January–March, 1951), 14–23.

———. "Railroad Costs in Relation to the Volume of Traffic," *American Economic Review*, Vol. 30 (June, 1940), 324–332.

———. "The Time Element in Transportation," *American Economic Review, Supplement*, Vol. 37 (May, 1947), 423–440.

Baker, George P. "The Possibilities of Economies by Railroad Consolidation and Co-ordination," *American Economic Review, Supplement*, Vol. 30 (March, 1940), 140–157.

Barton, Frank L., and Byron Nupp. "Regulation and Economic Performance in Transportation," *George Washington Law Review*, Vol. 31 (October, 1962), 186–197.

Behling, Burton H. "The Causes and Cure of Railroads' Ills," *Commercial and Financial Chronicle*, Vol. 192 (August 18, 1960), 651, 675–678.

Belsterling, C. S. "Freight Rates and Terminal Switching Services," *University of Pennsylvania Law Review*, Vol. 95 (June, 1947), 719–738.

Beverly, Phil. C. "Consideration of Antitrust Policy in Determination of Mergers and Consolidations under Section 5 of the Interstate Commerce Act," *I.C.C. Practitioners' Journal*, Vol. 29 (November, 1961), 169–178.

Bigham, Truman C. "Regulation of Minimum Rates in Transportation," *Quarterly Journal of Economics*, Vol. 61 (February, 1947), 206–231.

———. "The Transportation Act of 1940," *Southern Economic Journal*, Vol. 8 (July, 1941), 1–21.

Blair, J. P. "Process and Results of Railroad Unification," *Academy of Political Science Proceedings*, Vol. 13 (June, 1929), 339–349.

Bledsoe, Samuel T. "Consolidation and Coordination Problems," *Academy of Political Science Proceedings*, Vol. 17 (January, 1937), 250–262.

Bornemann, H. B. "Conditions for Protection of Employees in Railroad Abandonment Proceedings," *I.C.C. Practitioners' Journal*, Vol. 20 (September, 1953), 939–942.

Borts, George H. "Production Relations in the Railway Industry," *Econometrica*, Vol. 20 (January, 1952), 71–79.

———. "Increasing Returns in the Railway Industry," *Journal of Political Economy*, Vol. 62 (August, 1954), 316–333.

Bridgeman, Lester M. "The Relief from the Operation of the Antitrust Laws Provided by Section 5a of the Interstate Commerce Act," *I.C.C. Practitioners' Journal*, Vol. 29 (October, 1961), 3–14.

Brown, Carman E. "The Interstate Commerce Commission and Monopoly—A Study of the Commission's Powers and Duties in the Antitrust Field," *I.C.C. Practitioners' Journal*, Vol. 29 (February, 1962), 596–604.

Bruce, Harry J., and Stanley Zoints. "Research: The Forgotten 'R' in Transportation," *Transportation Journal*, Vol. 2 (Summer, 1963), 28–33.

Burkett, C. W. "Regulatory Problems Arising in Connection with the Adjustment of Rail Passenger Service," *Public Utilities Fortnightly*, Vol. 62 (November 6, 1958), 836–841.

Burck, Gilbert. "A Plan to Save the Railroads," *Fortune,* Vol. 58 (August, 1958), 82–86, 174–182.

Burstein, H. "Railroads and Motor Carriers—Competition or Coordination," *Villanova Law Review,* Vol. 7 (Summer, 1962), 563–586.

Church, Donald E. "Railway Freight Car Problem," *Survey of Current Business,* Vol. 21 (July, 1941), 10–15, 18.

"Competition as a Factor in the Judicial Review of Decisions of the I.C.C.," *Illinois Law Review,* Vol. 42 (November-December, 1947), 651–658.

County, A. J. "Consolidation of Railroads into Systems," *American Economic Review, Supplement,* Vol. 14 (March, 1924), 73–87.

Craven, L. "The Problem of Railroad Competition," *American Economic Review, Supplement,* Vol. 25 (March, 1935), 102–110.

Cummings, J. E. "The Need for Co-ordination of Our Transportation System," *Journal of Political Economy,* Vol. 35 (December, 1927), 852–861.

Cunningham, A. J. "The Separation of Railroad Operating Expenses Between Freight and Passenger Service," *Quarterly Journal of Economics,* Vol. 31 (February, 1917), 209–240.

Cunningham, W. J. "Correlation of Rail and Highway Transportation," *American Economic Review, Supplement,* Vol. 24 (March, 1934), 46–56.

———. "The Federal Coordinator's Contribution to Railroad Coordination," *Harvard Business Review,* Vol. 15 (No. 3, 1937), 265–274.

Daggett, Stuart. "The Decision of the Union Pacific Merger," *Quarterly Journal of Economics,* Vol. 27 (February, 1913), 295–328.

———. "Later Developments in the Union Pacific Merger Case," *Quarterly Journal of Economics,* Vol. 28 (August, 1914), 772-794.

———. "Our Changing Transportation System," *American Economic Review, Supplement,* Vol. 22 (March, 1932), 256–266.

———. "Railroad Traffic Associations and Antitrust Legislation," *American Economic Review, Supplement,* Vol. 38 (May, 1948), 452–464.

Daniels, W. M. "Economic Purposes and Limitations of Consolidation," *American Economic Review, Supplement,* Vol. 14 (March, 1924), 43–51.

Daniels, Winthrop M. "The Changing Attitude of Public Policy Toward Railroad Consolidation," *Academy of Political Science Proceedings,* Vol. 13 (June, 1929), 433–440.

———. "Railroad Unification in New England in Relation to the Four-Party Plan," *Harvard Business Review,* Vol. 10 (October, 1931), 8–14.

Dearing, C. L., and W. Owen. "The Reorganization of Transport Regulation," *American Economic Review, Supplement,* Vol. 40 (May, 1950), 261–270.

Dennis, Jack R. "Immunity of Rate Association Agreements from the Antitrust Laws," *Ohio State Law Journal,* Vol. 18 (Spring, 1957), 260–271.

Dewey, R. L. "Criteria for Establishment of an Optimum Transportation System," *American Economic Review, Supplement,* Vol. 42 (May, 1952), 644–653.

———. "The Transportation Act of 1940," *American Economic Review,* Vol. 31 (March, 1941), 15–26.

Due, John. "An Empirical Study of Abandonment Decisions," *Journal of Finance,* Vol. 14 (September, 1959), 361–372.

Duncan, C. S. "Some Business Aspects of 'Adequate Transportation Service,' " *Harvard Business Review,* Vol. 4 (January, 1926), 145–152.

Eastman, Joseph E. "Transportation Problems and Suggestions Toward a Constructive Solution," *Academy of Political Science Proceedings,* Vol. 17 (January, 1937), 239–249.

———. "Transportation by Rail and Otherwise," *American Economic Review, Supplement,* Vol. 72 (March, 1932), 247–255.

Edwards, Ford K. "Application of Cost Analysis to Rail Passenger Service," *I.C.C. Practitioners' Journal,* Vol. 18 (April, 1951), 599–609.

————. "Competitive Problems Arising from the Existence of Fixed Costs in the Transportation Industries," *I.C.C. Practitioners' Journal*, Vol. 12 (June, 1945), 1012–1014.

————. "Cost Analysis in Transportation," *American Economic Review, Supplement*, Vol. 37 (May, 1947), 441–461.

Esch, John J. "Advantages and Disadvantages of Consolidation," *Academy of Political Science Proceedings*, Vol. 13 (June, 1929), 383–395.

Fair, M. L. "The Interstate Commerce Commission and the Railroad Terminal Problem," *Quarterly Journal of Economics*, Vol. 44 (May, 1930), 462–492.

————. "The Unification of Railroad Terminals," *Harvard Business Review*, Vol. 10 (October, 1931), 85–96.

Fess, Simeon D. "The Proposed Railroad Consolidation Act of 1929," *Academy of Political Science Proceedings*, Vol. 13 (June, 1929), 441–444.

Fort, J. C. "Regulated Transportation and the Antitrust Laws," *I.C.C. Practitioners' Journal*, Vol. 14 (February, 1947), 445–447.

Freas, H. "Reflections on Regulation," *I.C.C. Practitioners' Journal*, Vol. 25 (March, 1958), 628–636.

Greenough, A. J. "Taking a Critical Look at Railroad Management," *Commercial and Financial Chronicle*, Vol. 191 (April 21, 1960), 1742.

Grunfeld, Yehuda. "The Effect of the Per Diem Rate on the Efficiency and Size of the American Railroad Freight-Car Fleet," *Journal of Business*, Vol. 32 (January, 1959), 52–73.

Guandolo, John. "Extension of Railroad Lines," *Transportation Journal*, Vol. 2 (Winter, 1962), 36–39.

Hale, George E., and Rosemary D. Hale. "Competition on Control I: The Chaos of the Cases," *University of Pennsylvania Law Review*, Vol. 106 (March, 1958), 641–683.

————. "Competition or Control III: Motor Carriers," *University of Pennsylvania Law Review*, Vol. 108 (April, 1960), 775–831.

————. "Competition or Control IV: Air Carriers," *University of Pennsylvania Law Review*, Vol. 109 (January, 1961), 311–360.

Hansbury, J. E. "Passenger Deficit Study on Class I Railroads, 1950 and 1951," *I.C.C. Practitioners' Journal*, Vol. 20 (February, 1953), 409–414.

Harbeson, Robert W. "New Patterns in Railway Consolidation," *Quarterly Review of Economics and Business*, Vol. 2 (February, 1962), 7–19.

————. "Some Aspects of Wage-Price Relationships in Regulated Industry: the Railways as a Case Study," *Journal of Business*, Vol. 25 (July, 1952), 175–186.

————. "The Transportation Act of 1940," *Journal of Land and Public Utility Economics*, Vol. 17 (August, 1941), 291–302.

————. "The Transportation Act of 1958," *Land Economics*, Vol. 35 (May, 1959), 156–171.

Healy, Kent T. "The Problem—Rational and Effective Allocation of Resources," *The Annals of the American Academy of Political and Social Science*, Vol. 345 (January, 1963), 39–46.

Hendrix, Roger B. "Railroads—Abandonments and Partial Discontinuance of Passenger Service," *North Carolina Law Review* (December, 1962), 137–147.

Hilton, George W. "Experience Under the Reed-Bulwinkle Act," *I.C.C. Practitioners' Journal*, Vol. 28 (September, 1961), 1207–1219.

Hines, Walker D. "The Public Interest in Railroad Unification and Consolidation," *Academy of Political Science Proceedings*, Vol. 13 (June, 1929), 329–338.

————. "The Relationship of the Burlington-Great Northern-Northern Pacific Group to the Federal Railroad Consolidation Law," *Harvard Business Review*, Vol. 1 (July, 1923), 398–413.

Horowitz, Morris A. "Some Effects of Labor Costs on the Railroad Industry," *Labor Law Journal*, Vol. 8 (February, 1957), 105–116.

Hotelling, Harold. "The General Welfare in Relation to Problems of Taxation and of Railway and Utility Rates," *Econometrica*, Vol. 6 (July, 1938), 242–269.

Hudson, Henry. "The Southern Railway and Steamship Association," *Quarterly Journal of Economics*, Vol. 5 (October, 1890), 70–94, 115–130.

Huntington, S. P. "The Marasmus of the I.C.C.: The Commission, the Railroads, and the Public Interest," *Yale Law Journal*, Vol. 61 (April, 1952), 467–509.

Hutchinson, Everett. "I.C.C. Organization and Procedure," *George Washington Law Review*, Vol. 31 (October, 1962), 29–36.

———. "Regulation—Stimulus or Stumbling Block," *I.C.C. Practitioners' Journal*, Vol. 27 (September, 1960), 1069–1073.

Johns, C. H. "The Interstate Commerce Commission and the Department of Justice," *George Washington Law Review*, Vol. 31 (October, 1962), 242–257.

Johnson, Emory R. "Obstacles to Railroad Consolidation in Eastern Territory," *Academy of Political Science Proceedings*, Vol. 13 (June, 1929), 359–368.

Koopmans, T. C. "Optimum Utilization of the Transportation System," *Econometrica*, Vol. 17 (July, 1949), 136–145, and Vol. 19 (April, 1951), 227.

Korbel, Herbert J. "The Interstate Commerce Commission and Monopoly—A Study of the Commission's Powers and Duties in the Antitrust Field: The Commission and Railroad Unifications—from Unrestrained Competition to Regulated Monopoly," *I.C.C. Practitioners' Journal*, Vol. 29 (December, 1961), 318–329.

Landon, Charles E. "Regional Transportation Coordination," *Southern Economic Journal*, Vol. 5 (July, 1938), 1–6.

Langdon, Jr., J. "Regulation of Competitive Business Forces: The Obstacle Race in Transportation," *Cornell Law Quarterly*, Vol. 41 (Fall, 1955), 57–92.

Liipfert, Eugene T. "Consolidation and Competition: The Need for an Effective and Consistent Policy," *George Washington Law Review*, Vol. 31 (October, 1962), 106–135.

Locklin, D. P. "Economic Implications of Current Transportation Policy Recommendations," *Journal of Farm Economics*, Vol. 38 (December, 1956), 1585–1589.

———. "Transport Coordination and Rate Policy," *Harvard Business Review*, Vol. 15 (No. 4, 1937), 417–428.

Magee, G. M. "U.S. Railroaders Inspect Japanese 'Super-Railroad,'" *Railway Track and Structures*, Vol. 59 (June, 1963), 23–28.

Mansfield, E., and H. H. Wein. "A Study of Decision-Making Within the Firm," *Quarterly Journal of Economics*, Vol. 72 (November, 1958), 515–536.

Mansfield, Harvey C. "The Minimum Rate Power and the Control of Carrier Competition," *Yale Law Journal*, Vol. 45 (June, 1936), 1406–1425.

Marshall, Donald Ross. "Railroad Certificates of Convenience and Necessity Issued Under the Interstate Commerce Act," *Oregon Law Review*, Vol. 22 (April, 1943), 215–267.

Martin, E. "Legal Problems of the Railroad Passenger Deficit, *I.C.C. Practitioners' Journal*, Vol. 22 (January, 1955), 275–284.

Mayer, H. M. "Localization of Railway Facilities in Metropolitan Centers as Typified by Chicago," *Land Economics*, Vol. 20 (November, 1944), 299–315.

McFarland, W. "Consolidation of Railroads," *I.C.C. Practitioners' Journal*, Vol. 13 (February, 1946), 363–375.

McGinnis, Patrick B. "Radical Cures for Railroad Ills," *Commercial and Financial Chronicle*, Vol. 186 (November 7, 1957), 2013, 2030–2031.

McGrath, J. H. "Relation of Department of Justice to I.C.C.," *I.C.C. Practitioners' Journal*, Vol. 18 (November, 1950), 83–89.

Melton, Lee J. "Transport Coordination and Regulatory Philosophy," *Law and Contemporary Problems*, Vol. 24 (Autumn, 1959), 622–642.

———. "An Integrated Approach to the Transportation Problem," *Southern Economic Journal*, Vol. 23 (April, 1957), 398–410.

Meyer, John R. "Some Methodological Aspects of Statistical Costing as Illustrated by the Determination of Rail Passenger Costs," *American Economic Review, Supplement*, Vol. 48 (May, 1958), 209–222.

Meyer, John R., and Gerald Kraft. "The Evaluation of Statistical Costing Techniques as Applied in the Transportation Industry," *American Economic Review, Supplement,* Vol. 51 (May, 1961), 313–334.

"Minimum Rate Regulation by the Interstate Commerce Commission," *Harvard Law Review,* Vol. 73 (February, 1960), 762–775.

Moore, Samuel W. "Our Lagging Railway Mergers," *Virginia Law Review,* Vol. 15 (June, 1929), 743–756.

Morton, N. "Carrier Consolidation," *I.C.C. Practitioners' Journal,* Vol. 30 (January, 1963), 425–448.

Moulton, Harold G. "Fundamentals of a National Transportation Policy," *American Economic Review, Supplement,* Vol. 24 (March, 1934), 33–46.

Munby, D. L. "The Reshaping of the British Railways," *Journal of Industrial Economics,* Vol. 11 (July, 1963), 161–182.

Nelson, James C. "Coordination of Transportation by Regulation," *Journal of Land and Public Utility Economics,* Vol. 14 (May, 1938), 167–181.

——. "Effects of Public Regulation on Railroad Performance," *American Economic Review, Supplement,* Vol. 50 (May, 1960), 495–505.

——. "Revision of Nation Transport Regulatory Policy," *American Economic Review,* Vol. 45 (December, 1955), 910–918.

——. "Highway Development, the Railroads, and National Transport Policy," *American Economic Review, Supplement,* Vol. 41 (May, 1951), 495–505.

——. "Patterns of Competition and Monopoly in Present-Day Transport and Implications for Public Policy, *Land Economics,* Vol. 26 (August, 1950), 232–248.

Newcomb, Harry Turner. "Railway Competition: A Problem in Statistics," *Journal of the American Statistical Association,* Vol. 5 (June, 1896), 65–77.

"Notes on the Determination of the Traffic Capacity of Single and Multiple Track Railways," *Proceedings* of American Railway Engineering Association, Vol. 22 (1921), 744–772.

Oldham, J. E. "The Problem of Railroad Consolidations," *Harvard Business Review,* Vol. 1 (January, 1923), 139–153.

Owen, Wilfred. "Transportation and Technology," *American Economic Review, Supplement,* Vol. 52 (May, 1962), 405–413.

Payne, J. S. "History of the 'Consolidation' Provisions of the Interstate Commerce Act," *I.C.C. Practitioners' Journal,* Vol. 19 (February, 1952), 453–462.

Pegrum, Dudley F. "Investment in the Railroad and Other Transportation Industries Under Regulation," *American Economic Review, Supplement,* Vol. 47 (May, 1957), 416–429.

Peterson, G. S. "Transport Coordination: Meaning and Purpose," *Journal of Political Economy,* Vol. 38 (December, 1930), 660–681.

Phillips, Jr., C. F. "Railroad Mergers: Competition, Monopoly, and Antitrust," *Washington and Lee Law Review,* Vol. 19 (Spring, 1962), 1–22.

Phillips, Edmund John. "Diversion of Freight Traffic from the Railroads," *Journal of Land and Public Utility Economics,* Vol. 16 (November, 1940), 403–415.

Priest, A. J. G. "Discontinuance of Railroad Service," *Public Utilities Fortnightly,* Vol. 61 (May 8, 1958), 656–665.

Prince, Gregory S. "Railroads and Government Policy—A Legally Oriented Study of an Economic Crisis," *Virginia Law Review,* Vol. 48 (March, 1962), 196–278.

Quarles, James. "Consolidation of Interstate Railroads," *Virginia Law Review,* Vol. 20 (December, 1933), 200–207.

"Railroad Consolidations and State Corporations," *Columbia Law Review,* Vol. 31 (April, 1931), 651–660.

"Railroad Terminal Consolidation in Chicago," *Illinois Law Review,* Vol. 46 (March, 1951), 138–155.

Raper, C. L. "Railroad Consolidation in Eastern Territory," *Journal of Business,* Vol. 7 (July, 1934), 200–223.

"Regulation of Railroad Service Competition," *Yale Law Journal*, Vol. 48 (November, 1938), 143–149.

Renshaw, Edward F. "Utility Regulation: A Reexamination," *Journal of Business*, Vol. 31 (October, 1958), 335–343.

Rice, William Thomas. "Why Not Merge and Survive," *Annals of the American Academy of Political and Social Science*, Vol. 345 (January, 1963), 103–108.

Riordan, H. P. "Railroad Merger—Dissected," *Business Lawyer*, Vol. 16 (April, 1961), 577–590; *Antitrust Bulletin*, Vol. 6 (July-December, 1961), 465–486.

Ripley, W. Z. "The Problem of Railway Terminal Operation," *Harvard Business Review*, Vol. 4 (April, July, 1926), 266–274, 385–392.

Roberts, Merrill J. "The Regulation of Transport Price Competition," *Law and Contemporary Problems*, Vol. 24 (Autumn, 1959), 557–585.

Robinson, Bird M. "The Relation of the Short Lines to Railroad Consolidation," *Academy of Political Science Proceedings*, Vol. 13 (June, 1929), 416–424.

Schrag, A. "Competing Modes of Transportation and the ICC," *University of Pennsylvania Law Review*, Vol. 94 (July, 1946), 378–399.

Schwendt, B. J. "Economic Relation Between Signals, Track Arrangement, Motive Power, and Method of Operation, *Economics of Railway Signaling* (March, 1937), 447–499.

Simpson, Sidney P. "The Interstate Commerce Commission and Railroad Consolidation," *Harvard Law Review*, Vol. 43 (December, 1929), 192–250.

Sjoberg, Arne. "Economic Aspects of (a) Discontinuing Service on Old Railway Lines; (b) Construction of New Railway Lines; with regard to the Possibility of Handling Transport with Other Means," *Bulletin of the International Railway Congress Association*, Vol. 29 (March, April, 1952), 201–342.

Smith, E. A. "The Interstate Commerce Commission, the Department of Justice and the Supreme Court," *American Economic Review, Supplement*, Vol. 36 (May, 1946), 479–493.

Sorrell, Lewis C. "Railroad Consolidations: Discussion," *American Economic Review, Supplement*, Vol. 14 (March, 1924), 102–104.

Splawn, W. M. W. "Legal Aspects of the Proposed Regulation of the Railroad Holding Company," *Harvard Business Review*, Vol. 10 (July, 1932), 471–481.

"State Power to Order Railroad Trackage Agreements, *Stanford Law Review*, Vol. 12 (May, 1960), 674–681.

Stevens, J. P. "Regulation of Railroads," *American Bar Association Section on Antitrust Law*, Vol. 19 (1961), 355–361.

Swaine, Robert T. "Reorganizational Corporations: Certain Developments of the Last Decade," *Columbia Law Review*, Vol. 28 (January, 1928), 29–63.

Thomas, Norman C. "Public Utilities: Discontinuance of Railroad Service," *Rutgers Law Review*, Vol. 14 (Winter, 1960), 345–355.

Trumbower, Henry R. "Railway Abandonments and Additions," *Journal of Political Economy*, Vol. 34 (February, 1926), 37–60.

Tucker, W. H., and J. H. O'Brien. "Public Interest in Railroad Mergers," *Boston University Law Review*, Vol. 42 (Spring, 1962), 160–186.

Tuggle, K. H. "Adequate and Efficient Car Service," *I.C.C. Practitioners' Journal*, Vol. 25 (November, 1957), 181–187.

Ward, L. E. and associates. "Determination of Maintenance of Way Expense Variation with Various Traffic Volumes and Effect of Using Such Variations, in Terms of Equated Mileage or Other Derived Factors, for Allocation of Available Funds to Maintenance of Way," American Railway Engineering Association *Bulletin* No. 574 (November, 1962), 113–115.

Waterman, Richard. "The Progress of Unification," *Academy of Political Science Proceedings*, Vol. 13 (June, 1929), 369–377.

Weisbrod, B. A. "The Per-Diem Freight-Car Rate and Railroad Efficiency: the Short-Run Problem," *Journal of Business*, Vol. 32 (October, 1959), 383–385.

Weissman, Jacob. "Railroad Abandonments: the Impact of Competition," *Iowa Law Review*, Vol. 44 (Spring, 1959), 492–512.

————. "Railroad Abandonments: the Competitive Ideal," *Minnesota Law Review*, Vol. 43 (December, 1958), 251–273.

Wells, David E. "Review of Interstate Commerce Commission 13a Decisions," *I.C.C. Practitioners' Journal*, Vol. 27 (May, 1960), 821–831.

White, Alan M. "Monopoly Under the Interstate Commerce Act," *I.C.C. Practitioners' Journal*, Vol. 29 (January, 1962), 470–473.

Willard, Daniel. "The Status of Railroad Consolidation," *Academy of Political Science Proceedings*, Vol. 13 (June, 1929), 445–451.

Williams, Ernest W. "An Evaluation of Public Policy toward the Railway Industry," *American Economic Review, Supplement*, Vol. 41 (May, 1951), 506–518.

————. "Railroad Traffic and Costs," *American Economic Review*, Vol. 33 (June, 1943), 360–365.

Wilson, G. W. "The Weeks Report Revisited," *American Economic Review*, Vol. 49 (March, 1959), 130–133.

GOVERNMENT DOCUMENTS

Great Britain. British Railways Board. *The Reshaping of British Railways*. London: 1963.

U.S., Board of Investigation and Research. *Technological Trends in Transportation*. S. Doc. 76, 79th Cong., 1st Sess., 1945.

U.S. Congress. House. *The Transportation System of Our Nation: Message from the President of the United States*. Document No. 384, 87th Cong., 2d Sess., 1962.

————. House Committee on Interstate and Foreign Commerce. *Independent Regulatory Commissions*. Report of the Special Subcommittee on Legislative Oversight, 86th Cong., 2d Sess., 1961.

————. ————. ————. Staff Report to the Special Committee on Legislative Oversight, 86th Cong., 2d Sess., 1960.

————. ————. *Investigation of ICC's Administration of Motor Carrier Act*. Hearing, 86th Cong., 2d Sess., 1960.

————. ————. *Investigation of Regulatory Commissions and Agencies*. Hearings, Part 14, 86th Cong., 1st Sess., 1959.

————. ————. *Passenger Train Service*. Hearings, 86th Cong., 2d Sess., 1960.

————. ————. *Railroad Problems*. Hearings, 85th Cong., 2d Sess., 1958.

————. ————. *Regulation of Stock Ownership in Railroads*, Hearings, 71st Cong., 2d Sess., 1931.

————. ————. *Transportation Diversification*. Hearings, 86th Cong., 2d Sess., 1960.

————. House Committee on the Judiciary. *Merger in a Regulated Industry: A Case Study of the Proposed Merger of the Louisville & Nashville and Nashville, Chattanooga & St. Louis Railroads*. Report, 84th Cong., 2d Sess., 1956.

————. Senate Committee on Commerce. *Freight Car Shortage*. Hearings, 87th Cong., 1st Sess., 1961.

————. Senate Committee on Interstate Commerce. *Investigation of Railroads, Holding Companies, and Affiliated Companies: Report on Railroad Combination in the Eastern Region*. Report No. 1182, 76th Cong., 3d Sess., 1940.

————. ————. *Investigation of Railroads, Holding Companies, and Affiliated Companies: the Van Sweringen Corporate System*. Report No. 714, 77th Cong., 2d Sess., 1942.

————. ————. *Amendments to the Transportation Act of 1958 (Train Discontinuance)*. Hearings, 86th Cong., 1st Sess., 1959.

————. Senate Committee on Interstate and Foreign Commerce. *National Transportation Policy*. Report, 87th Cong., 1st Sess., 1961.

————. ————. *Problems of the Railroads*. Hearings, 85th Cong., 2d Sess., 1958.

————. ————. ————. Report, 85th Cong., 2d Sess., 1958.

————. ————. *Proposed Passenger Train Act of 1960.* Hearings, 86th Cong., 2d Sess., 1960.

————. Senate Committee on the Judiciary. *Administrative Practice and Procedure.* Report No. 168, 86th Cong., 2d Sess., 1961.

————. ————. *Administrative Practice and Procedure.* Report No. 1484, 86th Cong., 1st Sess., 1960.

————. ————. *Federal Administrative Procedure.* Hearings, 86th Cong., 2d Sess., 1960.

————. ————. *Rail Merger Legislation.* Hearings, 87th Cong., 2d Sess., 1962.

————. ————. *The Railroad Merger Problem.* Report, 88th Cong., 1st Sess., 1963.

————. ————. *Report on Regulatory Agencies to the President Elect.* 87th Cong., 2d Sess., 1960.

————. Senate Select Committee on Small Business. *ICC Administration of the Motor Carrier Act.* Hearings, 84th Cong., 1st Sess., 1955.

————. ————. *Ratemaking Rule—ICC Act.* Hearings, 85th Cong., 2d Sess., 1958.

————. ————. *Trucking Mergers and Concentration.* Hearings, 85th Cong., 1st Sess., 1957.

U.S. Department of Commerce. *Federal Transportation Policy and Program.* 1960.

————. *Rationale of Federal Transportation Policy.* 1960.

U.S. Federal Coordinator of Transportation. *Passenger Traffic Report.* 1935.

————. ————. *Report on Economic Possibilities of Regional Coordination Projects.* 1935.

————. ————. *Report on Freight Car Pooling.* 1934.

————. ————. *Report on Transportation Legislation,* 1934.

U.S. Interstate Commerce Commission. *Annual Report of the Interstate Commerce Commission.* 1920–1963.

————. Bureau of Accounts. *Explanation of Rail Cost Finding Procedures and Principles Relating to the Use of Costs.* Statement No. 7–63, 1963.

————. Bureau of Statistics. *Railroad Coordination and Consolidation: A Review of Economics,* 1940.

————. Bureau of Transport Economics and Statistics. *A Brief History of the Separation of Railroad Operating Expenses Between Freight and Passenger Services.* Statement No. 577, 1957.

————. ————. *The Capacity and Capital Requirements of the Railroad Industry.* Statement No. 5227, 1952.

————. ————. *Railroad Abandonments, 1920–1943.* Statement No. 453, 1945.

————. ————. *Railroad Consolidation and the Public Interest—A Preliminary Examination.* Statement No. 6201, 1962.

————. ————. *Statistics of Railways in the United States,* 1920–1953.

————. ————. *Transport Statistics in the United States,* 1954–1962.

U.S. National Resources Planning Board. *Transportation and National Policy.* 1942.

U.S. Office of the President. *Criteria to Implement the Merger Provisions of the President's Transportation Message.* March 6, 1963.

U.S. Presidential Advisory Committee on Transport Policy and Organization. *Revision of Federal Transportation Policy.* 1955.

ANNUAL REPORTS

Atchison, Topeka and Santa Fe Railway Company
Atlantic Coast Line Railroad Company
Baltimore & Ohio Railroad Company
Central of Georgia Railway Company
Chesapeake and Ohio Railway Company
Chicago & Eastern Illinois Railroad Company
Chicago and North Western Railway Company
Chicago, Burlington & Quincy Railroad Company

Chicago Great Western Railway Company
Chicago, Milwaukee, St. Paul and Pacific Railroad
Chicago, Rock Island and Pacific Railroad Company
Delaware, Lackawanna & Western Railroad Company
Erie-Lackawanna Railroad Company
Erie Railroad Company
Great Northern Railway Company
Gulf, Mobile and Ohio Railroad Company
Illinois Central Railroad Company
Lehigh Valley Railroad Company
Louisville & Nashville Railroad Company
Missouri Pacific Railroad Company
New York Central Railroad Company
New York, Chicago and St. Louis Railroad Company
New York, New Haven and Hartford Railroad Company
Norfolk and Western Railway Company
Northern Pacific Railway Company
Pennsylvania Railroad Company
Peoria and Pekin Union Railway Company
Pullman Company
Rutland Railway Corporation
Seaboard Air Line Railroad Company
Soo Line Railroad Company
Southern Pacific Company
Spokane International Railroad Company
Terminal Railroad Association of St. Louis
Toledo, Peoria & Western Railroad Company
Union Pacific Railroad Company
Virginian Railway Company
Wabash Railroad Company
Western Pacific Railroad Company

Indexes

Index of Court Decisions

Alabama Public Service Com'n v. Southern Ry. Co., 269 Ala. 63, 111 So. 2d 214 (1959); 141

Alabama Public Service Com'n v. Southern Ry., 341 U.S. 341 (1951); 133, 138

Ann Arbor R. Co. v. Michigan Public Serv. Com'n, 91 F. Supp. 688, (E.D. Mich. 1950); 138

Application of Chicago & N.W. Ry. Co., 167 Neb. 61, 91 N.W. 2d 312 (1958); 138, 139

Application of Chicago, B. & Q. R. Co., 166 Neb. 567, 89 N.W. 2d 837 (1958); 138

Application of Chicago, B. & Q. R. Co., 172 Neb. 321, 102 N.W. 2d 369 (1961); 161

Application of Chicago, B. & Q. R. R., 166 Neb. 29, 87 N.W. 2d 630 (1958); 141

Application of Chicago, R.I. & P.R. Co., 169 Neb. 867, 101 N.W. 2d 448 (1960); 162

Application of Chicago, R.I. & Pac. R.R. 166 Neb. 32, 87 N.W. 2d 616 (1958); 140, 141

Arizona Corporation Com'n v. Southern Pacific Co., 87 Ariz. 310, 350 P. 2d 765 (1960); 162

Arnold v. Louisville & N.R.R., 180 F. Supp. 429 (M.D. Tenn. 1960); 62

Atchison, T. & S.F. Ry. v. State Corp. Comm'n, 182 Kan. 603, 322 P. 2d 715 (1958); 140

Atlantic Coast Line v. North Carolina Comm'n, 206 U.S. 1 (1907); 138

Atlantic Coast Line R. Co. v. King, Fla., 135 So. 2d 201 (1961); 161, 163

Atlantic Coast Line R. Co. v. Public Service Com'n, 77 F. Supp. 675 (E.D.S.C. 1948); 138, 147.

Atlantic Coast Line R.R. v. United States, 284 U.S. 288 (1932); 53

Attorney General v. New York, N.H. & H.R.R., 201 Mass. 370, 87 N.E. 621 (1909); 47

Attorney General v. New York, N.H. & H.R.R., 198 Mass. 413, 84 N.E. 737 (1908); 47

Baltimore & O.R.R. v. Public Util. Comm'n, 160 Ohio St. 67, 113 N.E. 2d 240 (1953); 141

Baltimore & O.R.R. v. United States, 345 U.S. 146 (1953); 149

Baltimore Transit Co. v. Hessey, 196 Md. 141, 75 A. 2d 76 (1950); 149

Bellamy v. Missouri & N.A.R.R., 215 Fed. 18 (8th Cir. 1914); 149

Board of Comm'rs v. Public Util. Comm'n, 107 Ohio St. 442, 140 N.E. 87 (1923); 144

Board of Public Utility Com'rs. of N.S. v. United States, 158 F. Supp. 98 (N.J. 1957); 133, 152

Boston & M.R.R. v. State, 102 N.H. 9, 148 A. 2d 652 (1959); 163

Brooks-Scanlon Co. v. R.R. Comm., 251 U.S. 396 (1920); 120, 144

Broth. of Maint. of Way Employees v. United States, 221 F. Supp. 19 (E.D. Mich. 1963); 78

Brotherhood of Locomotive Engineers v. United States, 217 F. Supp. 98 (N.D. Ohio 1963) 117

Brotherhood of Maintenance of Way Employees v. United States, 189 F. Supp. 942 (E.D. Mich. 1960); 65, 76

Bullock v. Railroad Comm'n, 254 U.S. 513 (1921); 144

Burke County, Ga. v. United States, 206 F. Supp. 586 (S.D. Ga. 1962); 102

Burlington Truck Lines v. I.C.C., 194 F. Supp. 31 (S.D. Ill. 1961); 177

Canadian Pac. Ry. v. United States, 158 F. Supp. 248 (D. Minn. 1958); 58, 167

Index of Railroads

Subject Index

Abandonments, 20, 102–103, 113–131; administrative problems, 127–128; burden of proof, 120–121, 169; burden on commerce, 124–125; carload shippers, 124; causes, 20, 115–118; condemnation, 119–120; conditions precedent, 125–127, 130–131; economic criteria, 118–120; legal criteria, 118–20; maintenance policy, 122–123; national planning, 172; partial deregulation, 169; profitable branch lines, 122; proposed statutory changes, 128–131; public interest standards, 119–120, 123; railroad lines, 20–21; recent decisions, 120–127; scheduled, 128; statistics, 113–115; statutory uncertainty, 127–128; tax aspects, 131; with trackage agreements, 102–103

Administrative regulation, 166–183; compulsory mergers, 172–173; I.C.C. procedures, 174–181; judicialized procedures, 175; major cases, 178–179; national merger plan, 49–50, 171–172; nationalization, 172–173; new economic standards, 169–171; official opinions, 177–178; oral hearings, 175; partial deregulation, 167–169; procedural rules, 175–177; voluntary mergers, 169–172. See also Regulatory policy

Air transport, 1, 20, 28, 40, 181, 182

Allegheny Corporation, 60

American Railway Engineering Association, 13–14

Association of American Railroads, 39

Bankruptcy reorganization, 71–72

Barriger, John, 6–7, 19

Beckmann, McGuire and Winsten: *Studies in the Economics of Transportation*, 12

Capacity, 1–2. See also Excess capacity, Route capacity, Yard and terminal capacity

Cassels, John M., on overinvestment, 18–19

Centralized traffic control, 4, 9–11

Chamberlin, Edward H., on long-run excess capacity, 16

Cherington, Charles R., 113, 114

Clayton Act: section 7, 61; section 11, 54–56

Competition, 25–41; absence of, 25–41, 166; enforcement of, 42–68; independent decision-units, 26; new forces, 168; public interest standard, 25, 42–43; rate, 1, 20. See also Air transport, Highway transport

Consent decrees, 47–48

Costs: branch-line allocation, 121–122; constant, 27; escapable, 118, 133; incidence on consumers, 166; long-run average, 26; long-run marginal, 27; maintenance, 21, 122–123; merger criteria, 169–171; savings from mergers, 86–90, 169–171, 172; wages, 21, 36, 116, 167. See also Freight costs, Passenger costs

Disinvestment, 20–21; regulation, 180–181. See also Abandonments, Service discontinuances

Doyle Report, 131

Economic efficiency, 36–38, 86–90, 168, 181; economies of scale, 26; electronic hump yards, 13–15; mergers, 169–171; optimal size firms, 36; optimal size yards, 33–34; technological change, 38–39, 179–180

Economic waste, 21

Electric interurban railroads, 21

Emergency Railroad Transportation Act of 1933, 57, 68

Engines, 5, 39

Excess capacity, 15–18, 21, 37, 167; all factors, 16–17, 25–26; Chicago to Omaha,